Drupal 6 Themes

Create new themes for your Drupal 6 site with
clean layout and powerful CSS styling

Ric Shreves

PUBLISHING

BIRMINGHAM - MUMBAI

Drupal 6 Themes

First published: September 2008

Production Reference: 1190908

Published by Packt Publishing Ltd.
32 Lincoln Road
Olton
Birmingham, B27 6PA, UK.

ISBN 978-1-847195-66-1

www.packtpub.com

Cover Image by Ric Shreves (ric@waterandstone.com)

Credits

Author

Ric Shreves

Reviewers

Alan Doucette

Bret Johnson

Dave Myburgh

Senior Acquisition Editor

Douglas Paterson

Development Editor

Ved Prakash Jha

Technical Editor

Ajay Shanker

Editorial Team Leader

Mithil Kulkarni

Project Manager

Abhijeet Deobhakta

Project Coordinator

Rajashree Hamine

Indexer

Monica Ajmera

Proofreader

Camille Guy

Production Coordinator

Aparna Bhagat

Cover Designer

Aparna Bhagat

About the Author

Ric Shreves is a partner in water&stone (`www.waterandstone.com`), a web development company that specializes in open source content management systems, including Drupal. Ric has been building websites professionally since 1999 and now works primarily as a web applications consultant. He lives in Bali with his wife Nalisa.

This book would not have been possible without the assistance and encouragement of the Packt Team, particularly Douglas Paterson, Damien Carvill, Ajay Shanker, Rajashree Hamine, and Ved Prakash Jha.

I would also like to thank the various individuals who took the time provide feedback on the previous edition of this text; their input had a positive impact on this version. Similarly, this work benefitted from the efforts of a number of reviewers, many of whom I have sadly never actually met. Thanks to all of you!

Looking a bit further afield, beyond the publishing realm, I would be remiss if I failed to mention my wife Nalisa, who's CSS skills are exceeded only by her patience with me during the course of this book.

Last but not least, my hat's off to the Drupal Team. Drupal 6 is a nice piece of work and shows clearly that the team is capable of continuing to deliver great code with a volunteer-driven, community-oriented project—no easy task, but they manage to make it happen (again and again). Cheers!

About the Reviewers

Alan Doucette is a partner of KOI (koitech.net), a web development company based in Jacksonville Beach, Florida, USA. He is passionate about PHP and open-source software. He is also very active in the web community as the Organizer of JaxPHP (jaxphp.org) and a contributor of Drupal.

> Thanks go to the awesome Drupal community for all their daily hard work creating great open-source software. I would also like to thank my business partner, Ben Davis, for his support and dealing with a Drupal fanatic.

Bret Johnson is a Network Analyst in his hometown of Austin, TX. About a year and a half ago, he developed a keen interest in web development and has been a diligent student ever since. After becoming involved with maintaining his team's intranet site, he decided to start developing websites in his spare time. While researching PHP scripts for a certain project, he stumbled across Drupal and has been working with it ever since.

> I would like to thank my family and friends for their support on all of my endeavors. I would also like to thank Packt Publishing for this great learning opportunity. Thanks also to the Drupal community, whose willingness to share their knowledge and advice, has become an invaluable asset.

Dave Myburgh started out in computers when entire operating systems ran on a single floppy disk and 640kb of RAM was a lot! He studied to become a molecular biologist, but never lost his passion for computers. Later, he ran a successful computer company for a couple of years in South Africa, before moving to Canada with his wife. He went back to science on his arrival in Canada, and since discovering Drupal two and a half years ago, he has once again started his own company, MybesInformatik. He loves working with Drupal, and is quite handy at theming. Since the birth of his son, his time is split between family and keeping his clients happy.

I would like to thank Dries and the Drupal community for making Drupal 6 such a great release. I'd also like to thank my wife and son for their support.

Table of Contents

Preface

Welcome to Drupal 6 Themes. This book is an updated and expanded version of our Drupal 5 Themes title. Not only has the content been updated to reflect the changes in Drupal 6, but it has also been expanded to include new examples, together with more information and resources.

The goal of this book is to explain the principles behind the Drupal theming system and to provide a reference work for theme developers. The book provides an explanation of the Drupal theme framework and shows how you can use it effectively to manage the presentation of your site. Throughout the text, we illustrate key points by demonstrating practical solutions to common problems.

The book begins with an overview of the default theming system and how you can squeeze the most out of it. In the middle sections, we discuss how to execute more extensive modifications by directly working with Drupal's theme functions and styling. In the latter chapters, we discuss more advanced topics, like how to make the site's presentation layer responsive to the users or the content and how to build templates from scratch.

As the PHPTemplate engine is now so closely integrated with Drupal, we tend to focus on techniques that rely on PHPTemplate. We devote little space to building themes with alternative template engines or directly in PHP. Also, as this work is concerned with the presentation layer of your Drupal site, we do not cover creating new modules or writing custom functionality.

Please note that the author comes from a design background and that many of the explanations and rational reflect the author's background. In that light, this book may not always satisfy hardcore programmers who expect the technical issues to be explained in detail. This book should, however, make the life of many designers a little easier. We also hope that the extensive reference materials included in this book will allow this title to find a lasting home on the shelves of many Drupal developers.

What This Book Covers

Chapter 1 examines the working of the theme system in Drupal, and the different approaches to working with Drupal themes.

Chapter 2 takes a look at all the various theming options that are available in the default Drupal system. By way of example, we take a default theme and customize it using only the options provided by the system.

Chapter 3 will cover how the PHPTemplate theme engine works and how you can use this powerful tool.

Chapter 4 identifies all the themable elements in the Drupal system and tells you where to find the elements together with an explanation of their functions.

Chapter 5 will cover employing of intercepts and overrides to modify the default styling in your Drupal theme.

Chapter 6 takes a look at how to implement extensive modifications to a default Drupal theme. This is a hands-on example of the techniques covered in previous chapters.

Chapter 7 examines how you can build from scratch a new theme employing the PHPTemplate theme engine.

Chapter 8 takes a look at how the Drupal system enables you to vary the styling between sections, pages or users.

Chapter 9 covers the styling of forms in Drupal, one of the more complex areas in the system.

Appendix A is an inventory of the contents of all the stylesheets in the Drupal system.

Appendix B is a listing of tools and extensions that make your work with themes easier and more efficient.

What You Need for This Book

Throughout this book, we will assume that you have the following package installed and available:

- Drupal CMS (version 6.x)

Who is This Book For

The main requirements of this book are knowledge of HTML, CSS, and a touch of creativity! Though this book aims to make Drupal theming accessible to designers, theming in Drupal 6 involves writing some PHP code, and a basic knowledge of PHP will be helpful.

Conventions

In this book, you will find a number of styles of text that distinguish between different kinds of information. Here are some examples of these styles, and an explanation of their meaning.

Code words in text are shown as follows: "We can include other contexts through the use of the `include` directive."

A block of code will be set as follows:

```
.title {
  color: #666;
  font-size: 1.8em;
  line-height: 2.0em;
  font-style: italic;
```

When we wish to draw your attention to a particular part of a code block, the relevant lines or items will be made bold:

```
function phptemplate_breadcrumb($breadcrumb) {
  if (!empty($breadcrumb)) {
    return '<div class="breadcrumb">'. implode(' > ', $breadcrumb) .'</div>';
  }
```

New terms and **important words** are introduced in a bold-type font. Words that you see on the screen, in menus or dialog boxes for example, appear in our text like this: "clicking the **Next** button moves you to the next screen".

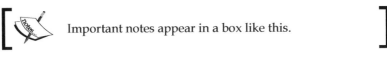

Important notes appear in a box like this.

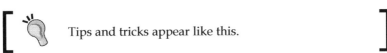

Tips and tricks appear like this.

Reader Feedback

Feedback from our readers is always welcome. Let us know what you think about this book, what you liked or may have disliked. Reader feedback is important for us to develop titles that you really get the most out of.

To send us general feedback, simply drop an email to feedback@packtpub.com, making sure to mention the book title in the subject of your message.

If there is a book that you need and would like to see us publish, please send us a note in the **SUGGEST A TITLE** form on www.packtpub.com or email suggest@packtpub.com.

If there is a topic that you have expertise in and you are interested in either writing or contributing to a book, see our author guide on www.packtpub.com/authors.

Customer Support

Now that you are the proud owner of a Packt book, we have a number of things to help you to get the most from your purchase.

Downloading the Example Code for the Book

Visit http://www.packtpub.com/files/code/5661_Code.zip to directly download the example code.

The downloadable files contain instructions on how to use them.

Errata

Although we have taken every care to ensure the accuracy of our contents, mistakes do happen. If you find a mistake in one of our books — maybe a mistake in text or code — we would be grateful if you would report this to us. By doing this you can save other readers from frustration, and help to improve subsequent versions of this book. If you find any errata, report them by visiting http://www.packtpub.com/support, selecting your book, clicking on the **let us know** link, and entering the details of your errata. Once your errata are verified, your submission will be accepted and the errata added to the list of existing errata. The existing errata can be viewed by selecting your title from http://www.packtpub.com/support.

Piracy

Piracy of copyright material on the Internet is an ongoing problem across all media. At Packt, we take the protection of our copyright and licenses very seriously. If you come across any illegal copies of our works in any form on the Internet, please provide the location address or website name immediately so we can pursue a remedy.

Please contact us at `copyright@packtpub.com` with a link to the suspected pirated material.

We appreciate your help in protecting our authors, and our ability to bring you valuable content.

Questions

You can contact us at `questions@packtpub.com` if you are having a problem with some aspect of the book, and we will do our best to address it.

1
The Elements of a Drupal Theme

In this chapter, we will introduce the concept of themes and explain the key role that themes play in the Drupal system.

The chapter covers the various types of themes, the basic elements of a theme, and the functions those elements fulfil. At the end of the chapter, we will also look at the themes contained in the Drupal distribution, and examine exactly what it is that makes each theme distinct.

The contents of this preliminary chapter provide the general comprehension necessary to grasp the big picture of the role of themes in Drupal. Think of the knowledge communicated in this chapter as a foundation upon which we can build the skills that follow in the subsequent chapters.

The Importance of Themes in Drupal

The theme of your Drupal site is responsible for the visitor's first impression of the site. Given the key role in shaping the presentation, a theme is arguably the most influential piece of your Drupal installation.

While the default Drupal distribution includes a set of themes that will prove sufficient for many users, I assume you are reading this book out of a desire to do more— whether it be only to install additional themes and then modify them to suit your needs, or whether you plan to build your own themes from scratch.

In order to grasp better some of the challenges (and opportunities) associated with Drupal themes, it is useful to look at three concepts that impact the way you use the system and the way in which you must plan your theme deployment. These three key concepts are basic to the approach throughout this book.

1. Theme it in Whole or in Part
2. Build with Blocks
3. Intercept and Override

Theme It in Whole or in Part

With Drupal, you can either set a single unified look for the entire site with a single template or you can control the look and feel of the individual parts of the site with multiple templates.

One source of confusion for many first time users of Drupal is that the default administrator interface is the same as the front-end interface seen by site visitors. Unlike other content management systems, there is not a purpose-built administration interface in Drupal.

 By setting the configuration within the admin interface, you can assign a specific theme to act as the interface for your administration system, however, this option is not active by default. Designating a separate admin theme is discussed in Chapter 8.

During the installation process, the system is configured to display the Garland template both for the front end (the public view) and the back end (the administrator's view). This is an example of using a single unified look for the entire site—the simplest approach to theming a Drupal site. If you want to work with just one template throughout the site, you can.

The seamless integration of the administrator interface into the site works well in some cases, but in others it may be problematic. There will be situations where the use of the same theme for the visitors and the administrators is undesirable, for example, on a marketing-oriented site where the artistic theme used for the site visitors may be impractical for site administrators.

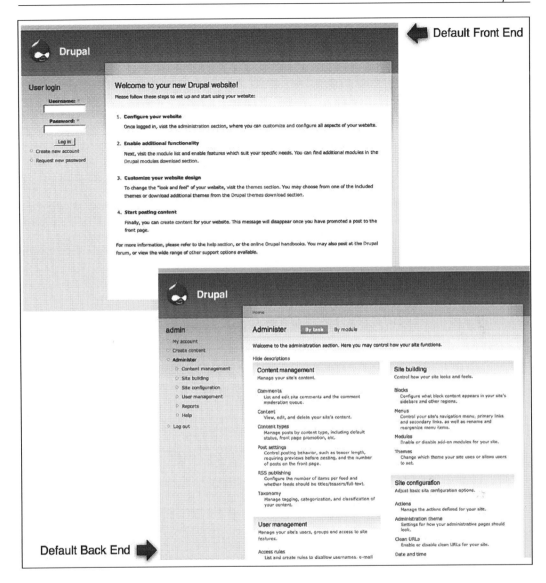

The system's default use of the same page template for both the front end and the back end conceals the existence of a great deal of flexibility and makes it non-obvious that you can do more with the themes. That's the bad news. The good news is that you can do more—much more!

The Drupal system allows you to specify different templates for different purposes on your site. You can, for example, build one page template for your homepage, another for your interior pages, and yet another for your administrator's use. Indeed, not only can you specify different templates for different pages, but you can also specify different templates for different parts of the same page. The sky is the limit as the theme engine also gives you the ability to provide styling for specific types of content or for the output of a particular module. The control is highly granular and with a little practice (and a little ingenuity), you will find the system to be very flexible.

In the following chapters, we will look at how to implement multiple themes and how to theme and configure all the various constituent parts of the Drupal system. You can quite literally, theme it all!

Build with Blocks

The code of a Drupal theme includes placeholders called regions. The regions are areas in a page where content is typically displayed. The site administrator can assign a variety of output to the regions through the block manager in the admin interface.

Modules are one of the most common sources of output in the Drupal system. Modules are standalone bits of code—mini applications in some cases—that extend the functionality of your site. The default distro includes a large number of modules. It is through modules that Drupal provides functions like the Forum, the Aggregator, and even additional administrative power, like the Throttle module.

Some modules produce output that appears on the screen, for example, the Forum module produces a threaded discussions functionality with extensive output. Other modules simply add functionality, for example the Ping module, which notifies other sites or services when your content has changed. The administrator is able to toggle modules on or off and able to assign the output of those modules—called blocks—to the various regions in the theme.

In addition to the blocks produced by modules, you can also create blocks specific to your installation. Manually created blocks provide an easy avenue for placement of additional information (for example, text or images), or, by inclusion of PHP code in the block, additional functionality.

Each of the blocks in the system, whether created by modules or manually created by the system administrator, can be themed individually, if you so desire.

The process of activating modules and assigning blocks to regions on the pages is one of the most basic and most important skills for a site administrator. Understanding how to administer the system and what options are available is key to building interesting and usable sites. A great deal of flexibility can be squeezed out of the system in this area alone.

This system, however, is not without complications. Module developers typically build their modules to be self-contained units. This independence also extends to the presentation layer of these discreet items of code. As a result, almost all the modules have distinct formatting and specific files that control that formatting. This approach to programming and modularization leads to a system in which a significant number of discrete units must be dealt with, adding greatly to the potential for complexity in changing the look and feel of a site to your specifications.

Each of the functional units—each module—is kept in a separate directory inside the `Modules` folder. Many contain their own CSS files, creating a large number of stylesheets scattered throughout the system. Add to that already daunting collection of modules any additional extensions you wish to install on your particular site and you can see how CSS juggling might come to dominate your life. Nevertheless, fear not, as styling all of this is manageable, using the technique discussed in this book.

Intercept and Override

The process of getting data from its raw form to its final displayed form provides several opportunities for you to affect the output prior to the data's arrival on the viewer's screen. While it is possible (even tempting!) to work at the lower levels—that is, hacking the files in the core files (or the modules or the theme engine)—I strongly advise against that. The recognized best practice approach to customizing themes emphasizes making changes at the higher levels, primarily to the theme files themselves.

The best practice approach to customizing themes involves intercepting and overriding files and styles—not altering the files in the Drupal core. In short, if you wish to style a particular block, instead of hacking the module that produces it, you will override the default module file with one of your own, or you will intercept the styles or functions of the module with those of your own (most likely, you will use a combination of both techniques). The new files and styles you create will be part of the theme itself—distinct from the core files.

By choosing to affect the system's output at the highest levels of Drupal's processes, we leave the core in its original state. This approach has several advantages— the most significant being that system upgrades and patches can be applied to the core without fear of losing modifications necessary to your presentation. Sites customized in this manner are easier to maintain, and your code remains portable and available for re-use in other deployments.

"override"—as used in this context, refers to creating a file, function, or style that is redundant with an existing file, function, or style and, courtesy of the order of precedence inherent in Drupal, the new file, function, or style will be in control. The use of intercepts and overrides to modify the look and feel of a Drupal theme is the subject of Chapter 5.

What Is a Theme?

In the context of Drupal, the term "theme" means a collection of interrelated files that are responsible for the look and feel of the website. Other content management systems (CMS) use different names for the files that perform the same function in their particular systems—the most common term used being "template"

Expressed conceptually, a theme is a visual container that is used to format and display data on the screen. Expressed in terms of its component parts, a theme is a collection of files that format data into the presentation layer viewed by site visitors and system administrators. Expressed in simple terms: The theme determines how your site looks!

A theme contains many files that are familiar to web designers, including stylesheets, images, and JavaScript. A theme may also include some files whose extensions may not be so familiar, for example *.theme, or *.tpl.php files. The former is used by pure PHP themes; the latter extension appears in themes that employ the PHPTemplate theme engine bundled with Drupal. In later chapters, we will look at theme engines and their files in detail.

Throughout this book, we will use "theme" to refer to the collection of files responsible for displaying the information on the page. We will use "template" to refer to specific files of the theme, that is, the .tpl.php files.

Here are some of the official Drupal online resources:

Resource	URL
Main Drupal Site	http://www.drupal.org
Drupal Theming Forum	http://drupal.org/forum/3
Drupal Theming on IRC	IRC @ #drupal-themes on the Freenode network
Download Extensions	http://drupal.org/project
Drupal 6 Theme Guide	http://drupal.org/theme-guide

What Is a Theme Engine?

A theme engine is a collection of scripts and files that serve to interpret the programming language used and process the commands contained therein. As data is drawn from the database and from outside sources (if any), the theme engine plugs the data into a predetermined format for display.

There are several popular theme engines, each of which is designed to interpret different templating languages. Drupal is distributed with the PHPTemplate engine. PHPTemplate is popular for a variety of reasons, not the least of which being that the language it relies on is good old PHP—a preferred choice for many Web developers today.

While PHPTemplate is distributed with the Drupal core, historically there were a variety of other theme engines that could also be installed and used with the Drupal system. Among the most popular were XTemplate, Smarty, and PHPTal. With the advent of Drupal 6, the PHPTemplate engine has been further integrated into the Drupal core and frankly it is hard to find a good reason to look for something other than the default theme engine. Alternative theme engines are discussed briefly in Chapter 3.

The Range and Flexibility of Drupal Themes

What can be done with a Drupal theme? How much presentation flexibility does the system have? These are key questions that arise when evaluating Drupal for your project.

The themes included in the default distribution, while useful, don't really offer much in the way of variety. But don't let the default themes narrow your vision; the default themes are simple and are best viewed as basic examples or starting points for your theming efforts. The system is flexible enough to be used to create a wide variety of layout styles, from traditional portal layouts to more cutting-edge sites.

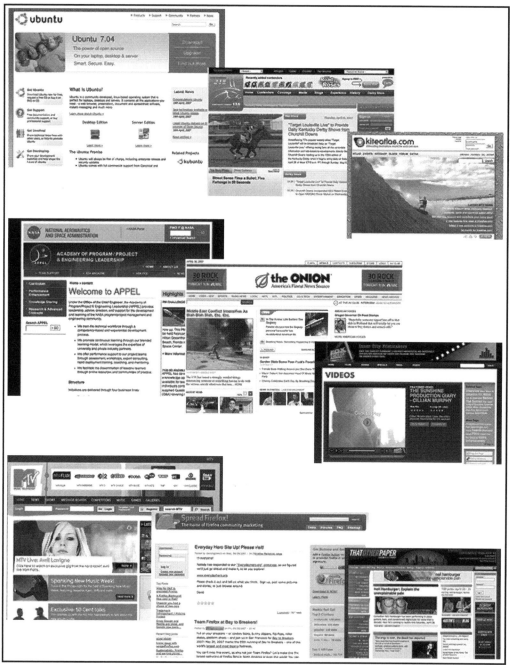

Just a few examples of the layout variety that can be achieved with Drupal themes.
For a current list of some of the high-profile sites using Drupal, view the case studies page on Drupal.org:

`http://drupal.org/cases`

When assessing a CMS in terms of suitability for purpose, programmers and designers often have different agendas.

- Programmers tend to focus on the development potential the system offers — the underlying language, the availability of hooks or the existence of tools, like theme engines.

- Designers, on the other hand, are typically more concerned with determining what restrictions a system imposes on their ability to design the interfaces desired by their clients. Designers want to know: Is the system easy to theme? Is the presentation layer easily accessible?

With Drupal, there is good news for both parties. For programmers, the inclusion of the PHPTemplate engine in the Drupal distribution means it is possible to tailor the output to match a variety of criteria. For designers, the flexibility of the Drupal approach to site building allows for the creation of attractive and brand-sensitive interfaces (not just a cookie-cutter portal or blog site).

The system offers the ability to create custom templates and to specify your modified files over the default files — all without having to actually hack the Drupal core. While it may take a while for a newcomer to become comfortable with the Drupal approach to the presentation layer, it is worth the effort, as a little knowledge can go a long way towards allowing you to tailor the system's output to your specific needs.

What You See on the Screen

When you access a Drupal website, what you see on the screen is the result of the site's active theme files. As the theme files call the functions that produce the data, the theme also sets the styling, the position, and the placement of the data on your screen. A lot of work for a small group of files….

Within a web page layout, a Drupal theme designer can designate certain general areas to fulfill certain functions. For example, in a typical 3-column theme, the center column is used to hold the primary content whereas the two smaller side columns contain secondary information. Screen space within each of those areas is also allocated according to the designer's priorities.

 In Drupal, that main content area is called the Content Column and those columns on the side are known as Sidebars.

Drupal theme files segregate the elements on the page through the definition of markers called *regions*. A theme developer can place the regions anywhere on the page by adding a short statement to the code of the appropriate file.

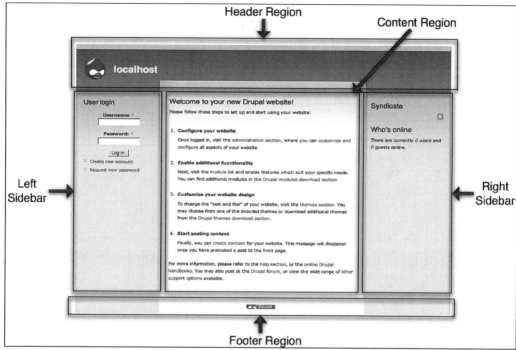

The default Garland theme, showing hard-coded regions.

 Adding or modifying the regions in a theme is discussed in Chapter 3.

Wherever regions have been specified, the site administrator can then assign module output, which in Drupal-speak is called a *block*.

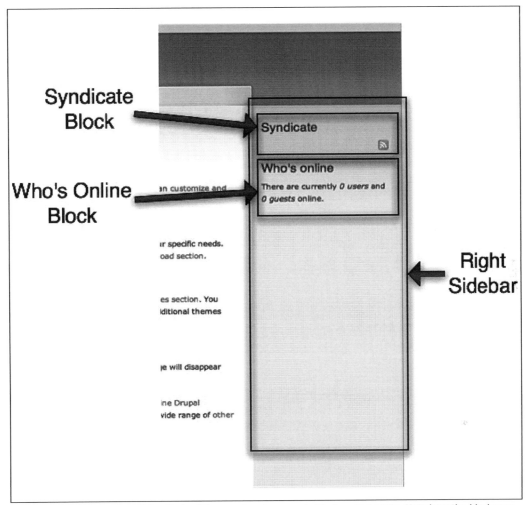

The Right Sidebar region of the Garland theme, showing sample block assignments. Note how the blocks are nested inside the region.

Regions are, in other words, placeholders inside the page layout where a site administrator can position functional output; this is most frequently done by assigning blocks to the desired region.

Regions must be coded into your theme files and are, therefore, primarily the province of the theme developer. Blocks, on the other hand, can be created and manipulated by the site administrator from within the admin interface (without having to modify the code).

Blocks can be created in two fashions:

- First, whenever the site administrator activates a module that produces visual output, one or more parallel blocks automatically become active. The administrator can then assign the block to wherever they want the module output to appear.
- Alternatively, the administrator can manually create and display a new block from within the block manager.

Regions that have no content assigned to them are inactive, but remain eligible for block assignment. Note in the illustration that the regions labeled **Header**, **Left Sidebar**, **Right Sidebar**, and **Content** all have output assigned to them. Those regions are active. The **Footer** region, in contrast, has no output assigned to it and is inactive on this particular page.

 Drupal themes can be created in a manner that allows inactive regions to be hidden from view—the Garland theme includes this feature. Where nothing is assigned to a left or right sidebar, the entire region collapses and hides from view.

To view the block placement in each of the default templates of your distro, log in to your Drupal site as an administrator and then go to **Administer | Site building | Blocks**. Click each of the themes' names to view the block placement, which will be overlaid on your screen.

The Big Picture: How Drupal Displays a Page

In order to appreciate the philosophy behind theming and the rationale for the approach to modifying and creating themes that is presented in this text, it is useful to see how Drupal functions at run time.

The shortest explanation of how a CMS functions can be expressed as follows: Text and pointers to other kinds of content are stored in the database; and that data is then dynamically retrieved, composed, and presented to a user in response to a request sent from a web browser. Drupal functions in the same manner, with the themes playing the crucial role in the formatting and presentation of the contents.

To illustrate the topic in more detail, consider the following:

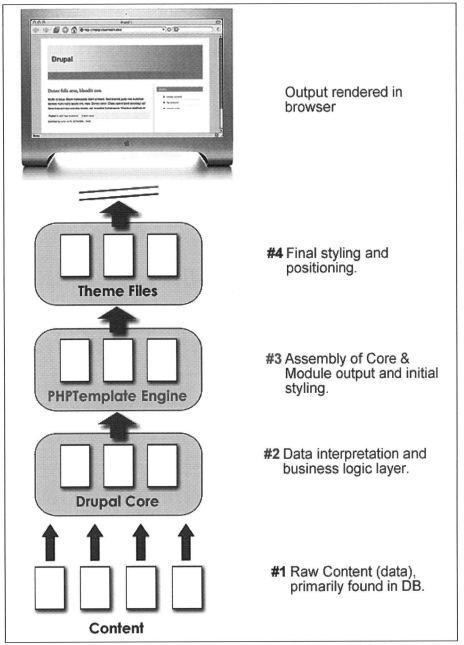

Output rendered in browser

#4 Final styling and positioning.

#3 Assembly of Core & Module output and initial styling.

#2 Data interpretation and business logic layer.

#1 Raw Content (data), primarily found in DB.

The diagram shows a hierarchy, wherein the lowest level is the raw data and the highest level is the final output displayed on the page. The diagram also shows an order of precedence in which the items at the top of the hierarchy, nearest the browser, take precedence over items lower in the order.

By way of further explanation:

1. The data, for the most part, is stored in basic form in the database of your installation. Formatting, if any, is present only as HTML tags that may have been specified in the content by the author.

2. The first significant step on the way to output occurs when the Drupal core extracts and pre-processes the data. No real formatting occurs at this level. Any HTML formatting specified in items stored in the DB is simply passed through for interpretation by the browser.

3. The next step on the way to output sees the theme engine begin to assemble the core and module output into something close to final form.

4. The final step before output occurs when the theme-specific files process the data. This last stage can have a wide range of impacts, from minimal to very significant. The variance in impact depends on the extent to which the theme's author has provided specific directions for the formatting and whether the author has chosen to override the formatting of the theme engine or of the default stylesheets in the Drupal distro—all topics we will cover in depth later in this book.

The Default Themes of the Drupal Distro

The default distribution of Drupal comes with a variety of themes ready for use. The themes not only provide some basic variety in look and style but can also be used to help you understand how themes work in Drupal. By studying the themes in the distro, you can learn from the functional examples they provide, and you can see how various theming techniques have been implemented successfully.

To view the various themes, log in to your site as an administrator, then go to **Administer | Site building | Themes**. This is the theme manager page. On this page, you will see a list of the themes installed and the controls that allow you to enable, activate, and configure each of the themes.

There are six themes in the default distribution:

*   Bluemarine
*   Chameleon
*   Garland
*   Marvin
*   Minnelli
*   Pushbutton

Four of the themes employ the PHPTemplate engine; two, Chameleon and Marvin, do not. The default theme that is automatically selected during the installation process is Garland. You can switch to any of the other themes easily from within the administration interface.

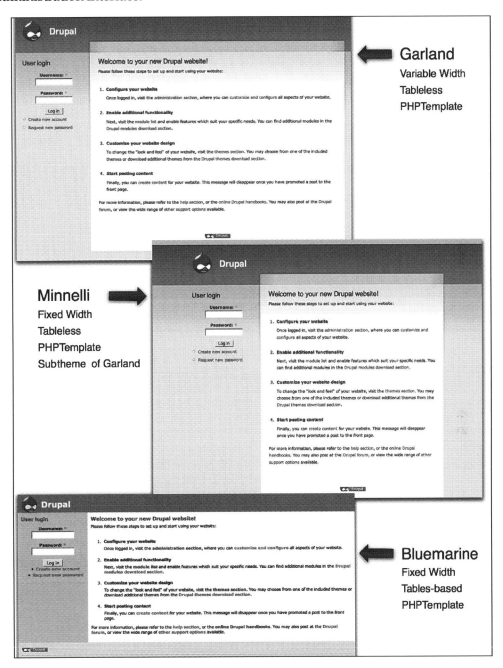

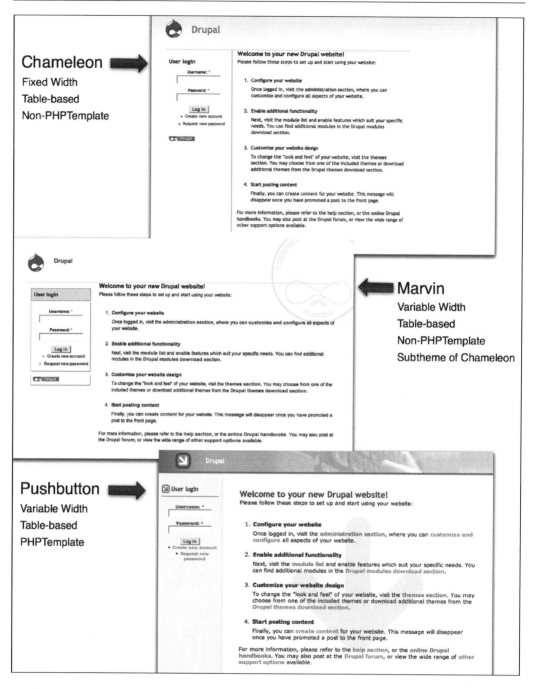

Chameleon

Fixed Width
Table-based
Non-PHPTemplate

Marvin

Variable Width
Table-based
Non-PHPTemplate
Subtheme of Chameleon

Pushbutton

Variable Width
Table-based
PHPTemplate

To change themes, simply access the theme manager in the admin interface and click the **Enabled** checkbox next to the theme you wish to activate. Select the radio button control marked **Default** if you wish to set the theme as the default. (The default theme will appear on all pages that are not specifically assigned to another theme.) The default theme will be immediately visible once your choice has been saved.

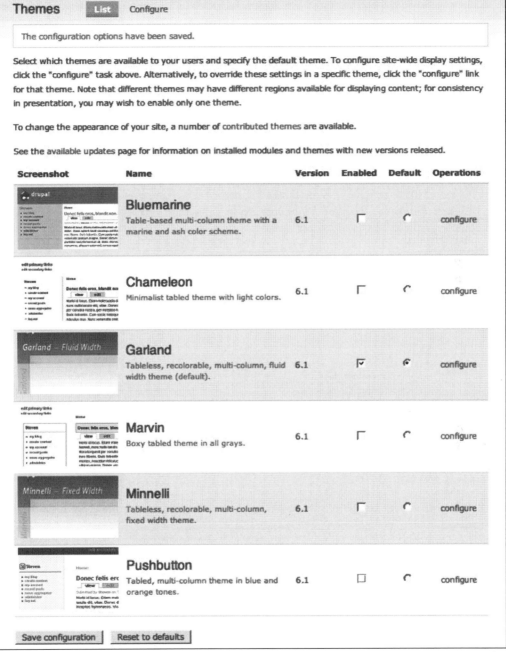

The admin screen showing the theme manager (**Administer | Site building | Themes**) with its controls for enabling and configuring themes.

All six of the default themes can support either two or three column layouts, though in the default configuration you will see only two columns displayed. The way in which these themes are designed creates the flexibility in the layout. The site administrator can assign items to a third column if desired; the third column will only appear when items are assigned to that position. When items are not assigned to the third column, the theme automatically collapses the unused region to show only two columns. The assignment of items to those columns is discussed in the next chapter.

The themes also vary in their approach to accessibility issues. Bluemarine, Chameleon, Marvin, and Pushbutton employ tables in their layout. Garland and Minnelli are tableless and depend entirely upon CSS to place and control the elements on the page.

Table-based layouts often make it difficult to create accessible web pages and their use is generally not preferred. If maximum accessibility is a consideration in your choice of themes, you should strive for layout using pure CSS.

The Drupal distribution also includes two examples of what are known as subthemes. Minnelli and Marvin are actually simple variations on other themes (specifically, Garland and Chameleon, respectively). Minnelli and Marvin are subthemes, that is, themes built on the same frameworks as their parents (note the visual similarity in the accompanying illustration). The subthemes are created by setting up alternative stylesheets inside the theme directory. While the subthemes use the same template files as their parents, the stylesheets use CSS to impart a different layout and a slightly different look. The presence of a dedicated `style.css` file in a subdirectory tells PHPTemplate to treat this as a separate theme, distinct from its parent.

The Theme Files

The themes and their respective files are kept in the directory named `themes` on your server. The default distro also comes bundled with the PHPTemplate engine. The PHPTemplate files are located in a sub directory inside the `themes` directory on your server.

Note that although the default themes are located in the `/themes` directory, if you create or install new themes, they should be placed in the `/sites/all/themes` directory.

To view the theme and theme engine files in your Drupal installation, access your server and navigate to the directory located at /themes.

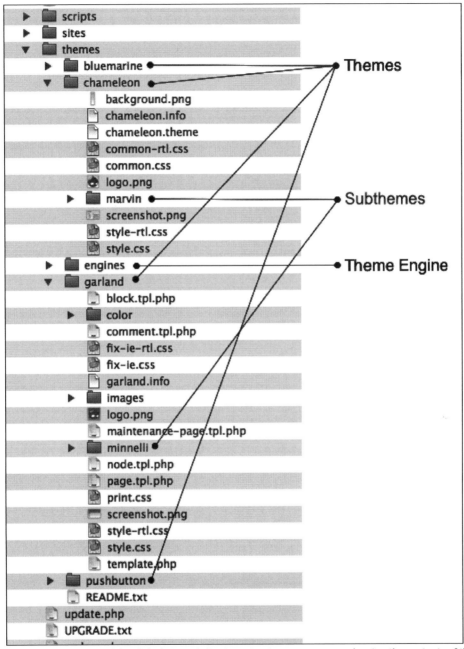

Screenshot of a section of the default Drupal directory structure on a server, showing the contents of the Themes directory.

The sample themes included in the distro demonstrate the two principal methods of creating themes. The themes Bluemarine, Garland, Minnelli, and Pushbutton all employ PHPTemplate. The themes Chameleon and Marvin are built without use of PHPTemplate; they are written directly in PHP. Themes that bypass the theme engine are sometimes referred to as "pure" PHP themes.

Should you use a theme engine or build a pure PHP theme? Which approach is better for you? It's hard to say; the answer varies from person to person and according to the intended use. The right answer will depend largely on your needs and your relative skill with the technologies. (Building a pure PHP theme can be a challenge for those who lack strong PHP skills!) Speaking generally, the theme engine approach is preferable as it is not only easier to master, but it is also more modular and reusable than a pure PHP approach to themes.

The Files of a PHPTemplate Theme

Let's look at the files of the default Bluemarine theme and their roles at run time:

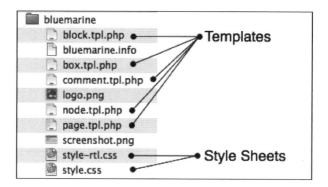

File Name	Description
block.tpl.php	A template to define the appearance of the blocks on a page.
bluemarine.info	A key file that sets a number of parameters for your theme, including the theme's name, description, and version information.
box.tpl.php	A template used in this theme to define a specific format—a box used to frame things (like comments in the Bluemarine theme).
comment.tpl.php	A template to define the appearance of the comments that follow items.

File Name	Description
logo.png	An image file containing the logo used in the theme.
node.tpl.php	A template to define the appearance of the nodes.
page.tpl.php	This template is the primary theme file; it is required by PHPTemplate theme and typically defines the appearance of most of the areas on any given page.
screenshot.png	An image file containing a screenshot of the theme; this is used as a reference.
style-rtl.css	The alternative stylesheet for this theme, for Right-To-Left oriented text.
style.css	The primary stylesheet for this theme.

Note that not all of these files are necessary for a PHPTemplate theme to function properly. The three key files are page.tpl.php, style.css, and bluemarine.info.

 While it is not necessary for the theme to function, it is best practice to always include screenshot.png, as this file is used in the admin interface to provide site administrators with a preview of the installed themes. The guidelines for screenshots can be found at http://drupal.org/node/11637

The file page.tpl.php does the heavy lifting in all PHPTemplate themes. The file incorporates, by reference, any theme-specific overrides contained in related files. In the case of the Bluemarine theme, those additional overrides are:

- block.tpl.php
- box.tpl.php
- comment.tpl.php
- node.tpl.php

Overrides are not required — the overrides in the Bluemarine theme represent a decision made by the author of the theme to style specific elements. As this is within the discretion of the theme developer, the presence and extent of overrides will vary from theme to theme.

The PHPTemplate-specific files all follow the same naming convention *.tpl.php. The prefix of each of those files is specific in that they are intended to override functions defined elsewhere. For the system to recognize that these files in the theme directory are intended to override the originals, the names must be consistent with the originals. The naming of some of the other theme files is flexible and within the discretion of the author.

We will take an in-depth look at the various PHPTemplate files and the concepts and rules relating to overrides in later chapters.

The Files of a Pure PHP Theme

Let's look at the files that comprise the Chameleon theme and their roles at run time.

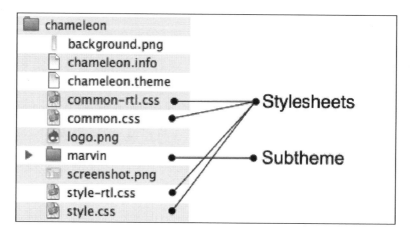

File Name	Description
background.png	An image file used as a page background.
chameleon.info	Sets a number of parameters associated with the theme, including the theme's name, description, and version information.
chameleon.theme	This is the primary theme file. This is the only required file in a pure PHP theme and it defines the appearance of the page.
common-rtl.css	An alternative stylesheet for this theme to handle Right-To-Left oriented text.
common.css	The stylesheet that covers the common Drupal elements in this theme.
logo.png	An image file containing the logo used in the theme.
style-rtl.css	An alternative stylesheet to set spacing in Right-To-Left orientation.
style.css	The stylesheet that covers the theme-specific elements in this theme.

In this theme, the key files are chameleon.theme, common.css, style.css, and chameleon.info. The *.theme file uses PHP statements to manage the page elements. The *.css files contain the styles necessary to support the presentation of those elements.

We will examine pure PHP themes in more detail in later chapters.

Summary

This chapter lays the groundwork for what comes ahead. You should now have some familiarity with the big picture—with the basic terminology used in Drupal, with the way Drupal presents data at runtime, with the general functions of themes, theme engines, and stylesheets, as well as with the location and nature of the key files and directories.

You should also be aware that despite the apparent complexity one sees at first glance, Drupal themes can be managed in a logical and relatively easy fashion by working with theme files (not hacking the core!) and through applying your own styling to intercept and override the default formatting of the Drupal system.

2
Theme Setup and Configuration

The large and active community of developers that has formed around Drupal guarantees a steady flow of themes for this popular CMS. The diversity of the Drupal community also assures that there will be a wide variety of themes produced. Add into the mix the existence of a growing number of commercial and open-source web designs, and you can be certain that somewhere out there is a design that is close to what you want. The issue becomes identifying the sources of themes and designs, and determining how much work you want to do yourself.

You can find both design ideas and complete themes on the Web. You will need to choose between working with an existing theme, converting a design idea into a theme, or creating a theme from scratch, unburdened by any preliminary constraints or alien code. For purposes of this chapter, we will be dealing with finding, installing, and configuring a pre-existing Drupal themes. In later chapters, we will look at converting designs and at building themes from scratch.

After we review the theme configuration options built into Drupal, we will take a default theme and run it through the entire customization process to see how far we can go with only the default resources at our disposal.

This chapter assumes you have a working Drupal installation, and that you have access to the files on your server. In terms of skills, for this chapter, you will need to know how to create content (for testing purposes) and some basic HTML.

Finding Additional Themes

There are two basic technical issues to consider when determining whether an existing theme is suitable for your needs: compatibility and system requirements.

The first issue is compatibility. Due to changes made to Drupal in the 6.x series, older themes will not work properly with Drupal 6.x.

To find the version information for your installation, go to **Administer | Reports | Status report**. The first line of the Status Report tabular data will show your Drupal version number.

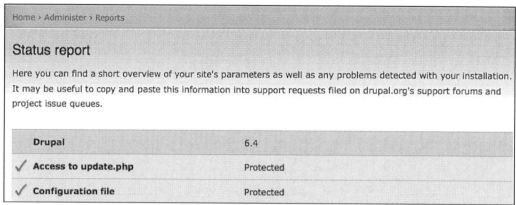

Home › Administer › Reports

Status report

Here you can find a short overview of your site's parameters as well as any problems detected with your installation. It may be useful to copy and paste this information into support requests filed on drupal.org's support forums and project issue queues.

	Drupal	6.4
✓	**Access to update.php**	Protected
✓	**Configuration file**	Protected

TThe Status Report screen showing Drupal version number. Note also this screen includes other useful information, like your MySQL and PHP version numbers

If you do not see the **Status report** option, then you are probably using a Drupal version earlier than 5.x. We suggest you upgrade your Drupal installation as this book is intended for Drupal 6.x.

If you know your Drupal version, you can confirm whether the theme you are considering is usable on your system. If the theme you are looking at doesn't provide versioning information, assume the worst. While it is extremely rare for a theme installation to cause problems, it's always a better practice to back up your site before installing anything that might be questionable.

To back up your Drupal site properly, you need to capture three things: the core files, the /sites directory, and the database. Simply copying the files via FTP is not enough; to properly back up your site you will need to back up the database. To back up your MySQL database, use phpMyAdmin, or whatever tools are provided by your webhost. Alternatively, there are extensions (Drupal modules) you can install on your Drupal site that allow you to perform backups from within Drupal. To learn more about the various backup techniques, visit http://drupal.org/node/22281 .

Once you're past the compatibility hurdle, your next concern is system requirements; does the theme require any additional extensions to work properly? Most themes are ready to use with your default Drupal installation. While many themes use the PHPTemplate engine, if you are running a recent version of Drupal, PHPTemplate is already installed. There are some themes, however, which may require either a different theme engine, or may require the installation of specific modules.

Check carefully whether the theme you've chosen requires you to download and install other extensions; this information is typically found on the theme's homepage or in the readme file included with the theme. If your theme does require additional extensions to work properly, track them down and install them first, before you install your theme.

> If you need a different theme engine for your theme to work properly, visit: `http://drupal.org/project/Theme+engines`.

A good place to start looking for a complete Drupal theme is, perhaps not surprisingly, the official Drupal site. At Drupal.org, you can find a variety of downloads, including some of the most popular themes. Go to `http://drupal.org/project/Themes` to find a listing of the current collection of themes. All the themes state very clearly the version compatibility and whether there are any prerequisites to run the theme.

> If you log in to the Drupal site, you can filter the Themes (and other extensions) by version—this makes finding compatible extensions a breeze.

In addition to the resources on the official Drupal site, there is an assortment of fan sites providing themes. Some themes are open source, others commercial, and a fair number are running other licenses (most frequently asking that footers be left intact with links back to the developer's site). If you wish to use an existing theme, pay attention to the terms of usage. You can save yourself (or your clients) major headaches by catching any unusual licensing provisions early in the process. There's nothing worse than spending hours on a theme only to discover its use is somehow restricted.

Some of the themes available from the community are great; most are average. If your firm is brand sensitive, or your personal style idiosyncratic, you will probably find yourself working from scratch. Most community-produced themes are fairly generic in nature and are meant to fit a wide variety of usages. Some are more flexible than others and can be tailored to your needs. Some, like the Zen theme we use in this book, are intended as a starting point for your use in the creation of subthemes.

Regardless of your particular needs, the theme repositories are a good place to start gathering ideas. Even if you cannot find exactly what you need, you can sometimes find something with which you can work. An existing set of properly formed theme files can jump start your efforts and save you a ton of time.

A rich source for designs is the Open Source Web Design site, `http://www.oswd.org`, which includes a repository of designs, all governed by open-source licensing terms. The downside of this resource is that all you get is the design—not the code, not a ready-made theme. You will need to convert the design into a usable theme.

For this chapter, let's search out a completed theme and, for the sake of simplicity, let's take one from the official Drupal site. I am going to download the Zen theme from Drupal.org. I'll refer to this theme as a working example of some of the steps below. You can either grab a copy of the same theme or you can use another—the principles are the same regardless.

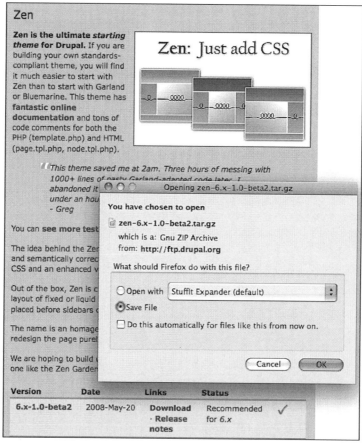

I downloaded Zen theme from `http://drupal.org/project/Themes`

Zen is described by the authors as "the ultimate starting theme for Drupal.". The theme is intended as a starting point for themers. With Zen, you are given a variety of common templates and supporting files upon which you can build—typically through the creation of a subtheme that uses the Zen resources.

The Zen theme has been around for a while and is under active development. There are a number of good resources associated with this theme and the theme is the subject of frequent discussions on the Drupal forums. This is a good place to start if you are new to theming and want a flexible framework that can help you learn how to theme a Drupal site.

 Zen, even has its own project page with good documentation. Visit the Zen project at `http://drupal.org/node/193318`

Installing an Additional Theme

Theme installation requires that you have the ability to move files from your local machine on to your server. Typically, this is done with an FTP client or through your web hosting control panel. The method you use is up to you. It makes no difference to Drupal which method you choose to employ.

Odds are your theme was delivered to you as a single file containing a compressed archive of files. When I downloaded Zen, above, I wound up with the file `zen-6.x-1.0-beta2.tar.gz`. The `.tar.gz` format (a.k.a. "tarball") is one of several commonly used archive formats.

The first step towards getting the theme installed is to uncompress the archive. Double-click the tarball and one of two things will happen: Either the file will uncompress and leave you with a new folder named "zen" or your system will prompt you to look for an application to open the archive file. In the latter case, you will need to track down and install a file compression program. There are lots of good ones out there. Most users, however, should have no problems as compression software is installed on many systems these days.

Once you have successfully extracted the files, take a look at what you have. If the theme you are working with includes a README file, read it now, making sure you haven't missed any system requirements or terms of use for the theme.

The next step is to get the extracted files up to your server. Use whatever means you prefer (FTP, control panel, etc.) to gain access to the directories of your Drupal site on the server.

Once you have access to your server, navigate to the directory `sites/all`; this is where you should place all third-party themes and extensions.

A note for old Drupal hands: The use of the sites/all directory is a change that was implemented in the version 5.x family. Using the sites/all directory, instead of the traditional themes directory, allows you to run multiple sites off a single Drupal installation. Placing all your extensions inside the sites/all directory means less complication with future upgrades.

Inside the sites/all directory, create a new subdirectory and name it themes. This new themes directory is where you will place all additional theme files. Finally, copy the zen directory and its contents inside sites/all/themes. Each theme should be kept in a separate directory. In this case, you should have wound up with a directory structure like this: sites/all/themes/zen.

▶ 📁 scripts	Aug 14, 2008, 8:10 AM	--	Folder
▼ 📁 sites	Today, 3:32 PM	--	Folder
▼ 📁 all	Today, 4:23 PM	--	Folder
📄 README.txt	Dec 23, 2006, 11:35 PM	4 KB	Plain text
▼ 📁 themes	Today, 4:23 PM	--	Folder
▶ 📁 zen	May 20, 2008, 9:20 PM	--	Folder
▶ 📁 default	Today, 3:32 PM	--	Folder
▶ 📁 themes	Aug 14, 2008, 8:10 AM	--	Folder
📄 update.php	Feb 4, 2008, 2:41 AM	28 KB	PHP: ...ument

Create the sites/all/themes directory to store the Zen theme files.

If all has gone according to plan, you are now ready to close the connection to your server and visit the admin interface of your Drupal site.

For the next steps, access the admin interface to your site via your browser and go to the theme manager (**Administer | Site building | Themes**). You should see your new theme listed alphabetically in the list of themes, as per the following illustration:

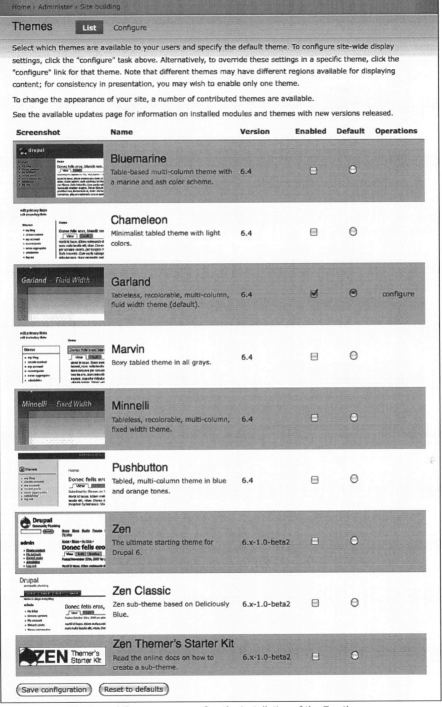

The Drupal theme manager after the installation of the Zen theme.

The theme manager provides a list of all the themes available on your site. Note the **Enabled** checkbox and the **Default** radio button; these controls are key to activating and configuring a theme for display on the site.

To use the new theme, we must first enable it. Once the theme is enabled, we can assign it to appear where we wish, and configure it.

To enable Zen, select the **Enabled** checkbox to the right of the theme name. Once you've selected **Enabled**, then click the **Save configuration** button at the bottom of the screen. Note that the appearance of the site does not change—that is because the new theme is neither assigned to any pages (nodes) nor is it set as the default.

Next, let's assign the theme to appear where we want. In this case, I want Zen to appear throughout the site, so I am going to select the **Default** radio button. The **Default** control is important; it sets the primary theme—the default theme—for the site. The default theme will be used by the system in all situations in which another theme is not specified. If we click the **Default** radio button next to our new theme and click **Save configuration**, the theme will be applied immediately, for both the front end and the back end (Admin system) of the site.

It is possible to override the default application of a theme to the back end of the site by specifying a separate theme for the administration system. This topic is dealt with in Chapter 8.

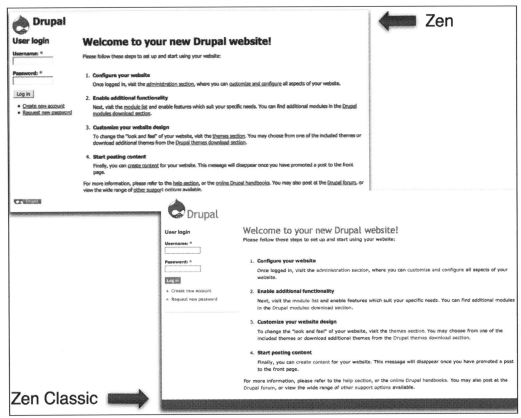

The Zen theme package includes both the basic starter theme, Zen, and a more polished subtheme, Zen Classic.

Note that you can enable more than one theme at a time. By enabling more than one theme, another function becomes possible. Registered visitors can choose which theme to use when they view the site. When multiple themes are enabled, a registered user can pick a theme as their default theme and the system will remember their choice.

When the multiple theme function is active, site visitors can select their preferred theme via the **Theme configuration** preferences on the **edit** tab of the **My account** page. The administrator can disable this functionality on the User Permissions page (**Administer | User management | Permissions**).

Note that once you enable a theme, another choice appears on the theme manager interface. Enabling a theme causes the **configure** option to become active (it will appear to the right of the **Default** radio button in the column labeled **Operations**). The Configuration Manager provides access to both global configuration options and theme-specific settings. In the next section, we take a look at both.

Configuring a Theme

In this section, we're going to go through the system and highlight the configuration options that are part of the default Drupal distro. We're not going to install any additional extensions or modify any code—we're going to focus exclusively on what can be done straight out of the box. We'll then apply this knowledge with an example configuration. For the example, let's use one of the default Drupal themes: Garland.

To begin, navigate to the theme manager (**Administer | Site building | Themes**). Access the configuration options of the Garland theme by clicking the **configure** link in the righthand column.

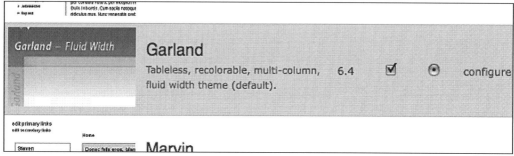

The Garland theme as it appears in the theme manager. The configure link is in the right-hand column

The Theme Configuration screen provides access to both global configuration and theme-specific configuration settings. As the name implies, global configuration is used to apply configuration choices consistently across the entire site—even across multiple themes. The theme specific configuration options relate only to that particular theme.

 If there is a conflict between the theme-specific configuration settings and the global configuration settings, the theme-specific settings will take precedence.

Theme-Specific Configuration Options

The initial view on your screen is the theme-specific configuration options. In Garland, this looks like the following illustration:

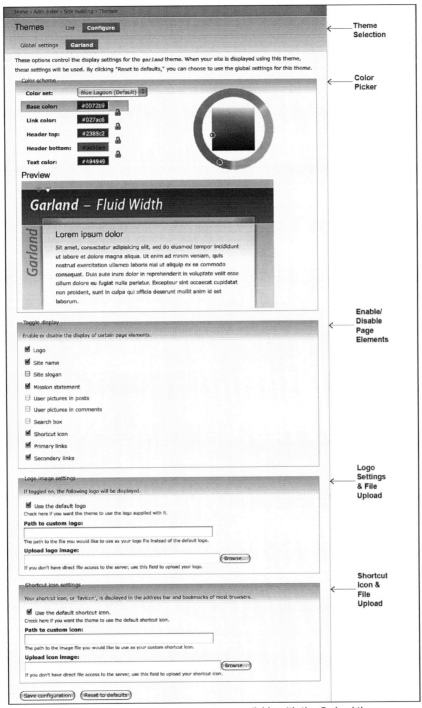

The theme-specific configuration options available with the Garland theme

Let's break this down and look at what each section of the Theme Configuration manager can do.

Color Picker

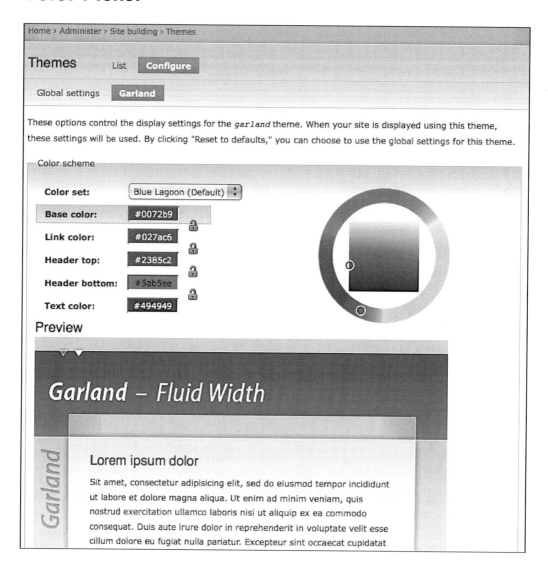

The Color Picker is a nifty little tool made possible by the Color module (modules/color/color.module), which is included by default in the core. The Color Picker is designed to make it easy for you to change the colors of a theme without coding. If the theme supports the Color Picker, all you need to do is visit the theme configuration page and you can change the colors to suit your needs. Not all themes support this configuration option, but when they do, this is a dead easy way to modify the colors used throughout the theme.

The best way to learn this tool is to just get in and play with it. It is a simple tool and the range of choices and the limitations become apparent pretty quickly.

The padlock icons on the Color Picker color fields are used to lock in the relationship between two or more color choices. This allows you to experiment with different color combinations, all the while keeping the relationship between the various colors intact.

If you don't want to use the Color Picker, you can feel free to disable the Color module on the module manager page.

Enable/Disable Page Elements

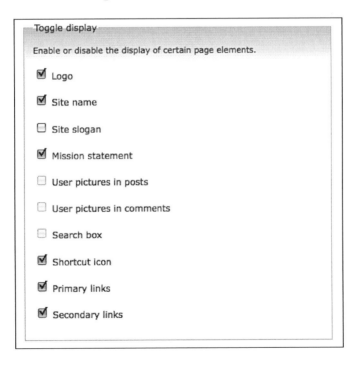

The Page Elements section contains a set of options that can be toggled on or off. Many of the options in this section relate to fundamental elements related to the look and feel of the site, like the logo, the site name, the slogan, and the mission statement. Other options are specific to certain types of functionality, for example, whether to show or hide the users' pictures in posts or comments. Note that the **Search box** option that appears on this page is dependent on the Search module being active. If the Search module is disabled, the search box option will not be available. Note also that two of the checkboxes in this section, **Logo** and **Shortcut icon**, affect the two sections that appear below.

[You can enable/disable the Search module from the modules manager, located at **Administer | Site building | Modules**.]

Logo Settings

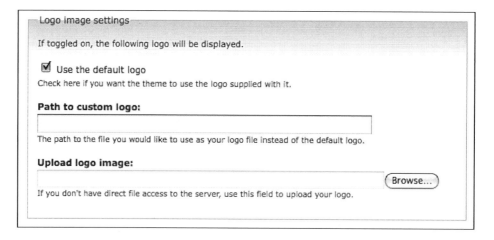

The Logo section allows you to select which logo the site theme will use. This section is dependent on the **Logo** checkbox being selected in the Page Elements section, above. If the **Logo** checkbox is selected, then the administrator has the choice between using the default logo included with the theme, or of providing an alternative logo. An upload option allows the administrator to upload a new logo image directly from the admin interface, without having to resort to another application. Once the logo is uploaded, note that the location and name the system has given to the logo file appears in the box labeled **Path to custom logo**.

Shortcut Icon Settings

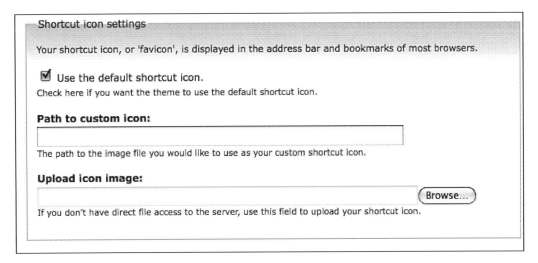

The Shortcut icon section allows you to select an icon that will appear in the address bar and bookmarks of certain browsers. Like the Logo section, this section is dependent on the **Shortcut icon** checkbox being selected in the Page Elements section, above. If the Shortcut icon checkbox is selected, then the administrator has the choice between using the default icon included with the template, or of providing an alternative. An upload option allows the administrator to upload a new icon directly from the admin interface, without having to resort to another application. Once the image is uploaded, the location of the file will appear in the box labeled **Path to custom icon**.

Global Configuration Settings

The options discussed above are, as noted above, theme-specific. The options will vary from theme to theme, depending on the choices made by the theme developer when they created the theme. Compare for example, the options available in the Garland theme with those in the Chameleon and Marvin themes.

In addition to the theme-specific configuration options, the administrator can also access and change the global configuration settings by selecting the **Global** tab at the top of the Theme Configuration page.

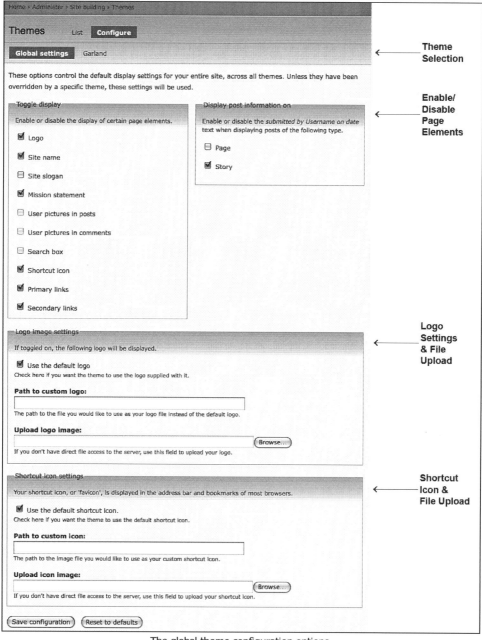

The global theme configuration options

You will note there is a great deal of similarity between the global configuration options and the theme configuration options. Basic choices function in a consistent manner in both sections; the exception being the **Color Picker**, which is absent from the global configuration, and the **Enable/Disable Page Elements** section that includes the option **Display post information on**.

Display post information on is unique to the Global Configuration Manager. The three controls in this box control allow you to select whether the text "**submitted by (Username) on (date)**" appears to viewers of certain types of content.

Managing Modules and Blocks

Modules are plugins that extend the functionality of the Drupal core. The modules you select and the positioning of their output (blocks) greatly affects the look and feel of your site. Effective management of the various modules and blocks is one of the keys to controlling the user experience on your site.

The standard Drupal distribution includes a number of modules, only some of which are active in the default configuration. You can enable additional modules or disable some of the optional ones to achieve the functionality you desire.

[A variety of additional modules can be found on the official Drupal site at `http://drupal.org/project/Modules`]

The Module Manager

The module manager (**Administer | Site building | Modules**) includes a list of all available installed modules. The default modules are categorized as **Core – optional** and **Core – required**. As you add additional modules to your installation, other group names may appear.

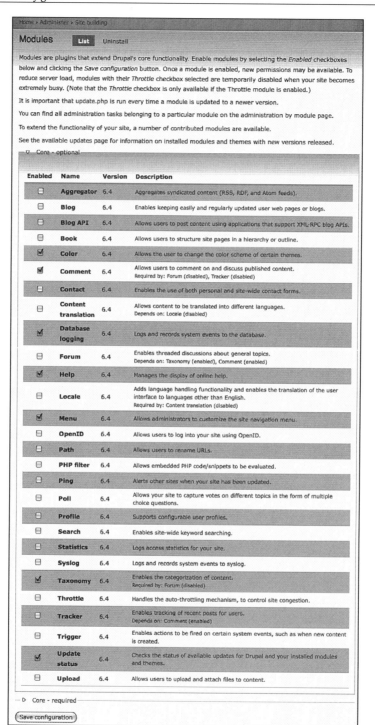

The module manager

To enable a module, simply access the module manager and then click the checkbox to the left of the module's name. De-select the box to disable the module. Once you have made your choices, click the **Save configuration** button at the bottom of the page.

Additional modules can be downloaded and installed easily. Note that while you can disable any module, you should not delete any of the Required Core modules or else you will lose critical or important functionality on your site.

> Enabling a new module may result in additional user permissions that need to be set, or other configuration decisions that need to be taken by the administrator.

Blocks are output generated by the various components in the system. In many cases, enabling a module automatically creates one or more related blocks. Accordingly, your next step after enabling a module should be a visit to the blocks manager.

> Note that some modules may require you to set permissions if you wish users other than User #1 to see all the options available. If you wish to expand permissions beyond User #1, you will need to visit the Permissions page (**Administer | User management | Permissions**) and adjust the settings for your new module accordingly.

The Blocks Manager

The tasks relating to block management are accessed through the blocks manager, which can be found at **Administer | Site building | Blocks**.

The blocks manager interface looks like this:

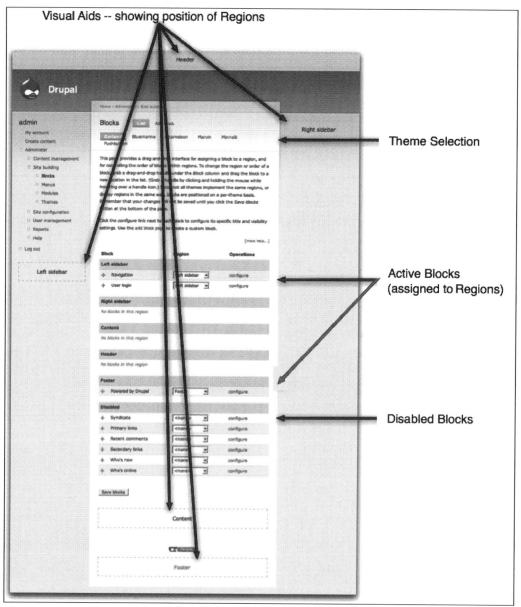

The blocks manager. Note that the system helps with block assignment by showing
all the active regions in the theme

The blocks manager gives you control over a number of useful aspects relevant to your theme. First and of primary importance is the ability to publish blocks to the regions of your theme, thereby allowing you to position the output on the screen.

For a block to be visible, the block must be both enabled and assigned to an active region on the page.

To assign a block to a region, select the target region from the combo box immediately to the right of the block's name. Click the **Save blocks** button. When the page reloads, the block will have been moved to reflect the new assignment; if all things necessary for output to appear have been satisfied, the output will now also appear on the page.

Hiding a block is just as easy: Simply select **<none>** from the combo box and then click **Save blocks**; the block will be immediately hidden from view.

 Remember that the name, number, and placement of regions may vary from theme to theme. If you are using multiple themes on your site, be sensitive to block placement across themes, else unexpected results may occur.

You can also use the blocks manager to manage the ordering of blocks inside each region. Immediately to the left of each block's name is a "cross" of four arrows; click and drag this spot to change the ordering of the blocks.

Configuring Individual Blocks

The blocks manager gives access to the configuration options for each block. Blocks can be configured at any time. Simply click the block's **configure** link in the far right **Operations** column.

Let's crack open the **User Login** block and look at the configuration options presented there, as they are typical of the group.

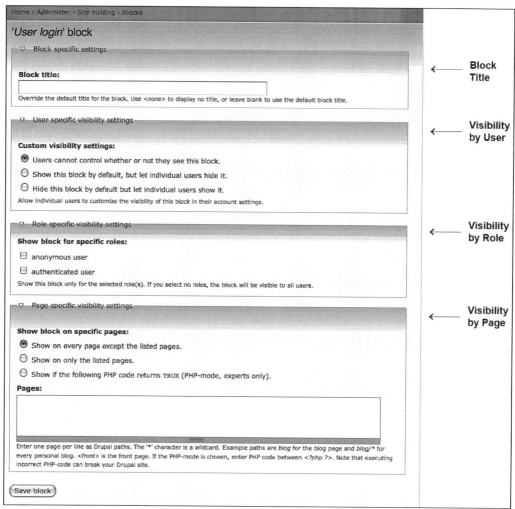

Configuring the User Login block—a typical block configuration screen

The Block Configuration interface provides options for naming and displaying the block. All parameters on this page are optional.

Block Title

The first option, **Block title**, gives you a free text field into which you can enter a specific name that will override the default block name. If nothing is entered, the default name (supplied by the system for the default blocks) will appear. If you wish for no title to appear with the block, then enter <none> in the text field provided.

The remaining options all relate to the visibility of the block. You are able to control when the block will appear to a user by setting and applying the conditions on this screen.

User Specific Visibility Settings

The first option, labeled **User specific visibility settings**, allows you to give users the freedom to show or hide blocks and to set their own preferences regarding whether the block displays by default. If you do not wish to grant users this discretion, leave the default setting (**Users cannot control whether or not they see this block.**).

Role Specific Visibility Settings

The second option is labeled **Role specific visibility settings**. The system presents you with 2 boxes, but in reality 3 choices. If you want everyone to see the block, leave the default state. Alternatively, you can show the block only to authenticated users (that is, users who have logged in) or only to anonymous users (that is, users who have not logged in).

 In addition to the parameters on this page, blocks can also be hidden during busy periods to decrease the load on your server. The Throttle module controls this specialized visibility setting.

Page Specific Visibility Settings

The final option is labeled **Page specific visibility settings**, but the label is actually a bit of a misnomer, as you can do much more here than simply tie block visibility to the page on the screen. The first two options allow you to list pages to include, or exclude, in the display of the block. To enable this function, select the appropriate radio button and then enter the URLs of the pages you wish to specify in the box below.

Let's look at the syntax required for this window, as the Drupal system requires you to specify things in a particular fashion. Note that there are also some good shortcuts available here that will save you from having to enter a number of URLs to capture every single page of a particular content area or functionality:

Term	Designates
<front>	The homepage
admin	The Admin main page
admin/*	All URLs that include admin/
aggregator	The RSS Aggregator main page
aggregator/x	The RSS Aggregator with the ID of x (where x is an integer)

Term	Designates
aggregator/*	All URLs that include aggregator/
blog	The blog main page
blog/x	The blog with the ID of x (where x is an integer)
blog/*	All URLS that include blog/ (every personal blog main page)
contact	The default system Contact form
forum	The Forum main page
forum/x	The Forum with the ID of x (where x is an integer)
forum/*	All URLs that include forum/ (every forum main page)
node/x	An item with the node ID of x (where x is an integer)
user/*	The User pages.
user/x	The main page of the user with the ID of x (where x is an integer)

Note that you can use more than one statement at a time. To use multiple statements, simply input them on separate lines in the text box. One consideration to keep in mind is that you cannot specify at the same time pages on which a block will appear as well as pages on which the block does not appear—those options are mutually exclusive.

The third radio button on this section is where the fun begins. If you select the third button, then you are able to enter PHP code to control the visibility of the block in almost literally any fashion you choose. Don't be fooled by the label they put on it—**Pages**—this is about more than just pages; it's a wild card field in which you can apply PHP code that can be used to establish logic that determines visibility according to various criteria.

Adding PHP to Blocks

Through the use of a little PHP, blocks management becomes much more interesting. You can add custom visibility settings of any variety: tie visibility to a user, a role, a content type or whatever combination is needed for your site.

Note the examples below, which control visibility according to whether a condition is met. If the condition is True, a block is visible; if it is False, the block will not be displayed.

Display a block only to the user who's User ID = 1:

```php
<?php
global $user;
if ($user->uid == 1){
  return TRUE;
}
else {
  return FALSE;
}
?>
```

Display a block only for a specific node (in this example, the node = story):

```php
<?php
$match = FALSE;
$types = array('story' => 1);
if (arg(0) == 'node' && is_numeric(arg(1))) {
  $nid = arg(1);
  $node = node_load(array('nid' => $nid));
  $type = $node->type;
  if (isset($types[$type])) {
    $match = TRUE;
  }
}
return $match;
?>
```

Display a block throughout all Forums:

```php
<?php
if (arg(0) == 'forum') {
  return TRUE;
}
if (arg(0) == 'node' && ctype_digit(arg(1))) {
  $node = node_load(arg(1));
  if ($node->type == 'forum') {
    return TRUE;
  }
}
return FALSE;
?>
```

A variation: Display a block throughout all Blogs:

```php
<?php
if (arg(0) == 'blog') {
  return TRUE;
}
if (arg(0) == 'node' && ctype_digit(arg(1))) {
  $node = node_load(arg(1));
  if ($node->type == 'blog') {
    return TRUE;
  }
}
return FALSE;
?>
```

There is a great deal of flexibility here and you should explore creative use of this feature. While you cannot combine the page syntax with the option to include PHP, you can control your block display to a very high degree.

In addition to the default blocks, administrators can also use the blocks manager to define custom blocks—through use of the **Add Block** tab at the top of the blocks manager. We'll look at an example of this technique in the course of the example in the next section.

Theming in Action: Dressing Up Garland

Now, just for the sake of practice, let's take what's been covered in this chapter and apply it to costomize an existing theme. We'll start with the default theme and apply the various options available in the system in an effort to turn our "off the rack" theme into something more tailored.

For the following example, assume we have a hypothetical client named "Fluid Carbon" and they want to build a fan site for Italian sports cars. This is a hobbyist's site, so the owner has a very limited budget and doesn't want to pay for custom design work or custom component development; the budget restrictions basically force us to work with Drupal straight out of the box.

Here are the client's requirements...

Look & Feel:

- Fluid 3 column layout
- Color scheme to match existing client I.D
- Must use client's logo in header
- The client wants a clean look—not too much clutter
- Vertical main nav, in the right column

Functionality:

- A blog for the site editor (only one blog)
- A forum (only one needed)
- The ability to display third-party RSS feed content
- Polls
- A contact form
- Must support user-generated comments
- Must display button ads
- Site search

The client's requirements are squarely within the capabilities of the default Drupal distro, with only one exception. The only thing we need to deal with outside of Drupal is the requirement for button ads. To handle the button ads, normally, you would want to go ahead and install one of the many ad management extensions available on the Drupal site, but as this client has no budget, we're forced to apply only the most basic solution.

Here are the major tasks we need to accomplish:

- Modify theme colors to match client I.D.
- Configure theme to match client requirements
- Get client logo into theme
- Enable necessary modules
- Enable new blocks
- Assign blocks to create 3 column layout
- Set block visibility rules
- Create Menu items
- Set user access controls

Along the way, we'll also look at a few little tweaks that will help the usability of the site and add some variety as well. The client is going to load his own content, so for our testing purposes, we'll only create dummy content as needed along the way.

Let's assume for this exercise that we have a fresh installation of Drupal. To begin, go to the theme manager (**Administer | Site building | Themes**) and click on the **configure** button by the Garland theme. Garland is a fluid design, which supports either 2 or three columns. It is simple and clean and consistent with the client's general wishes. Garland also supports the Color module, which makes it easy for us to change the theme color scheme to match the client's existing logo.

Set the Color Scheme

First, let's work on the color scheme. In the configuration manager, select **Custom** from the **Color set** combo box and enter the values you see in the illustration:

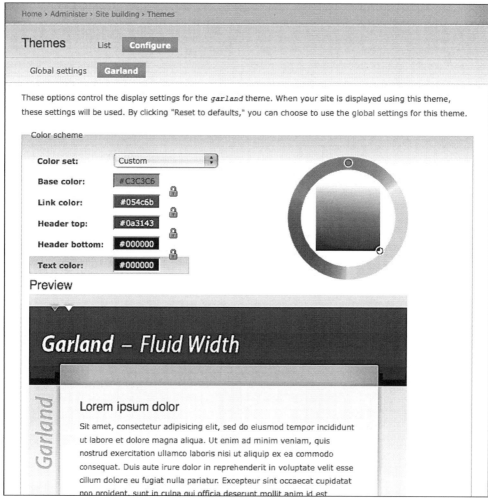

The Color module lets you set theme colors from within the admin interface.
As you modify the colors, the Preview image updates.

Set Page Elements (Toggle Display Settings)

Next, scroll down the configuration screen and change the **Toggle display** settings to enable the **Logo** option. We will want to use the **Primary Links** to hold part of the navigation scheme for this design, so enable that option as well. Unselect any other items as we don't want them cluttering up the interface.

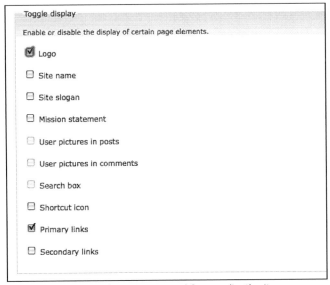

The Page Elements we need for our client's site.

Upload Logo

The next step is to upload the client's existing logo, by way of the **Logo image setting** controls further down the page in the Theme Configuration Manager. Unselect the box **Use the default logo**, then click the **Browse** button to find the client logo on your local machine (Note: I created a very simple logo for use in our example.).

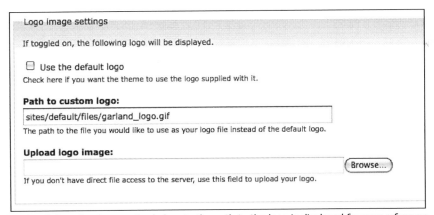

The client's logo has been uploaded; note the path to the logo is displayed for your reference.

The client doesn't have a shortcut icon of his own, and the budget leaves no room to dream one up, so we're through with the Theme Configuration Manager. Let's save our work and leave this page and move on to Global Configuration.

Global Site Information

Go to **Administer | Site configuration | Site information**. On this page, enter a name for the site, a slogan (even though you may not intend to set a slogan to appear on the theme, the system still uses it for several purposes, including some page titles!), and the footer, as per the illustration. Note that for the footer copy, I have specified the URL for the contact link, even though we have yet to set up a Contact form; we can do this with confidence as the default Drupal Contact form is always located at `/contact`. Once the changes are made, save and exit.

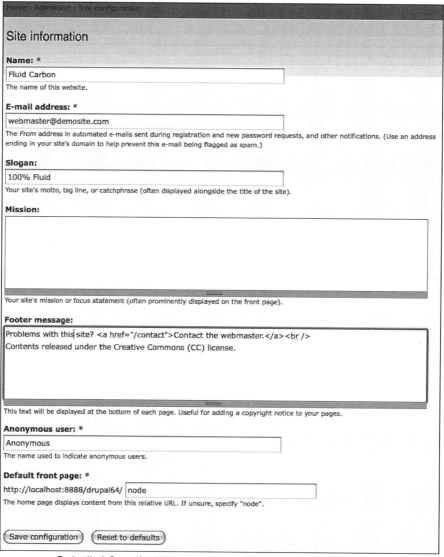

Basic site information is necessary to set the footer and the page titles.

Enable Modules

Next, let's enable the modules we need. Go to the module manager (**Administer |
Site building | Modules**) and match the settings shown in the following illustration:

The modules enabled for this example.

Manage Blocks

After enabling the modules, it's time to turn to the blocks. Go to the blocks manager (**Administer | Site building | Blocks**). Then, select the settings for Garland by clicking on the **Garland** link near the top of the page (underneath the word **Blocks**).

First, the client requests three columns with right side nav, so I'm going to start by moving the **Navigation** block from the Left Sidebar region to the Right Sidebar region.

Next, let's move the **User login** and **Syndicate** blocks to the Right Sidebar, as well. Let's also put the **Search** form on the right and let's activate the **Who's online** block and put it on the right side as well (that last item is not in the brief but if the client doesn't like it, we can always disable it easily enough!). To cut down on clutter, let's hide the block titles for the following blocks: **Navigation**, **User login**, **Search**, and **Syndicate**.

To hide block titles, access the Block Configuration page for each of the blocks and enter <none> in the **Block title** box at the top of the page.

To balance out our three column layout, let's enable the following and assign them all to the Left Sidebar: **Most recent poll**, **Recent comments**, **Recent blog posts**, and **Active forum topics**.

[To enable a block, you just need to assign it to an active region.]

To get the placements just right in the layout, you can experiment with different orderings for the blocks inside each region.

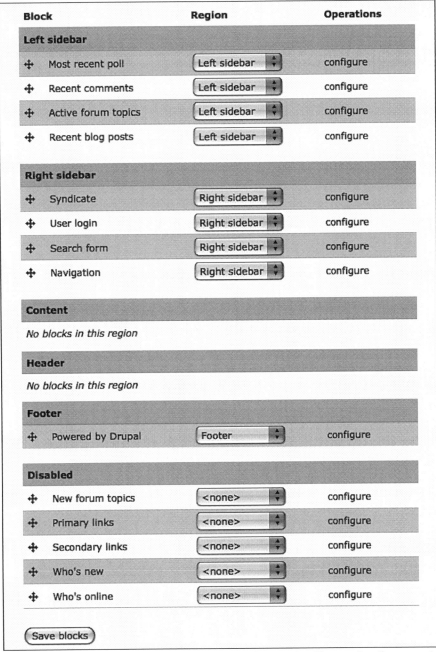

Shows whether each block is disabled or enabled and assigned to a region. You can drag the arrows to the left of the block name to set the block order within each region.

Add Some Dummy Content and Links

At this stage in the build, it's time to set up some basic containers and materials to give us something to work with when we create our menu items. For this client, we need to provide one Contact form and one Forum.

To set up a site-wide Contact form, go to **Administer | Site building | Contact form** and create a contact form with the necessary details.

Next, create a sample forum for use during development. Go to **Administer | Content management | Forums** and create one forum.

Let's get started on the navigation links so we can move around the site and assess our navigation menu placement. From the Menu Manager (**Administer | Site building | Menus**), I am going to work on both the **Primary Links** and the **Navigation**.

On the **Primary Links** menu, click **Add item** to create a new Menu Item. Set the **Menu link title** to "Home" and **Path** to <front>; this will link to our homepage. Next, add another new Menu Item and set the **Path** to contact — this will automatically link to our Contact Form.

On the **Navigation** menu, we're going to enable and rename the Forums link. When you click on the **Navigation** option in the Menu Manager, you will note that the Navigation Menu Manager interface is very different from that we saw in the Primary Links Manager, above. While the Primary Links Manager requires us to create any links we want to use, the Navigation Menu already has a number of presets in place. We will take advantage of that with this site, using the default settings with one exception. Click the **edit** link in the right column of the Forums item. Change **Menu link title** to "The Forum" and check the **Enabled** checkbox. Click **Save**. We now have a link to the Forums functionality.

For the next phase, let's load up some sample data to make finalizing the site easier and facilitate testing. I'm going to create a dummy homepage by going to **Create Content | Page**. I'll just use standard Lorem text (generic filler text, typically begins with "Lorem ipsum dolor...," hence the name) and a picture I have of a Ferrari grill to give the page some life (add whatever you wish here to fill these slots for purpose of this example). Use the **Publishing** options for this item to specify **Promoted to front page**.

Now that we have a homepage, let's populate the page with a couple of Blog entries, a couple of comments, a temporary Poll, and a couple of Forum topics — all simply for the sake of checking the blocks in action and testing as we go.

Set Access Levels

Now that we have some sample content, we need to make sure it is visible to all the right people. This means checking the site's Permissions settings. Go to **Administer | User management | Permissions.** Configure the settings to enable the following additional functionality for access by anonymous users:

- Access news feeds
- Access comments
- Post comments
- Access site-wide contact form
- Create forum topics
- Edit own forum topics
- Vote on polls
- Search content
- Use advanced search

Create a Custom Block

At this stage, the site is coming together and getting close to final form. The open issue on the client's wish list was for button ads. For this one, given the budget, he's getting the low tech solution; I'm going to create a new block and code the image placement and URL link directly into the block.

Go to the Blocks Manager and choose **Add Block**. Type a descriptive name for the **Block title** and then use HTML to specify the image and the URL that it links to.

We also need to set the visibility for our new block. Under the heading **User specific visibility settings**, choose **Users cannot control whether or not they see this block**. Under the heading **Page specific visibility settings**, choose the first option, **Show on every page except the listed pages.** Then input into the **Pages** text box on one line `admin` and on another line `admin/*`. The first command bans the block from the main admin page; the second bans the block from any of the interior admin pages.

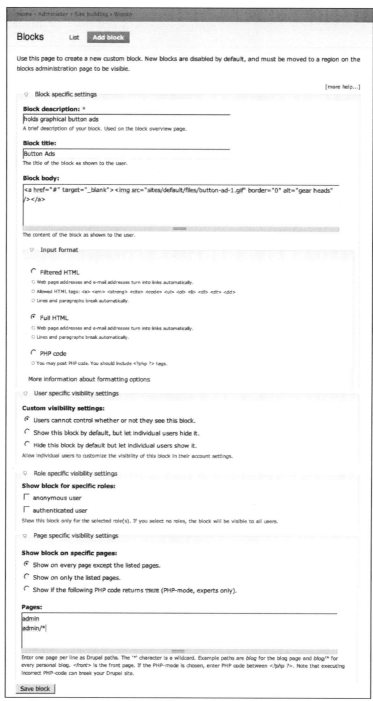

Adding a new (very simple!) custom block to hold the client's button ad image. Note the Input format option is set to **Full HTML** in the example, in order to give more flexibility in use of code in the block body.

Finally, let's go the blocks manager and assign this new block to the Right Sidebar region, as the two side columns still look a bit unbalanced in our layout.

Set Block Visibility

The only thing left at this stage is to configure the visibility of two other blocks in a common sense fashion. Let's do the following:

1. Display the User Login block on the homepage only
2. Display the Recent Blog Posts block throughout the Forum posts

First, the User Login block. Go to the blocks manager and click the **Configure** link on the User Login block. Change the Page specific visibility settings to the second option, **Show on only the listed pages**. In the Pages text box enter <front>; this restricts this block to displaying only on the front page of the site.

In order to get the Recent Blog Posts block to display throughout the Forum posts, but nowhere else, we have to add a bit of logic to help the block determine exactly which pages are part of the Forum. On the block configuration page, we will need to set the control to the third option, **Show if the following PHP code returns true**, and then add the following code to the **Pages** text box:

```php
<?php
if (arg(0) == 'forum') {
  return TRUE;
}
if (arg(0) == 'node' && ctype_digit(arg(1))) {
  $node = node_load(arg(1));
  if ($node->type == 'forum') {
    return TRUE;
  }
}
return FALSE;
?>
```

Taken together, the changes wrought above should produce a site that meets our hypothetical client's initial requirements. Compare the new Fluid Carbon front page with the default Garland front page for an appreciation of the difference.

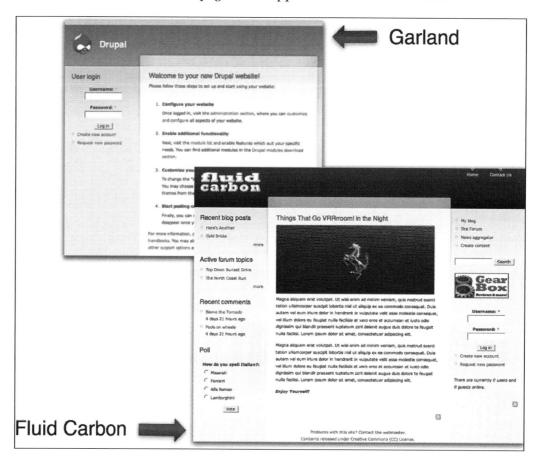

Uninstalling Themes

Uninstalling themes is a simple process, essentially the reverse of installing. First, go to the themes manager and make sure that the theme you wish to uninstall is not currently enabled. Once you have verified that it is disabled, then access your server. On the server, find the directory containing the theme files and delete the files and the directory. That's all there is to it!

Note that Drupal is very forgiving, and erroneous deletion of an active theme will not crash your site, it will simply result in the content being shown without any styling.

Summary

We started this chapter by looking at how to find and install themes and we ended by trying to extract as much as we could from a basic theme through use of the default Drupal configuration options.

Given the flexibility of the system, it is perhaps not surprising that a number of people work exclusively from the default themes. The Fluid Carbon example in this chapter shows that you can get quite a bit out of the basic setup, simply by understanding the options in the Drupal site and theme configuration management screens.

As you will see in the chapters ahead, the techniques we covered in this chapter are just the beginning of what you can do with Drupal themes. Nonetheless, the configuration principles in this chapter, particularly as they relate to the use of modules and blocks and the control of visibility settings, are important for all theme work. We will come back to some of these points when we get more into heavy customization and building custom themes.

Working with Theme Engines

3

In this chapter, we will explore theme engines in general and Drupal's default PHPTemplate theme engine in detail.

Our exploration of the PHPTemplate engine lays an important foundation for understanding how to create themes or how to extensively modify existing themes. In the examples below, we show:

- The key files used in the theming process
- How these files impact themes
- The order of precedence among theme files
- The availability of alternatives to the PHPTemplate engine

Though you don't need to be fluent in PHP to understand this chapter fully, a little familiarity with the programming language will certainly make things easier. The code examples in this chapter come from the default themes Bluemarine and Garland, contained in the Drupal distribution.

What is PHPTemplate?

PHPTemplate is one of a family of applications known as theme engines (referred to often elsewhere as "template engines"). These applications serve a middleware function and determine the coding syntax that can be used to create the theme. As the name implies, PHPTemplate supports the popular PHP programming language for theme creation.

PHPTemplate was created specifically for use with Drupal. It is the most widely supported theme engine for Drupal and is compatible with Drupal 4.6 and up. With Drupal 6, PHPTemplate has taken a step forward in evolution and is now very closely integrated with the Drupal core. Indeed, according to the Drupal.org site, "the job now of PHPTemplate is to only discover theme functions and templates on behalf of the theme. It is less of an engine and more of a theme helper."

One of the most significant changes in Drupal 6 was a change in the way the default template files are distributed. Previously, a limited number of default templates were located directly inside the `engines` directory, but in Drupal 6, all those files have been removed. Default template files are now more numerous and are located throughout the distribution, more closely associated with the modules and other functionalities that they affect.

The primary PHPTemplate engine file is located on the server in the directory `themes/engines/phptemplate`; default templates are scattered throughout the distro (see, Chapter 4 for a complete list). Additional templates and theme-related files appear in the theme directory of each individual PHPTemplate-enabled theme.

[PHPTemplate files follow a naming convention ending with the file extension `.tpl.php`. For example: `block.tpl.php`, `comment.tpl.php`, `node.tpl.php`, `page.tpl.php`.]

How Does It Work?

A theme engine helps separate the tasks of the programmer from the tasks of the designer. As a tool, PHPTemplate makes it possible for web programmers to work on the business logic of an installation without having to worry too much about the presentation of the content. In contrast, web designers can focus entirely on the styling of discrete bits of content and items comprising the layout and the interface. Developers and designers can divide their tasks and optimize their work.

By comparison, other approaches to Drupal theming exhibit less flexibility. While themes can be created directly in PHP without the use of a theme engine, those pure PHP themes are difficult for people less fluent in the PHP programming language. Pure PHP themes are hard to decipher, more difficult to code, and awkward to preview.

Building themes with a theme engine represents a more manageable way of handling dynamic web applications. Every PHPTemplate theme file contains an HTML skeleton together with some simple PHP statements that include the dynamic data. The theme files are linked to the CSS files, allowing the dynamic data to be styled and formatted with ease. Moreover, PHPTemplate gives multiple options for styling your website: use simple CSS, work with themable functions, or create dedicated template files.

The theme engine works in conjunction with the default templates and functions with the theme-specific template files and function overrides (if any) to produce the output that the end user sees on the screen. The PHPtemplate theme engine file can be found in the PHPTemplate directory on the server (`themes/engines/phptemplate`). Default templates and functions are located throughout the system. The theme-specific elements are located in the active theme's directory.

PHPTemplate theme files are written in PHP and contain a series of includes and conditional statements designed to detect the presence of elements that must be added into the final output. The includes and conditional statements relate to things like the content of the site title, the presence and location of a logo file, the number of active regions, boxes, and so on. Whether a statement is satisfied and the content is displayed is often the product of decisions made by the site administrator in the process of configuring the site and during the creation of content and functionality. The good news here is that much of the code you will see in a template file is very basic and relates purely to the formatting—CSS styling and simple HTML.

The key file in any PHPTemplate theme is `page.tpl.php`. The `page.tpl.php` file is one of only two required files (the other being the `.info` file). The file contains all the key attributes needed for PHPTemplate to display a Drupal theme.

For example, the segment of code below shows the head of a typical `page.tpl.php` file.

```
<head>
  <title>
    <?php print $head_title; ?>
  </title>
    <?php print $head; ?>

    <?php print $styles; ?>

    <?php print $scripts; ?>

</head>
```

The highlighted lines, above, show the include statements in action; in this case, calling into the template file a variety of information including: the page title (`$head_title`), the head information (`$head`), the stylesheets (`$styles`), and any necessary scripts (`$scripts`).

The example below shows a typical application of a conditional statement, again from inside the `page.tpl.php` file:

```
<?php if ($site_slogan);?>
<div id="site-slogan">
<?php print $site_slogan; ?>
</div>
<?php endif; ?>
```

In this segment, you see a conditional statement testing whether the `$site_slogan` returns as true (it exists) and if so, it displays the site slogan (`print $site_slogan`).

You will also note that the site slogan is wrapped by a `div` with an `id` of `site-slogan`. This is our first taste of how CSS integrates with the templates to control the presentation on the screen.

The example code, above, dealt with Drupal's site slogan function. Whether the site slogan is displayed is determined by a parameter specified by the administrator in the theme configuration manager (discussed in Chapter 2). The slogan text is set by the administrator in the site information manager. This parameter's value is stored in the database of your Drupal site.

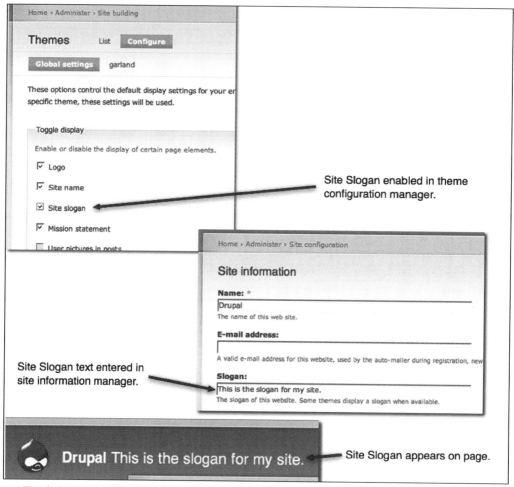

The choices made by the administrator are stored in the database as `$site_slogan` with the value: This is the slogan for my site. `$site_slogan` is then displayed courtesy of a conditional statement in the `page.tpl.php` file.

Putting it all together, it works like this:

1. `page.tpl.php` looks in the database for a string named `$site_slogan`.
2. If there is a value for `$site_slogan`, then that value prints on the screen.
3. The user's browser applies to the resulting site slogan, the styling specified by the `div` with the `id` "site-slogan".

The `div` styling in this case is located in the file `style.css`, which is also included in the specific theme's directory. Note also that `style.css` is present courtesy of the actions of the PHPTemplate. The stylesheets are designated by the `.info` file and included via the statement:

```
<?php print $styles; ?>
```

which appears in the head of the `page.tpl.php` file, as was shown in the previous example.

In summary, a complete Drupal theme consists of a number of template files that are combined at run time to present a coherent web page. The exact number of templates involved and the nature of their contents will vary from theme to theme. The output of the template files is styled by the CSS included with the theme.

Getting Started with PHPTemplate

Let's take a look at the key files involved in a PHPTemplate theme: the `.info` file and the `page.tpl.php` file. To illustrate how they work, we will then look at how two different themes approach their implementation with PHPTemplate.

The Role of the .info File

The `.info` file is required, as of Drupal 6. This file has a configuration function and syntax similar to a `.ini` file.

.info files are discussed at length in Chapter 7, but to give you a sample of what is happening, here is the bluemarine.info file, which accompanies the Bluemarine theme.

```
; $Id: bluemarine.info,v 1.4 2007/06/08 05:50:57 dries Exp $
name = Bluemarine
description = Table-based multi-column theme with a marine and ash
color scheme.
version = VERSION
core = 6.x
engine = phptemplate
; Information added by drupal.org packaging script on 2008-07-09
version = "6.3"
project = "drupal"
datestamp = "1215640509"
```

Note how the file addresses basic configuration issues: the theme's name, description, version and compatibility info, and what theme engine is required.

> To learn more about .info file, visit the Drupal site at
> http://drupal.org/node/171205

The Role of the page.tpl.php File

The page.tpl.php file, located inside the individual theme directory, plays a critical role in any PHPTemplate theme. You can build a PHPTemplate theme with just a .info file and a page.tpl.php file, if you so wish. Some themes use only the basic page.tpl.php file, together with creative use of CSS, to achieve the look and functions the developer desires. Other themes contain a wide variety of additional optional template files that style specific content or screen space, like the comments on a page, or the blocks placeholder.

> Where alternative templates are not specified, the default Drupal templates files are applied. The default templates provide the most basic level of formatting necessary for the styling of various page elements, and are supplemented by the stylesheets. In some cases, you may find that you can achieve the customizations you require by working only with the stylesheets that affect these default templates—without having to create your own template overrides.

Let's look at the `page.tpl.php` file from Drupal's Bluemarine theme and then examine the functional elements:

```php
<?php
// $Id: page.tpl.php,v 1.28 2008/01/24 09:42:52 goba Exp $
?><!DOCTYPE html PUBLIC "-//W3C//DTD XHTML 1.0 Strict//EN" "http://
www.w3.org/TR/xhtml1/DTD/xhtml1-strict.dtd">
<html xmlns="http://www.w3.org/1999/xhtml" lang="<?php print
$language->language ?>" xml:lang="<?php print $language->language ?>"
dir="<?php print $language->dir ?>">

<head>
  <title><?php print $head_title ?></title>
  <?php print $head ?>
  <?php print $styles ?>
  <?php print $scripts ?>
  <script type="text/javascript"><?php /* Needed to avoid Flash of
Unstyle Content in IE */ ?> </script>
</head>

<body>

<table border="0" cellpadding="0" cellspacing="0" id="header">
  <tr>
    <td id="logo">
      <?php if ($logo) { ?><a href="<?php print $front_page ?>"
title="<?php print t('Home') ?>"><img src="<?php print $logo ?>"
alt="<?php print t('Home') ?>" /></a><?php } ?>
      <?php if ($site_name) { ?><h1 class='site-name'><a href="<?php
print $front_page ?>" title="<?php print t('Home') ?>"><?php print
$site_name ?></a></h1><?php } ?>
      <?php if ($site_slogan) { ?><div class='site-slogan'><?php print
$site_slogan ?></div><?php } ?>
    </td>
    <td id="menu">
      <?php if (isset($secondary_links)) { ?><?php print
theme('links', $secondary_links, array('class' => 'links', 'id' =>
'subnavlist')) ?><?php } ?>
      <?php if (isset($primary_links)) { ?><?php print theme('links',
$primary_links, array('class' => 'links', 'id' => 'navlist')) ?><?php
} ?>
      <?php print $search_box ?>
    </td>
  </tr>
  <tr>
    <td colspan="2"><div><?php print $header ?></div></td>
  </tr>
</table>

<table border="0" cellpadding="0" cellspacing="0" id="content">
```

```
<tr>
  <?php if ($left) { ?><td id="sidebar-left">
    <?php print $left ?>
  </td><?php } ?>
  <td valign="top">
    <?php if ($mission) { ?><div id="mission"><?php print $mission
?></div><?php } ?>
    <div id="main">
      <?php print $breadcrumb ?>
      <h1 class="title"><?php print $title ?></h1>
      <div class="tabs"><?php print $tabs ?></div>
      <?php if ($show_messages) { print $messages; } ?>
      <?php print $help ?>
      <?php print $content; ?>
      <?php print $feed_icons; ?>
    </div>
  </td>
  <?php if ($right) { ?><td id="sidebar-right">
    <?php print $right ?>
  </td><?php } ?>
</tr>
</table>

<div id="footer">
  <?php print $footer_message ?>
  <?php print $footer ?>
</div>
<?php print $closure ?>
</body>
</html>
```

Let's break down this template file, and look at it in bite-sized functional units (we'll leave the CSS until next chapter).

The code below creates the head of the resulting page. The PHP statements, in this excerpt, include the page title and the various bits of head data, including the metadata, the stylesheets, and the scripts:

```
<head>
  <title><?php print $head_title ?></title>
  <?php print $head ?>
  <?php print $styles ?>
  <?php print $scripts ?>
  <script type="text/javascript"><?php /* Needed to avoid Flash of
Unstyle Content in IE */ ?> </script>
</head>
```

This next excerpt begins just inside the beginning of the body of the page. The PHP statements here are all conditional—they will only produce output visible to the viewer when the conditions are true. This section includes a number of the optional items controlled by the site administrator, such as the search box, the logo, the site name, and the site slogan. If the administrator has not enabled any of these items, they will not be displayed on the page:

```
        <?php if ($logo) { ?><a href="<?php print $front_page ?>"
title="<?php print t('Home') ?>"><img src="<?php print $logo ?>"
alt="<?php print t('Home') ?>" /></a><?php } ?>
        <?php if ($site_name) { ?><h1 class='site-name'><a href="<?php
print $front_page ?>" title="<?php print t('Home') ?>"><?php print
$site_name ?></a></h1><?php } ?>
        <?php if ($site_slogan) { ?><div class='site-slogan'><?php print
$site_slogan ?></div><?php } ?>
```

The following lines relate to the display of the primary and secondary links:

```
        <?php if (isset($secondary_links)) { ?><?php print
theme('links', $secondary_links, array('class' => 'links', 'id' =>
'subnavlist')) ?><?php } ?>
        <?php if (isset($primary_links)) { ?><?php print theme('links',
$primary_links, array('class' => 'links', 'id' => 'navlist')) ?><?php
} ?>
```

The template file also prints on the screen the various regions that will be active in this theme. In the order in which they appear are the following regions: header, left sidebar content, right sidebar, and footer regions. The statements that place them on the page appear as below:

```
        <?php print $header ?>
        <?php print $left ?>
        <?php print $content; ?>
        <?php print $right ?>
        <?php print $footer ?>
```

 In later chapters, we will look at how to enable these regions and make them eligible for block assignment.

Note how this theme uses a conditional statement to place the columns on each side of the page. First, the left sidebar region:

```
        <?php if ($left) { ?><td id="sidebar-left">
          <?php print $left ?>
        </td><?php } ?>
```

Then the right sidebar region:

```
<?php if ($right) { ?><td id="sidebar-right">
  <?php print $right ?>
</td><?php } ?>
```

The use of the conditional statement means that the sidebar columns will only display if something is assigned to the sidebar region. If nothing is assigned, then the column neatly collapses and disappears from view. In later chapters, we'll examine the CSS needed to implement this technique smoothly.

Two Contrasting Examples

As you can probably see, PHPTemplate presents a number of options that can be used to support the creation of themes. You can almost literally do as much or as little as you like.

A look at the range of techniques used by the themes in the market shows a wide variety of approaches to theming. Some themes, like the Bluemarine theme, keep it simple and implement only a few templates. Other themes, like Garland, are more complex, and include a wide range of optional templates, stylesheets and subthemes. You can even find themes that employ only the `page.tpl.php` file with no additional templates.

A Basic PHPTemplate Theme—Bluemarine

The Bluemarine theme, in contrast to Garland, shows the relatively direct and basic approach to the creation of a PHPTemplate theme. If you check the `themes/bluemarine` directory on the server, you will find the following files:

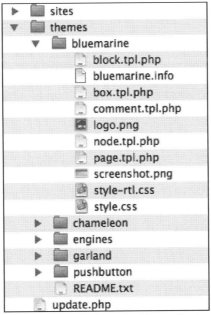

The contents of the Bluemarine theme directory.

Notice that the author of Bluemarine has chosen to create his theme using only a basic selection of common templates: the required `page.tpl.php` file, as well as the box, block, comment, and node templates. There is also a bare minimum of stylesheets: the basic `style.css` file and an alternative file that will be used if the site uses a language that needs to be read from right-to-left (`style-rtl.css`).

The files `block.tpl.php`, `box.tpl.php`, `comment.tpl.php`, and `node.tpl.php` are alternative versions of default templates included in the core. The system will give precedence to the template files in the theme directory over the default versions of the templates. Accordingly, the block, comment, and node elements will be handled by the alternative files in the theme directory, while other elements are still governed by the default templates located in the core. Put another way, the author of the Bluemarine theme is intercepting and overriding templates, a technique we shall explore in detail in this book.

The Drupal system will give precedence to files located in the `theme` directory. If the `theme` directory contains a version of one of the default template files, the version in the theme will be used in place of the original version. By taking advantage of the feature of the Drupal system, we are able to easily intercept and override default templates and functions.

A More Complex PHPTemplate Theme—Garland

By comparison, Garland shows a more complex approach to the creation of a PHPTemplate theme. If you check the `themes/garland` directory on the server, you will find the following files:

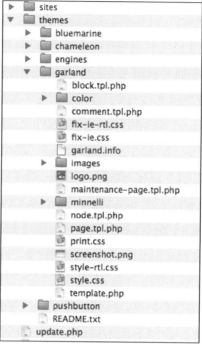

Note here that the theme developer has included not only the required `page.tpl.php` file, but has also included his own version of the `maintenance-page.tpl.php` file, a `template.php` file, an alternative `.css` files, and a subtheme.

The Garland theme developer has provided the basic `page.tpl.php` file, in addition to the following optional templates:

- `block.tpl.php`
- `comment.tpl.php`
- `node.tpl.php`
- `maintenance-page.tpl.php`

The Garland theme modifies only a few of the many default templates distributed with Drupal. A list of all the system's templates and themeable functions is included in the Chapter 4.

The author of this theme also provides us with examples of two other powerful Drupal theming techniques. First, the author has created a new template to handle a specific type of page. Note the presence of the file `maintenance-page.tpl.php`; the author has created this file to handle the site's maintenance page. Second, the author has included the file `template.php`. As you will see in later chapters, the `template.php` file is used to hold overrides to themable functions in the Drupal system.

[Overrides to one or more of the system's themable functions are usually placed in the `template.php` file.]

The second theming technique employed by the author is the creation of a subtheme. Note the presence of the subdirectory named `minnelli`.

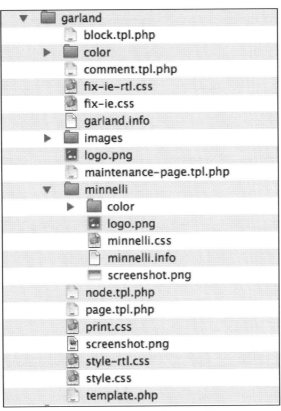

The Minnelli directory is nested inside the Garland directory. The presence of the `minnelli.info` file tells you this is subtheme.

The `Minnelli` directory contains a `.info` file—all that is needed to set up a subtheme. The `.info` file tells the Drupal system that the contents of this directory should be treated as a distinct theme. Subthemes inherit their parent theme's resources (including stylesheets, JavaScripts, template files, and theme function overrides). The author of this theme has added an additional `.css` (`minnelli.css`) file to create a customized version of the original theme.

Subtheming is a powerful technique that allows you to create something unique, without having to start from scratch. Subthemes can provide simple variations on the base theme, like we see in Garland/Minnelli, or themes that are very different than their parent. In the latter case, a developer may elect to create a subtheme as a way to fast track the creation of a new theme. By employing the templates and other assets of the base theme, the developer can save a great deal of time.

 Subtheming also presents interesting opportunities for creating multiple themes for a single site; design resources can be shared across the site to make editing easier, and your work more efficient.

Alternative Theme Engines

While previous Drupal releases offered a number of theme engine options, not all of the alternative engines were yet compatible with Drupal 6. Engines that functioned with the 5.x series are not compatible with the 6.x series.

PHPTAL

PHPTAL is a PHP implementation of the ZPT system. ZPT stands for Zope Page Templates. ZPT is an HTML/XML generation tool created for use in the Zope project (`http://www.zope.org`). ZPT employs TAL (Tag Attribute Language) to create dynamic templates. Visit the Zope site to learn more about the origins of the system, and how it all works.

TAL is attractive for several reasons. TAL statements come from XML attributes in the TAL namespace that allow you to apply TAL to an XML or plain old HTML document and enable it to function as a template. TAL generates pure, valid XHTML and the resulting template files tend to be clean and easier to read than those created with many other theme engines. One of the biggest advantages, however, is that TAL templates can be manipulated using a standard WYSIWYG HTML/XML editor and previewed in your browser, making the design-work on your theme a relatively easier task.

There are several minor drawbacks to PHPTAL. For purists, it is one level of abstraction further away from PHP, and therefore, performs a bit slower than PHPTemplate (though this difference is unlikely to be noticed by anyone and can be overcome by proper caching). Second, installation of PHPTAL requires Pear5 and PHP5 on your server. If you lack either of these, you should explore other alternatives.

 Download PHPTAL for Drupal 6.x at `http://drupal.org/project/ phptal`. The Drupal extension includes a variety of extras including at least one PHPTAL theme. You can get the most current PHPTAL snapshot, as well as supporting documentation, from `http://phptal. sourceforge.net/`

Smarty

The Smarty theme engine allows you to create themes using the Smarty syntax. This popular theme engine is widely used and there are a number of pre-existing themes that are based on Smarty.

Smarty is a mature system and there exists a number of resources to help you learn Smarty's syntax and conventions. Though the system implements another scripting language inside the Drupal system (the Smarty tags), it performs very well. Smarty parses the template files at run time and does not recompile unless the template files change. Smarty also includes a built-in caching system to help you fine tune performance even further. There are also a variety of plug-ins available, which allow you to extend Smarty's feature set.

 Download Smarty for Drupal 6.x at `http://drupal.org/project/ smarty`. Smarty's homepage and the most current version of the files can be found at `http://download.berlios.de/drupal-smarty/ smarty-4.6.0+libs_rel2.tar.gz`

PHP XTemplate

PHP XTemplate was once the default theme engine in Drupal but has fallen by the wayside as development of the application slowed. For many users, XTemplate was a popular system. It separates the HTML from the PHP and makes it easy for designers to work with themes. Also, as it is written in PHP and can handle either PHP4 or PHP5, it tends to perform well with Drupal.

Unfortunately, at this stage, it seems unlikely to be making a comeback in the near future, and those of you who previously enjoyed using this system should consider alternatives. XTemplate is also released under a different license than Drupal, which may present issues for some users.

Download PHP XTemplate for Drupal 4.7.x at `http://drupal.org/project/xtemplate`. You can visit the project's new homepage at `http://www.phpxtemplate.org`.

Installing Additional Theme Engines

Additional theme engines can be installed easily. After obtaining the theme engine files, access your server, and create a new directory inside of `sites/all/themes`. Name the new directory `engines` and place the theme engine directory inside. Your new theme engine should, in other words, exist inside `sites/all/themes/engines`.

Summary

In this chapter, we've looked in depth at the default PHPTemplate theme engine. You should now have an awareness of the key files involved in a PHPTemplate theme and some appreciation of how those files interact. The discussion of the order of precedence among various theme files lays down a fundamental principle. You have seen examples of how to override default theme files by placing alternative template and CSS files inside the theme directory.

In this chapter, we also spoke about alternative theme engines and how to add them to your system.

4

Identifying Templates, Stylesheets, and Themable Functions

The output of the Drupal system is subject to formatting via three primary elements: templates, stylesheets, and themable functions. These various elements are scattered throughout the Drupal distribution and may not, at first glance, be obvious. Accordingly, one of the most important keys to the success of your theming efforts is the ability to identify and locate the elements that impact the appearance. In this chapter, we'll take you on a guided tour of all the system's various templates, stylesheets, and themable functions, as a precursor to learning how to intercept and override these elements in later chapters.

Putting Together the Pieces—Templates, Stylesheets, and Functions

The inclusion of a wide variety of default templates within the Drupal core was one of the big changes in Drupal 6. However, templates are only one piece of the picture—or if you prefer, only one tool in your toolkit. To have the fullest control over your site's look and feel, you need to be fluent with the system's many stylesheets and themable functions.

Taken together, templates, stylesheets, and themable functions provide everything the vast majority of people will need to customize a site to their needs. It is important to note that you are not restricted by these pre-existing elements, as you can modify them extensively, for example, by adding variables to existing templates or by adding new selectors to a themable function.

As you theme your site, it is likely that you will use a combination of the elements to achieve the result you desire. If you are working with an existing theme, you may only modify the stylesheets to change the styling, or you may need to override a default template with a customized version of your own. Alternatively, you may want to go further and dig into the themable functions to address specific needs. You can do all these things (and more!) by using the elements discussed in this chapter.

Default Templates and Variables

The default templates included in Drupal 6 address many of the most common needs. Among the most powerful templates are the block and page templates, but there are many other templates located within the directories of the various modules they impact. The templates are a welcome improvement in the system as they save a great deal of time and remove quite a bit of complexity from the theme customization process.

The templates provide you with a quick and easy starting place for common customizations. If you wish to change one, simply copy it into your theme directory and modify it as needed. Modifications can be simple, such as changing selectors, or more complex, such as adding new variables to the template.

[Overriding templates is discussed in detail in the next chapter.]

In the section below, we identify the templates associated with each functionality, describe their purpose, and list the variables available to that template. Note that, in addition to the template-specific variables outlined in each section, below, there exists a set of default variables that are available for all templates in the system.

The default variables available for all templates are:

Variable	Description
$db_is_active	Returns as True when the database is running. This is provided for use in theming in maintenance mode.
$directory	The theme's path, relative to the base Drupal installation.
$id	Provides an ID for the template.
$is_admin	Returns True when the visitor is a site administrator.
$is_front	Returns True when viewing the front page.
$logged_in	Returns True when the visitor is logged in and authenticated.

Variable	Description
$user	Contains data on the user.
$zebra	Provides an "odd/even" marker for templates. Alternates each time the template is used.

Default Stylesheets

The default Drupal installation includes a mind-boggling assortment of stylesheets. If you have installed additional extensions, you may well find that they come with their own stylesheets, increasing the confusion factor even more.

While the Drupal approach to stylesheets may initially appear to be overkill in the extreme, or at the very least a rather literal application of modularization, there is a method behind the apparent madness. The use of multiple stylesheets not only makes it easier to maintain individual modules, but also helps you find what you need more quickly than having to deal with one or two massive files. The net result of the approach is actually quite effective—that is, once you come to grips with the mass of stylesheets lurking in your system!

 In order to reduce the potential threats of conflicting stylesheets and absurd loading times, Drupal provides a CSS pre-processing engine. This engine identifies the required stylesheets, strips out the line breaks and spaces from all the files, and delivers the styles in a combined single file. The use of this feature is disabled by default; if you wish to use it, you must access **Administer | Site configuration | Performance** and enable the option labeled **Optimize CSS** files.

 While working on the themes of your Drupal site, you should make sure the CSS compression is disabled. If the compression is enabled, you may not be able to immediately see the impact of changes to your site's CSS.

In the section below, we list the default Drupal stylesheets, where they are found, and briefly explain their functions. The contents of each of the stylesheets are detailed in the Stylesheet Map included as Appendix A.

The Themable Functions

Drupal 6 relies less on themable functions than previous versions, yet they still play a key role in theming. A large number of themable functions remain in the system and as you will see below, they relate to a wide variety of functionality.

The default Drupal system does not provide an automated tool for the identification of the various themable functions in Drupal. You can, however, identify them by their names; all themable functions employ a consistent naming convention. Themable functions use the prefix `theme_`. The naming convention makes it possible to work your way through the various files to isolate all the functions. You can search for them easily by setting up Dreamweaver (or a similar program) to do the searching for you. Better still, you can employ the Theme Developer tools in the Devel module to help you identify themable functions.

The Devel extension, and other useful theming tools, are explained in more detail in Appendix B, The Themers' Toolkit. The Devel module can be downloaded at: `http://drupal.org/project/devel`

A Guide to Theming Elements

With the large assortment of templates, stylesheets and themable functions available to you in the default Drupal distro, finding exactly what you need can sometimes be a bit of a challenge. In an effort to simplify the process of isolating relevant theming elements, we present in the pages that follow a list of the elements organized relative to the functionality they affect.

Common Theme System Functions

The `theme.inc` file controls the Drupal theme system. In addition to the initializing of loading the theme system, the file contains a number of themable functions that relate specifically to various key elements in Drupal. The functions can be found in two files: `includes/theme.inc` and `includes/theme.maintenance.inc`.

Here is a table of the functions and a description of each one:

Function	Path	Description
theme_box	includes/theme.inc	Creates a themed box (container).
theme_breadcrumb	includes/theme.inc	Handles the breadcrumb trail.
theme_closure	includes/theme.inc	Formats the `hook_footer()` at the end of the page.
theme_feed_icon	includes/theme.inc	Enables a feed icon.
theme_image	includes/theme.inc	Themes an image.
theme_indentation	includes/theme.inc	Provides a div for standardizing indentation.
theme_item_list	includes/theme.inc	Returns a themed list of items.

Function	Path	Description
theme_links	includes/theme.inc	Styles a list of links (such as primary and secondary links).
theme_mark	includes/theme.inc	Returns a themed marker for content (spell out, new, updated).
theme_more_help_link	includes/theme.inc	Produces the more help link.
theme_more_link	includes/theme.inc	Produces the more link seen in blocks.
theme_placeholder	includes/theme.inc	Formats text for display in a placeholder.
theme_progress_bar	includes/theme.inc	Displays the percentage complete progress bar.
theme_status_ messages	includes/theme.inc	Formats status and error messages.
theme_table	includes/theme.inc	Formats a table.
theme_table_select_ header_cell	includes/theme.inc	Controls the header cell of tables that have a select-all functionality.
theme_tablesort_ indicator	includes/theme.inc	Produces the sort icon.
theme_task_list	includes/theme. maintenance.inc	Formats the list of maintenance tasks.
theme_username	includes/theme.inc	Formats the user name.
theme_xml_icon	includes/theme.inc	Generates an XML icon.

Theming the Aggregator Module

The aggregator module provides a variety of functions related to the aggregation and display of syndicated content feeds (spell out, RSS, RDF, and Atom).

Default Templates

Theming the aggregator module is made easier in Drupal 6 through the addition of several dedicated template files:

- aggregator-feed-source.tpl.php
- aggregator-item.tpl.php
- aggregator-summary-item.tpl.php
- aggregator-summary-items.tpl.php
- aggregator-wrapper.tpl.php

The default templates are located at modules/aggregator/

aggregator-feed-source.tpl.php

Provides a template for formatting the source of a feed. When a user is browsing the feed, they will see the output above the feed listings. The available variables include:

Variable	Description
$last_checked	When the feed was last checked (locally).
$source_description	The description text—from the source of the feed.
$source_icon	This is the feed's icon—from the source of the feed.
$source_image	The image associated with the feed—from the source of the feed.
$source_url	The URL to the source of the feed.

aggregator-item.tpl.php

Format an individual feed item. The available variables include:

Variable	Description
$categories	Categories assigned to the feed.
$content	The content of the individual feed item.
$feed_title	The title of the feed item—from the source of the feed.
$feed_url	The URL of the feed item—from the source of the feed.
$source_date	The date of the item—from the source of the feed.
$source_title	The title of the provider of the feed—from the source of the feed.
$source_url	The URL to the source of the feed.

aggregator-summary-item.tpl.php

Theme a linked feed item for summaries. The available variables include:

Variable	Description
$feed_age	The age of the remote feed.
$feed_title	The title of the feed item—from the source of the feed.
$feed_url	The URL of the feed item—from the source of the feed.
$source_title	The title of the provider of the feed—from the source of the feed.
$source_url	The URL to the source of the feed.

aggregator-summary-items.tpl.php

Themes a presentation of feeds as list items. The available variables include:

Variable	Description
$summary_list	The unordered list of feed items.
$source_url	The URL to the local source (or category).
$title	The title of the feed (or category).

aggregator-wrapper.tpl.php

Wraps aggregator content. The available variables include:

Variable	Description
$content	The entire aggregator contents.
$page	Pagination links.

Default Stylesheets

Two stylesheets are dedicated to the formatting of the aggregator modules. Both are located at /modules/aggregator

File	Description
aggregator.css	Affects the RSS/Newsfeed Aggregator Module and its contents.
aggregator-rtl.css	A stylesheet that is used when the site employs right-to-left text orientation.

Themable Functions

There are a number of themable functions that relate to the aggregator. The functions can be found in two files: modules/aggregator/aggregator.module and modules/aggregator/aggregator.pages.inc.

Function	Path	Description
theme_aggregator_block_item	modules/aggregator/aggregator.module	Formats an individual feed item displayed in a block.
theme_aggregator_page_opml	modules/aggregator/aggregator.pages.inc	Allows you to theme the output of the OPML feed.
theme_aggregator_page_rss	modules/aggregator/aggregator.pages.inc	Allows you to theme the output of the RSS feed.

Theming the Block Module

The block module provides the mechanism for managing the blocks on the page.

Default Templates

The system includes only two template files dedicated to blocks:

- `block.tpl.php`
- `block-admin-display-form.tpl.php`

The `block.tpl.php` template can be found at `modules/system/`

The `block-admin-display-form.tpl.php` template can be found at `modules/block/`

block.tpl.php

This is the key template for formatting blocks. The available variables include:

Variable	Description
`$block->content`	The block content.
`$block->delta`	The numeric ID associated with the module.
`$block->module`	The module that generated the block.
`$block->region`	The region that contains the block.
`$block->subject`	The block title.
`$block_id`	ID unique to the block in the region.
`$block_zebra`	Provides an "odd/even" marker for block. Alternates for each block used within a region.
`$id`	Similar to `$block_id` but not dependent upon the region.
`$is_admin`	Returns True if user is an administrator.
`$is_front`	Returns True if user is viewing the front page.
`$logged_in`	Returns True if user is logged in and authenticated.
`$zebra`	Provides an "odd/even" marker for block but is not region dependent.

block-admin-display-form.tpl.php

The template controls the admin system's block configuration interface. The available variables include:

Variable	Description
$block_listing	An array of blocks keyed to region and delta.
$block_regions	The title of the region of the block.
$form_submit	The submit form button.
$throttle	Flag indicating whether the throttle option is selected.

Default Stylesheets

There is one stylesheet dedicated to the block module. It is located at:
/modules/block

File	Description
block.css	Provides basic selectors for the styling of the block management admin interface.

Themable Functions

The key themable function for blocks is located at includes/theme.inc.

Function	Path	Description
theme_blocks	includes/theme.inc	Controls output of all Blocks in a particular region.

Theming the Book Functionality

The book functionality creates a node that allows users to collaboratively author a work. The book module provides the functions that impact book content and output.

Default Templates

The default system includes four default template files dedicated to the book functionality.

- book-all-books-block.tpl.php
- book-export-html.tpl.php
- book-navigation.tpl.php
- book-node-export-html.tpl.php

The templates can be found at modules/book/

book-all-books-block.tpl.php

This template renders book outlines within a block. The available variables include:

Variable	Description
$book_menus	An array of the book outline. Presented as an unordered list.

book-export-html.tpl.php

This template handles the printed version of the book outline. The available variables include:

Variable	Description
$base_url	The URL to the homepage.
$content	The nodes within the book outline.
$head	The header tags.
$language	The code indicating the language used.
$language_rtl	Returns True when the site uses right-to-left text orientation.
$title	The node's title.

book-navigation.tpl.php

Provides a template for formatting the navigation associated with a book node. The available variables include:

Variable	Description
$book_id	The ID of the current book being viewed.
$book_title	The title of the current book being viewed.
$book_url	The URL of the current book being viewed.
$current_depth	The current node's depth inside the outline.
$has_links	Returns True whenever the parent, previous or next function has a value.
$next_title	The title of the next node.
$next_url	The URL of the next node.
$parent_title	The title of the parent node.
$parent_url	The URL of the parent node.
$prev_title	The title of the previous node.
$prev_url	The URL of the previous node.
$tree	The children of the current node, rendered as an unordered list.

book-node-export-html.tpl.php

Provides a template for formatting a printer-friendly version of the node. The available variables include:

Variable	Description
$children	All the child nodes associated.
$content	The content of the node.
$depth	The current node's depth inside the outline.
$title	The title of the node.

Default Stylesheets

Two stylesheets are dedicated to the formatting of books. Both are located at /modules/book

File	Description
book.css	Controls the formatting of Book node content.
book-rtl.css	A stylesheet that is used when the site employs right-to-left text orientation.

Themable Functions

There are only two themable functions that relate to books. The functions can be found in two locations: modules/book/book.module and modules/book/book. admin.inc

Function	Path	Description
theme_book_ admin_table	modules/book/book.admin.inc	Themes the book administration page.
theme_book_ title_link	modules/book/book.module	Provides the HTML output for the link to the book title, when it is used as a block title.

Theming the Color Module

The color module provides the color change functionality seen in the theme configuration manager of some themes.

Default Templates

There are no default templates provided for the color module.

Default Stylesheets

Two stylesheets are dedicated to the color module. Both are located at `/modules/color`

File	Description
color.css	Controls the color module used with some themes.
color-rtl.css	A stylesheet that is used when the site employs right-to-left text orientation.

Themable Functions

There is only one themable function associated with the color module.

Function	Path	Description
theme_color_ scheme_form	modules/color/color. module	Controls formatting of the Color Module form.

Theming the Comment Functionality

The comment functionality allows users to add comments to published content.

Default Templates

Theming the comments is made easier in Drupal 6 through the addition of three dedicated template files:

- comment-folded.tpl.php
- comment-wrapper.tpl.php
- comment.tpl.php

The default templates are located at `modules/comment/`

comment-folded.tpl.php

Provides a template for formatting the comments in folded view. The available variables include:

Variable	Description
$author	The name of the author of the comment.
$comment	The full comment.
$date	The date and time the comment was posted.
$new	Designates a new comment.
$title	The title of the comment, with link to the full comment body.

comment-wrapper.tpl.php

This template is used to wrap all the comments. It is a container that controls the overall formatting of the comment area. The available variables include:

Variable	Description
$content	Handles all the comments for a particular page.

comment.tpl.php

This is the primary template for controlling the appearance of a comment. The available variables include:

Variable	Description
$author	The name of the author of the comment.
$content	The main body of the comment.
$date	The date and time the comment was posted.
$links	The links associated with the functionality.
$new	A marker that indicates a new comment.
$picture	The author's picture.
$signature	The author's signature.
$status	The status of the comment (i.e., published, unpublished, etc.)
$submitted	**Submitted by** text with date and time.
$title	The title of the comment, linked to the comment body.

Default Stylesheets

Two stylesheets are dedicated to the formatting of the comments. Both are located at `/modules/comment`

File	Description
comment.css	This is a very limited stylesheet that essentially only provides the indent style for comments.
comment-rtl.css	A stylesheet that is used when the site employs right-to-left text orientation.

Themable Functions

There are a number of themable functions that relate to the comment functionality. The functions can be found in two files: `modules/comment/comment.module` and `modules/comment/comment.admin.inc`

Function	Path	Description
`theme_comment_admin_ overview`	`modules/comment/ comment.admin.inc`	Formats the admin comment form.
`theme_comment_block`	`modules/comment/ comment.module`	Formats the list of recent comments displayed within a block.
`theme_comment_controls`	`modules/comment/ comment.module`	Formats the controls that provide the comment display options.
`theme_comment_flat_ collapsed`	`modules/comment/ comment.module`	Produces comment in flat collapsed view.
`theme_comment_flat_ expanded`	`modules/comment/ comment.module`	Produces comment in flat expanded view.
`theme_comment_post_ forbidden`	`modules/comment/ comment.module`	Controls the **you can't post comments** function.
`theme_comment_submitted`	`modules/comment/ comment.module`	Formats the **Submitted by**... text.
`theme_comment_thread_ collapsed`	`modules/comment/ comment.module`	Produces comment thread in collapsed view.
`theme_comment_thread_ expanded`	`modules/comment/ comment.module`	Produces comment thread in expanded view.
`theme_comment_view`	`modules/comment/ comment.module`	Function for rendering display of a comment. Controls display of first new comment.

Theming the DBLog Module

The DBLog records system events and allows administrators to monitor their system. There is no front end functionality associated with this module, hence the theming options are limited.

 In Drupal 5.x and earlier, this module was known as Watchdog.

Default Templates

There are no default templates provided for the dblog module.

Default Stylesheets

Two stylesheets are dedicated to the formatting of the dblog. Both are located at `/modules/dblog`

File	Description
dblog.css	Provides the styles for the dblog admin interface.
dblog-rtl.css	A stylesheet that is used when the site employs right-to-left text orientation.

Themable Functions

There is only one themable function associated with the dblog module.

Function	Path	Description
theme_dblog_filters	modules/dblog/ dblog.module	Formats the filter selection interface in the admin system.

Theming the Filter Module

The filter module allows administrators to specify the text input formats for the site and filter out things that are potentially malicious or harmful. As there is no front end output from this module, the theming options are limited.

Default Templates

There are no default templates provided for the filter functionality.

Default Stylesheets

There are no stylesheets dedicated to the filter module.

Themable Functions

There are several themable functions associated with the filter module. The functions can be found in two files: `modules/filter/filter.module` and `modules/filter/filter.admin.inc`

Function	Path	Description
theme_filter_admin_order	modules/filter/ filter.admin.inc	Formats the filter order configuration form.
theme_filter_admin_overview	modules/filter/ filter.admin.inc	Themes the admin overview form for filters.
theme_filter_tips	modules/filter/ filter.pages.inc	Formats the filter tips.
theme_filter_tips_more_info	modules/filter/ filter.module	Formats the filter tips **more info** link.

Theming the Form Functionality

Handles the various forms and their elements.

Default Templates

There are no default templates provided for the form functionality.

Default Stylesheets

There are no stylesheets dedicated to the form functionality.

Themable Functions

There exist a large number of themable functions associated with forms. The functions can be found at: includes/form.inc

Function	Path	Description
theme_button	includes/form.inc	Formats a button.
theme_checkbox	includes/form.inc	Formats an individual checkbox.
theme_checkboxes	includes/form.inc	Handles a set of checkboxes.
theme_date	includes/form.inc	Formats the date selection element.
theme_fieldset	includes/form.inc	Formats a group of form items.
theme_file	includes/form.inc	Formats a file upload field.
theme_form	includes/form.inc	Provides an anonymous `<div>` for forms to help satisfy XHTML compliance requirements.

Function	Path	Description
theme_form_element	includes/form.inc	Returns a themed form element, including the **this field is required** message.
theme_hidden	includes/form.inc	Formats a hidden form field.
theme_image_button	includes/form.inc	Handles formatting of a form image button.
theme_item	includes/form.inc	Formats a form item.
theme_markup	includes/form.inc	Formats HTML markup for use in more advanced forms.
theme_password	includes/form.inc	Formats a password field.
theme_password_confirm	includes/form.inc	Formats the password confirmation item.
theme_radio	includes/form.inc	Formats a radio button.
theme_radios	includes/form.inc	Formats a set of radio buttons.
theme_select	includes/form.inc	Formats a drop-down menu or scrolling selection box.
theme_submit	includes/form.inc	Formatting of the submit button on a form.
theme_textarea	includes/form.inc	Formats a text area within a form.
theme_textfield	includes/form.inc	Formats a text field within a form.
theme_token	includes/form.inc	Assists with delivery of a themed HTML string, containing the contents of a hidden form field.

 Forms are discussed in greater length in Chapter 9.

Theming the Forum Module

The forum module handles the threaded discussion forums in Drupal. As this is a fairly complex module with a significant role on the front end of the system, it is not surprising that there are a number of options available for theming this functionality.

Default Templates

The default system includes six default template files dedicated to the forum functionality.

- `forum-icon.tpl.php`
- `forum-list.tpl.php`
- `forum-submitted.tpl.php`
- `forum-topic-list.tpl.php`
- `forum-topic-navigation.tpl.php`
- `forums.tpl.php`

The templates can be found at `modules/forum/`

forum-icon.tpl.php

Displays the icon associated with a post (e.g., new, sticky, closed, etc.). The available variables include:

Variable	Description
`$icon`	The icon to be displayed.
`$new_posts`	Indicates whether the topic includes any new posts.

forum-list.tpl.php

Template to control the display of the list of forums and containers. The available variables include:

Variable	Description
`$forum_id`	The ID of the current forum.
`$forums`	An array of forums and containers.

forum-submitted.tpl.php

This template controls the **submitted by...** information. The available variables include:

Variable	Description
`$author`	The name of the author of the post.
`$time`	When the post was made.
`$topic`	The raw post data.

forum-topic-list.tpl.php

This template displays a list of the forum topics. The available variables include:

Variable	Description
$header	The table header.
$pager	The pagination elements.
$topic_id	Numerical ID for current topic.
$topics	An array of the topics.

forum-topic-navigation.tpl.php

Displays the topic navigation at the bottom of posts. The available variables include:

Variable	Description
$next	The node ID of the next post.
$next_title	The title of the next post.
$next_url	The URL of the next post.
$node	The raw node being viewed.
$prev	The node ID of the previous post.
$prev_title	The title of the previous post.
$prev_url	The URL of the previous post.

forums.tpl.php

The template for the forum as a whole. The available variables include:

Variable	Description
$forums	The forums to be displayed.
$forums_defined	A flag to indicate whether the forum has been defined.
$links	An array of links relating to the user and posting.
$topics	The topics to be displayed.

Default Stylesheets

Two stylesheets are dedicated to the formatting of the forums. Both are located at /modules/forum

File	Description
forum.css	Affects the contents of the forum module.
forum-rtl.css	A stylesheet that is used when the site employs right-to-left text orientation.

Themable Functions

There are no additional themable functions associated with the forums.

Theming the Help Module

The help module powers the context sensitive help information, most often seen in the admin interface.

Default Templates

There are no default templates dedicated to the help functionality.

Default Stylesheets

There are two stylesheets dedicated to the help module. Both are located at `/modules/help`

File	Description
help.css	Contains two selectors to style the help function.
help-rtl.css	A stylesheet that is used when the site employs right-to-left text orientation.

Themable Functions

There is one themable function related to the help messages.

Function	Path	Description
theme_help	includes/theme.inc	Formats the help message.

Theming the Locale Functionality

The locale module enables administrators to manage a site's interface languages.

Default Templates

There are no default templates dedicated to the locale functionality.

Default Stylesheets

There is only one stylesheet dedicated to the locale module. It is located at /modules/locale

File	Description
locale.css	Provides a selector for the Locale module.

Themable Functions

There is one themable function related to the locale functionality.

Function	Path	Description
theme_locale_languages_overview_form	includes/locale.inc	Themes the locale admin manager form.

Theming the Menu Functionality

The menu module allows administrators to customize the site navigation menu.

Default Templates

There are no default templates dedicated to the menu module.

Default Stylesheets

There are no stylesheets unique to the menu module.

Themable Functions

There are a number of themable functions that relate to the menu module. The functions can be found in three locations: includes/menu.inc, module/menu/menu.admin.inc, and includes/theme.inc.

Function	Path	Description
theme_menu_item	includes/menu.inc	Formats the HTML output for a single menu item.
theme_menu_item_link	includes/menu.inc	Formats the HTML representing a particular menu item ID.
theme_menu_local_task	includes/menu.inc	Returns a single rendered local tasks.

Function	Path	Description
`theme_menu_local_tasks`	`includes/menu.inc`	Returns the rendered local tasks. The default implementation renders them as tabs.
`theme_menu_tree`	`includes/menu.inc`	Outputs the HTML for a menu tree.
`theme_menu_overview_form`	`module/menu/menu.admin.inc`	Themes the menu overview form.
`theme_submenu`	`includes/theme.inc`	Returns a themed submenu, typically, displayed under the tabs.

Theming the Node Functionality

The node module allows content to be submitted to the site, in various forms.

Default Templates

The node module provides a single dedicated template file, but it is key. This one template provides many formatting options and handles all node content:

- `modules/node/node.tpl.php`

The default templates are located at `modules/node/`

node.tpl.php

This template controls node display. This is a powerful and important template and accordingly, there are a number of variables associated with it:

Variable	Description
`$comment`	The comment settings for the node.
`$comment_count`	The number of comments tied to the node.
`$content`	The node body and/or teaser.
`$created`	The time the node was published.
`$date`	The creation date of the node.
`$id`	The position of the node.
`$is_admin`	Returns True when the current user is an administrator.
`$is_front`	Returns True when the current page is the front page.
`$links`	Themes links relative to the node (e.g., **read more**).

Variable	Description
`$logged_in`	Returns True when the current user is logged in and authenticated.
`$name`	The username of the node's author.
`$node`	The full node object.
`$node_url`	The URL of the current node.
`$page`	Flag indicating full page state.
`$picture`	The picture of the node's author.
`$promote`	Flag indicating from page promotion state.
`$readmore`	Flag indicating length of node exceeds teaser limit.
`$status`	Flag indicating published state.
`$sticky`	Flag indicating sticky state.
`$submitted`	The **submitted by...** information.
`$teaser`	Flag indicating the teaser state.
`$terms`	Themed list of the taxonomy term links.
`$title`	The node's title.
`$type`	The node type (e.g., story, blog, etc.)
`$uid`	The user ID of the node's author.
`$zebra`	Outputs odd or even identifier for node.

Default Stylesheets

Two stylesheets are dedicated to the node module. Both are located at:
`/modules/node`

File	Description
node.css	Provides selectors for nodes.
node-rtl.css	A stylesheet that is used when the site employs right-to-left text orientation.

Themable Functions

There are a number of themable functions that relate to the node functionality. The functions can be found in three files: `modules/node/node.module`, `modules/node/node.admin.inc`, and `modules/node/node.pages.inc`

Function	Path	Description
`theme_node_add_list`	`modules/node/node.pages.inc`	Displays the list of available node types.
`theme_node_admin_nodes`	`modules/node/node.admin.inc`	Formats the node administration overview.

Function	Path	Description
theme_node_filters	modules/node/node.admin.inc	Formats the node administration filter selection.
theme_node_filter_form	modules/node/node.admin.inc	Formats the node administration filter form.
theme_node_form	modules/node/node.pages.inc	The node submission form.
theme_node_list	modules/node/node.module	Formats a listing of links to nodes.
theme_node_log_message	modules/node/node.module	Styles the log message that appears during node creation and editing.
theme_node_preview	modules/node/node.pages.inc	The node preview used during content creation and editing.
theme_node_search_admin	modules/node/node.module	Renders the admin node search form.
theme_node_submitted	modules/node/node.module	Formats the **submitted by…** information for the node.

Theming the OpenID Module

The OpenID module enables authentication with the OpenID protocol.

Default Templates

There are no default templates provided for the OpenID module.

Default Stylesheets

There is one stylesheet dedicated to the OpenID module; located at:
/modules/openid

File	Description
openid.css	Provides selectors specific to authentication with the OpenID system.

Themable Functions

There are no additional themable functions associated with the OpenID module.

Theming the Pagination Functionality

The pagination (or "pager") function in Drupal handles the display of multi-paged content and the enabling navigation.

Default Templates

There are no default templates provided for the pagination function.

Default Stylesheets

There is no stylesheet dedicated to the pagination function.

Themable Functions

There are a number of themable functions that relate to the pager functionality. The functions can be at `includes/pager.inc`

Function	Path	Description
theme_pager	includes/pager.inc	Controls display of paged query results.
theme_pager_first	includes/pager.inc	Formats a **first page** link.
theme_pager_last	includes/pager.inc	Formats a **last page** link.
theme_pager_link	includes/pager.inc	Formats a link to a specific query result page.
theme_pager_next	includes/pager.inc	Formats a **next page** link.
theme_pager_previous	includes/pager.inc	Formats a **previous page** link.

Theming the Poll Module

Controls the formatting and display of the polls module, including the voting forms and the results.

Default Templates

Theming the polls module is made easier in Drupal 6 through the addition of a number of dedicated template files:

- `poll-bar-block.tpl.php`
- `poll-bar.tpl.php`
- `poll-results-block.tpl.php`
- `poll-results.tpl.php`
- `poll-vote.tpl.php`

The default templates are located at `modules/poll/`.

poll-bar-block.tpl.php

Provides a template for formatting the results bar of a single poll answer choice, applicable when poll is in block position. The available variables include:

Variable	Description
$percentage	The percentage of total votes received by this answer choice.
$title	The title of the poll.
$total_votes	The number of votes cast for this answer choice.
$vote	The current user's vote on the poll.
$voted	Returns True if the user had voted on this poll.
$votes	The total number of votes cast in the poll.

poll-bar.tpl.php

Displays the bar for a single choice in the poll. The available variables are the same as those for the template `poll-bar-block.tpl.php`, above.

poll-results.tpl.php

Provides a template for the display of poll results. The available variables include:

Variable	Description
$cancel_form	The form for a user to cancel their vote.
$links	Links in the poll.
$nid	The NID of the poll.
$raw_links	Raw array of links in the poll.
$results	The results of the poll.
$title	The title of the poll.
$vote	The current user's vote on the poll.
$votes	The total number of votes cast in the poll.

poll-results-block.tpl.php

Provides a template for the display of poll results, applicable in block position. The available variables are the same as those for `poll-results.tpl.php`

poll-vote.tpl.php

Provides a template for the voting form for a poll. The available variables include:

Variable	Description
$block	Returns True if this is being displayed in a block.
$choice	The radio buttons for voting on the choices in the poll.
$rest	A catch-all to pick up anything else that may have been added via hooks.
$title	The title of the poll.
$vote	The **vote** button.

Default Stylesheets

Two stylesheets are dedicated to the formatting of the polls module. Both are located at /modules/poll

File	Description
poll.css	Styling for Polls.
poll-rtl.css	A stylesheet that is used when the site employs right-to-left text orientation.

Themable Functions

There is only one themable function associated with the poll module.

Function	Path	Description
theme_poll_choices	modules/poll/poll. module	The admin poll form.

Theming the Profile Module

The profile module deals with the user profile pages.

Default Templates

Drupal 6 provides three dedicated template files to assist with formatting the profile functionality:

- profile-block.tpl.php
- profile-listing.tpl.php
- profile-wrapper.tpl.php

The default templates are located at modules/profile/

profile-block.tpl.php

Handles the display of a user's profile within a block. The available variables include:

Variable	Description
$picture	The image associated with the user.
$profile	Array of all profile fields that have data.

profile-listing.tpl.php

Provides a template for the user information on the member listing page. The available variables include:

Variable	Description
$name	The name of the user.
$picture	The image associated with the user.
$profile	Array of all profile fields that have data.

profile-wrapper.tpl.php

The template that is used for displaying a list of users. The available variables include:

Variable	Description
$content	The user account profiles.
$current_field	The field being browsed.

Default Stylesheets

There are no stylesheets dedicated to the profile functionality.

Themable Functions

There is only one themable function that is related to the profile functionality.

Function	Path	Description
theme_profile_admin_ overview	modules/profile/ profile.admin.inc	Themes the profile field overview.

Theming the Search Module

The search module powers the various search options for Drupal, including the theme search box, the search block, and the search form located in the main content area.

Default Templates

There are four default templates for theming the search forms:

- `search-block-form.tpl.php`
- `search-result.tpl.php`
- `search-results.tpl.php`
- `search-theme-form.tpl.php`

The default templates are located at `modules/search/`

search-block-form.tpl.php

Provides a template for displaying a search form within a block. The available variables include:

Variable	Description
`$search`	The complete search form.
`$search_form`	An array of search form elements.

search-result.tpl.php

This template renders a single search result. The available variables include:

Variable	Description
`$info`	String of all the meta information.
`$info_split`	Contains the same data as `$info`, but it is split into an array.
`$snippet`	The small preview contained in the result.
`$title`	The title of the result.
`$type`	The type of search.
`$url`	The URL of the result.

search-results.tpl.php

Provides a template for rendering the set of search results. The available variables include:

Variable	Description
$search_results	All results.
$type	The type of search.

search-theme-form.tpl.php

Provides a template for styling the theme search form. The available variables are the same as for search-theme-block.tpl.php, above.

Default Stylesheets

Two stylesheets are dedicated to the formatting of the search functionality. Both are located at /modules/search

File	Description
search.css	Styling for the Search module.
search-rtl.css	A stylesheet that is used when the site employs right-to-left text orientation.

Themable Functions

There are no additional themable functions associated with the search function.

Theming the Syslog Module

The syslog module handles the function of logging error messages.

Default Templates

There are no default templates provided for the syslog module.

Default Stylesheets

There is no stylesheet dedicated to the syslog module.

Themable Functions

There is only one themable function associated with the syslog module.

Function	Path	Description
theme_syslog_format	modules/syslog/ syslog.module	Provides the formatting for a system log entry.

Theming the System Module

The system module plays an important role in Drupal. The module provides key functionality for generating pages as well as handling the various configuration controls that help administrators modify the workings of the site.

Default Templates

The system module contains some of the most important templates in Drupal. The page and box templates are instrumental to theming your site.

- box.tpl.php
- maintenance-page.tpl.php
- page.tpl.php

The default templates are located at:modules/system/

box.tpl.php

Provides a template for creating a box around items. The available variables include:

Variable	Description
$content	The box contents.
$title	The box title.

maintenance-page.tpl.php

Provides a template for formatting the "site under maintenance" page. The available variables are the same as those applicable to the page.tpl.php file, below.

page.tpl.php

Provides an important template for controlling the output on a Drupal page. The available variables include:

Variable	Description
$base_path	The base path of the Drupal installation.
$body_classes	The CSS classes for the `<body>` tag.
$breadcrumb	The breadcrumb trail for the current page.
$closure	The closing markup for the page.
$content	The main content of the current page.
$css	An array of the CSS files for the current page.
$directory	The directory where the theme is located.
$feed_icons	A string of the feed icons relevant to the page.
$footer	The footer region.
$footer_message	The footer message set in the admin system.
$front_page	The URL of the front page.
$head	The markup for the `<head>` section.
$head_title	The page title, as used in the title metatag.
$help	The help text.
$is_admin	Returns True if user is an administrator.
$is_front	Returns True if current page is the front page.
$language	The language settings for the page.
$left	The left sidebar.
$logged_in	Returns True if user is logged in and authenticated.
$logo	The path to the logo image.
$messages	The status and error messages.
$mission	The mission statement, as defined in the admin system.
$primary_links	An array containing the primary navigation links.
$right	The right sidebar.
$scripts	Loads the JavaScript files.
$search_box	Displays the search box.
$secondary_links	An array containing the secondary navigation links.
$site_name	The name of the site, as defined in the admin system.
$site_slogan	The site slogan, as defined in the admin system.
$styles	Loads the stylesheets.
$tabs	The tabs linking to sub-pages (e.g., **edit**).
$title	The page title.

Default Stylesheets

There is a large number of stylesheets associated with the system module, however, the primary styling of the key templates discussed above is typically managed from within the `styles.css` file located in the `theme` directory. The stylesheets listed below are located at: `modules/system`

File	Description
`admin.css`	Concerns the admin system interface, status reports, and theme configuration.
`admin-rtl.css`	A stylesheet that is used when the site employs right-to-left text orientation.
`defaults.css`	Provides styling for basic default HTML elements used throughout the system.
`defaults-rtl.css`	A stylesheet that is used when the site employs right-to-left text orientation.
`maintenance.css`	Provides styling for the maintenance page.
`system.css`	Covers a wide variety of common styles, and also includes menus, tabs, and progress bars.
`system-menus.css`	Covers a wide variety of common styles, and also includes menus, tabs, and progress bars.
`system-menus-rtl.css`	A stylesheet that is used when the site employs right-to-left text orientation.
`system-rtl.css`	A stylesheet that is used when the site employs right-to-left text orientation.

Themable Functions

There are a number of themable functions that relate to the system module. The functions can be found in two files: `modules/system/system.module` and `modules/system/system.admin.inc`

Function	Path	Description
`theme_admin_block`	`modules/system/system.admin.inc`	Handles the admin system block display.
`theme_admin_block_content`	`modules/system/system.admin.inc`	Formats the contents of the admin block.
`theme_admin_page`	`modules/system/system.admin.inc`	Formats the administration page.
`theme_status_report`	`modules/system/system.admin.inc`	Themes the admin system's status report page.

Function	Path	Description
`theme_system_admin_by_module`	`modules/system/system.admin.inc`	Controls the formatting of the admin dashboard page.
`theme_system_modules`	`modules/system/system.admin.inc`	Handles the theming of the admin modules form.
`theme_system_modules_uninstall`	`modules/system/system.admin.inc`	Formats the table containing the uninstalled modules.
`theme_system_powered_by`	`modules/system/system.module`	Formats the **Powered by Drupal** text.
`theme_system_themes_form`	`modules/system/system.admin.inc`	Formats the themes form in the admin system.
`theme_system_theme_select_form`	`modules/system/system.admin.inc`	Formats the theme selection form.

Theming the Taxonomy Functionality

Enables the organization of content into categories, according to a hierarchical vocabulary.

Default Templates

There are no default templates provided for the taxonomy functionality.

Default Stylesheets

There is one stylesheet dedicated to the taxonomy module; it is located at: `modules/taxonomy`

Variable	Description
`taxonomy.css`	Provides four selectors for the taxonomy module.

Themable Functions

There are four themable functions that relate to the taxonomy functionality. The functions can be found in two files: `modules/taxonomy/taxonomy.module` and `modules/taxonomy/taxonomy.admin.inc`

Function	Path	Description
theme_taxonomy_ overview_terms	modules/taxonomy/ taxonomy.admin.inc	Themes the sortable list of terms.
theme_taxonomy_ overview_ vocabularies	modules/taxonomy/ taxonomy.admin.inc	Themes the sortable list of vocabularies.
theme_taxonomy_ term_page	modules/taxonomy/ taxonomy.pages.inc	Formats a taxonomy term's page.
theme_taxonomy_ term_select	modules/taxonomy/ taxonomy.module	Handles the field for selecting taxonomy terms.

Theming the Tracker Module

The tracker module enables the tracking of recent posts from users.

Default Templates

There is no default template provided for the tracker module.

Default Stylesheets

There is one stylesheet dedicated to the tracker module; it is located at:
modules/tracker

File	Description
tracker.css	Provides two selectors for theming the tracker table.

Themable Functions

There are no themable functions dedicated to the tracker module.

Theming the Trigger Module

The trigger module enables functions to be stored and executed at a later time—that is, when triggered.

Default Templates

There is no default template provided for the trigger module.

Default Stylesheets

There are no stylesheets dedicated to the trigger module.

Themable Functions

There is only one themable function dedicated to the trigger module.

Function	Path	Description
theme_trigger_ display	modules/trigger/ trigger.admin.inc	Formats the form for assigning actions to hooks.

Theming the Update Module

The update module checks for available updates to the Drupal core and modules and notifies the administrator if any are available.

Default Templates

There are no default templates dedicated to the update functionality.

Default Stylesheets

Two stylesheets are dedicated to the formatting of the update functionality. Both are located at /modules/update

File	Description
update.css	Numerous selectors for the update module interface in the admin system.
update-rtl.css	A stylesheet that is used when the site employs right-to-left text orientation.

Themable Functions

There are two themable functions associated with the update functionality. The functions can be found at: modules/update/update.report.inc

Function	Path	Description
theme_update_report	modules/update/update. report.inc	Formats the project status report.
theme_update_version	modules/update/update. report.inc	Formats the version display.

Theming the Upload Module

This module takes care of uploading and attaching files within nodes.

Default Templates

There are no default templates provided for the upload module.

Default Stylesheets

There are no stylesheets dedicated to the upload module.

Themable Functions

There are three themable functions that relate to the upload functionality. The functions can be found at: `modules/upload/upload.module`

Function	Path	Description
theme_upload_attachments	modules/upload/upload.module	Displays file attachments in a table.
theme_upload_form_current	modules/upload/upload.module	Themes the attachments list.
theme_upload_form_new	modules/upload/upload.module	Themes the attachment form.

Theming the User Functionality

Enables the user registration and login system.

Default Templates

Theming the user pages is made easier in Drupal 6 through the addition of four dedicated template files:

- `user-picture.tpl.php`
- `user-profile-category.tpl.php`
- `user-profile-item.tpl.php`
- `user-profile.tpl.php`

The default templates are located at: `modules/user/`

user-picture.tpl.php

Handles the presentation of the image associated with the user's account. The available variables include:

Variable	Description
$account	An array of the account information.
$picture	The image set by the user for the account.

user-profile.tpl.php

Provides a template for presenting all the user data. The available variables include:

Variable	Description
$profile	An array of the profile data (keyed).
$user_profile	All of the user's profile data.

user-profile-category.tpl.php

Provides a template for formatting the presentation of user profiles in category view. The available variables include:

Variable	Description
$attributes	The HTML attributes.
$profile_items	All the items for the group.
$title	The category title for the group.

user-profile-item.tpl.php

Handles the presentation of the user profile data. Loops through to present each item. The available variables include:

Variable	Description
$attributes	The HTML attributes.
$title	The field title for the profile item.
$value	The value for the profile item.

Default Stylesheets

Two stylesheets are dedicated to the formatting of the user data. Both are located at
`/modules/user`

File	Description
user.css	Styles for the User module and Profile module; includes styles for user administration.
user-rtl.css	A stylesheet that is used when the site employs right-to-left text orientation.

Themable Functions

There are a number of themable functions that relate to the user functionality. The functions can be found in two files: `modules/user/user.module` and `modules/user/user.admin.inc`

Function	Path	Description
theme_user_admin_account	modules/user/user.admin.inc	Formats the admin overview of user accounts.
theme_user_admin_new_role	modules/user/user.admin.inc	Handles the new role form.
theme_user_admin_perm	modules/user/user.admin.inc	Themes the permissions page.
theme_user_filter_form	modules/user/user.admin.inc	Formats the user's filter selection form.
theme_user_filters	modules/user/user.admin.inc	Formats the administrator's filter selection form.
theme_user_list	modules/user/user.module	Produces a list of users.
theme_user_signature	modules/user/user.module	Handles the output of the user's signature.

Summary

This chapter is meant as a resource for your ongoing use. The contents provide an extensive roadmap to the themable elements in your Drupal system. Each of the templates, stylesheets, and themable functions are catalogued relative to the system's functionalities and explained.

This chapter also marks the end of the introductory materials in this book. These first four chapters have equipped you with all the basic knowledge that you need to begin in earnest to modify Drupal themes, and have provided you with the building blocks necessary for creating your own themes.

In Chapter 5, we take the next step and begin to work with each of the elements with the aim of customizing them to suit your particular needs.

5

Intercepts and Overrides

In this chapter, we dive into the most powerful technique for customizing the output of a Drupal site—the use of intercepts and overrides. The logical consistency of the Drupal architecture lays the foundation for the approaches discussed in this chapter. Through the application of simple naming conventions, you can intercept and override the system's default styling. By creating your own templates and selectors and then naming them properly, it is a relatively easy matter to gain control over the output of the Drupal site. The techniques discussed in this chapter enable you to customize the site as a whole or through any of its components; you can even vary the styling by type of content, page or user.

Intercepts and overrides can be applied in three different but closely intertwined concepts: Drupal's default templates, the cascading stylesheets (CSS), and the themable functions. Though the applications may vary, the underlying principle that empowers the use of intercepts and overrides is exactly the same.

For the purpose of illustrating the examples in this chapter, we will be using the Garland theme, that is bundled with your default Drupal distro.

Overriding the Default CSS

Drupal contains a large number of stylesheets—more than forty at the last count! If you are employing third-party themes or modules, you are also likely to encounter additional stylesheets that are particular to that specific extension.

While there are certainly a lot of stylesheets to juggle, with good planning and use of overrides you can avoid having to track down and modify individual stylesheets. Indeed, as you will be placing your new styles in the theme directory, you won't need to work much with the multitude of the system's default stylesheets.

 Remember, you always want to avoid modifying the default files, and that includes both the CSS files in the core and those in any additional installed modules.

Drupal deals gracefully with the complexity of its multilayered approach to CSS. The system includes a CSS compression option (see, **Administer | Site configuration | Performance**) that will automatically compile the various stylesheets into one coherent list of styles at run time. This option not only eliminates any potential redundancies in style definitions but also improves the performance of the site.

To enable CSS Compression on your site, simply log in to the admin system and then go to the Performance page at **Administer | Site configuration | Performance**. Set the **Optimize CSS files** option to **Enabled** and click the **Save configuration** button at the bottom of the page. Note that during development you want to keep this option switched off, else you will experience difficulties in previewing your work.

The order in which the stylesheets are compiled creates a hierarchy among the stylesheets. While it is not necessary for you to be fluent with the details of the manner in which the stylesheets are compiled, it is important to appreciate the importance of the order of precedence established by the hierarchy. It is this hierarchy that enables you to easily intercept and override the default styles. The key to intercepting and overriding styling is to take advantage of the order of precedence by defining your custom styles in last stylesheet compiled. The last file compiled is highest in the hierarchy and any styles in that stylesheet will override any conflicting style definitions.

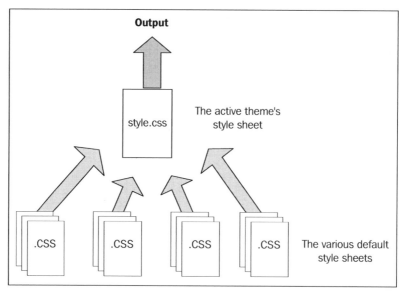

The theme's `style.css` file has the last word, that is, the CSS inside the active theme directory takes precedence over all other stylesheets. If there are conflicting style definitions, the definition included in the theme's stylesheet will have control. Where there is no conflict, the definitions in the default Drupal stylesheets will be applied.

As the name implies, Cascading Stylesheets set style precedence by cascade. The last item in the cascade has the last word in the final output.

 If you wish to add additional stylesheets, you may do so by creating new stylesheets, placing them inside the theme's directory, then incorporating them by reference inside your `.info` file. This topic is discussed further in Chapters 6 and 8.

CSS Overrides in Action

Let's take a basic example to illustrate the concept, and show a CSS override in action.

Drupal styles the page titles with the selector `.title`. The default Garland theme, however, contains no definition for the class `.title`. As there is no definition in the theme's stylesheet, the system will apply the default styling to the page title.

The page title of a default Garland installation appears as you see it in the following illustration:

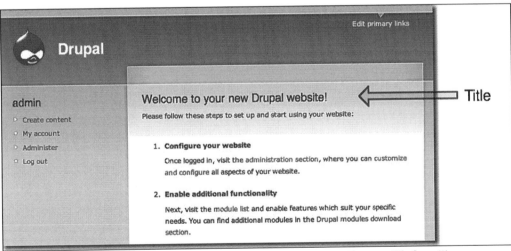

Default Garland theme with no additional style definitions. Note the page title formatting.

Let's now override the default styling; to do so we simply need to add our own definition for the `.title` class into the Garland theme's `style.css` file.

Add the following code to the Garland theme's stylesheet (`/themes/garland/style.css`):

```css
.title {
  color: #666;
  font-size: 1.8em;
  line-height: 2.0em;
  font-style: italic;
}
```

Now save the file to your server, overwriting the original `style.css` file. Our `.title` definition will now override the default styling. The results of the new styling will be seen when you reload the page in your browser, as shown in the following illustration:

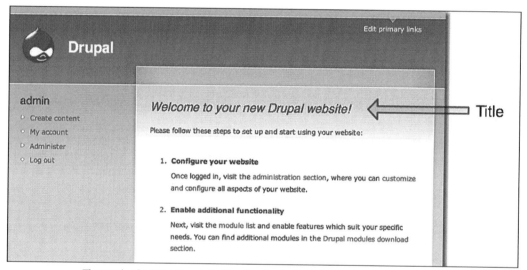

The result of adding the `.title` class to Garland theme's `style.css` file.

This simple example illustrates how the order of precedence allows us to easily override default style definitions—and it really is that simple. All we need to do is put our changes in the theme's `style.css` file and our styles will take precedence over the default style definitions. There's no need to make changes to the core files and no need to hunt through dozens of stylesheets to find what you need.

To override an existing style:

1. Find the styling applied to the item you want to change.
2. Write a new style definition.
3. Place the definition in the `style.css` file.
4. Repeat as needed!

Tools like Firebug, or the Web Developer extension for the Firefox browser, make it easy to locate relevant styling and even experiment with changes right from inside your browser. In Appendix B, The Themer's Toolkit, we provide the URLs for these extensions and for several other tools that can help make your work with templates easier.

Overriding Templates and Themable Functions

As discussed in Chapter 3, the templates and themable functions in Drupal control the HTML formatting for the final display of the contents. While CSS gives you one level of control over look and feel, to make significant changes to the functionality or the page layout you will need to work with the templates or the functions.

The default template and themable functions are located in a variety of places inside the distro (see Chapter 4 for a listing). If your site is using a theme engine other than PHPTemplate, you may also find templates and functions located inside the theme engine directory. Finally, because a theme developer can also create theme-specific templates and themable functions, you may find these items located inside the active theme's directory.

Like CSS styles, all templates and themable functions in a Drupal site can be overridden. As we saw with stylesheets, there is a hierarchy at work inside Drupal. The system will seek out themable functions in a specific order, and apply the first one it finds.

Various Approaches to Overriding Default Styling

In addition to working with the CSS, there are several other ways to override the default Drupal styling. Each of the alternatives has advantages and disadvantages and you, as the theme developer, will need to decide which approach best suits your needs.

The various approaches are:

- Substituting templates
- Overriding templates
- Placing function overrides in the `template.php` file
- Overriding themable functions with dedicated template files

In the following sections, we will look at each of these approaches.

The Theme Registry

Drupal's Theme Registry provides the system with information on the available functions and templates. When you add or remove theme functions or templates, you need to force the system to update the Theme Registry. (Simply editing an existing function or template, however, does not require you to clear the Registry.)

To update the Registry:

1. Go to **Administer | Site configuration | Performance**

2. Select **Clear cached data**

This is an important step that should not be skipped, else you may not be able to see your changes (and in some cases you may even get error messages).

Substituting Templates

This is an easy and powerful technique for managing customization. The essence of this approach is to create a duplicate file for one or more of the default template files. The substitute files must be placed in the individual theme's directory where they will be found by Drupal and displayed instead of the default templates.

The default templates and their purpose are detailed in Chapter 4.

Intercepting the default template files allows the theme developer to specify variations from the default presentation of key areas such as blocks, comments, and more.

As we shall see later in this Chapter, the Garland author uses this technique to provide alternative formatting for blocks, comments, and nodes and to provide an alternative template for the maintenance page.

The process of applying this technique is a straightforward matter of creating a duplicate for the file, and then modifying the code inside the new file:

1. Copy the template you wish to customize.
2. Paste the template into the theme directory, being careful to maintain the original file name.
3. Make your changes to the code in the new template file and save the file.
4. Clear the Theme Registry.

By applying the technique in this manner, you are able to specify your changes without having to modify the original core files. In the future, you benefit from this when it comes to upgrading your Drupal site, because you do not have to worry about the core upgrade overwriting your modifications. Additionally, your modified files are portable: should you wish to apply these changes to another theme, you only need to copy the appropriate files into the theme's directory.

Overriding Templates

Up to this point, we have limited the discussion to handling the overriding of the default (global) template files and individual functions; however, in Drupal, you can extend the intercept and override concept further to achieve highly granular control of the page templates that are called in various situations. You can, in other words, intercept and override on a conditional basis.

For example, if you wish to have different templates used for different types of content, you can create template files that are displayed only when that content is displayed. You can also style individual incidents of modules and other events using the techniques described in this chapter.

The page.tpl.php file is one of the most important in a PHPTemplate theme. This file is largely responsible for the results that appear in the browser—it defines the overall layout of the pages of your site. As you might expect given the name of the file, it appears in a wide variety of situations—it is the default page template.

Given the ubiquity of the file, there could be times when you want to customize a particular page (or set of pages) to add variety to your site or to enhance usability. Accordingly, the issue then becomes how to intercept the page.tpl.php template and override it to display the customized template when certain conditions are met.

Once again, Drupal relies on hierarchies and naming conventions to determine which template is called. By way of example, let's assume you wish to customize the user page. In the absence of any special definitions, Drupal will call page.tpl.php when a user clicks on the **My account** link on the main menu of the default distro.

If you want a custom page to be displayed, you will need to intercept the default page and display the page of your choosing. To do so, you will need to create a new template named page-user.tpl.php and place it in the active theme's directory. The system will give the file named page-user.tpl.php precedence over the default page.tpl.php.

Taking this one step further, let's say you want to show a particular user a customized user page. In that case, you would create a new template based on the `page.tpl.php` file and name it `page-user-1.tpl.php` (in this case, displaying the template to the user whose ID=1 when they view the user page).

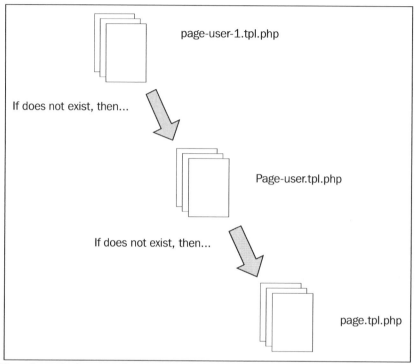

The hierarchy works from specific to general, where the specific takes precedence over the general.

Drupal is consistent, and the same logic is applied throughout the system. The system prefers the specific to the general. Drupal looks first for the most specific definition, and where that is absent, cascades downward, finally displaying the default instance where nothing else is found.

The logical, hierarchical nature of the system gives theme developers a great deal of control over pages or elements of pages.

By extension, the same principle can be applied to any `tpl.php` file. For example, a common request is for node-specific styling. To achieve variable styling according to node, you employ the same approach: Create the needed `tpl.php` files (applying the naming convention) and place them in the theme directory. At run time, Drupal will call the appropriate files.

For more information on this subject, as well as examples, please see the discussion of *Dynamic Theming* in Chapter 8.

Placing Function Overrides in the template.php File

The `template.php` file is an optional file in a PHPTemplate theme. When this file is present, Drupal will look in this file for extra instructions. This file provides a convenient place to define overrides of functions (among other things).

 The use of `template.php` is the most common approach to overriding themable functions. As we shall see later in this Chapter, this approach is implemented by the Garland theme to override the functions relating to the breadcrumb trail, the comments functionality, and the menu.

Here's a quick overview on the process used to implement this technique:

1. Create a new file named `template.php` inside your theme directory (use proper PHP syntax).

2. Find the functions you wish to customize.

3. Copy the original functions and paste them into the `template.php` file in their entirety.

4. Rename the functions (as discussed below).

5. Make your changes to the renamed functions in the `template.php` file and save the file.

6. Clear the Theme Registry

Again, note that by putting the changes inside a file in your theme directory, you can add customization to a site without having to touch the core files. Another significant advantage of this approach is simplicity: You have one file (`template.php`) holding multiple overrides in one location.

This approach makes it easy to locate your themable function overrides and manage them. The downside is that this is a theme-specific approach to the issue of overrides; should your site employ more than one theme, this approach may not be optimal.

Overriding Themable Functions with Dedicated Template Files

The final technique to master is the creation of individual template files that are dedicated to overriding specific themable functions. Transforming a function into a new template file gives you more flexibility than simply modifying the function inside the `template.php` file.

In this fashion, you employ the function in `template.php` to call a template file, rather than producing the output itself. This approach is a bit more complicated to set up, but in some cases may be preferable to other approaches.

Drupal functions can be a bit overwhelming for those less schooled in PHP. By creating templates out of themable functions, you can strip down the function to the themable elements and make the theming more accessible. Separate templates tend to be easier to work with.

 If you are a developer working with a designer, you can use this approach to break the themable elements into bite-sized pieces, and then pass them over to the designer for work on the look and feel. You can focus on the code; the designer can focus on the output.

Creating dedicated files requires additional steps, because you not only have to copy and modify the function, but you must also make a small change to the name.

The steps are as follows:

1. Create a new `.tpl.php` file inside your theme directory.
2. Name the new file by taking the function name, dropping the prefix, and changing the underscores to dashes (aka "hyphens"). (e.g., the function `theme_comment_view` would become the template `comment-view.tpl.php`)
3. Paste into the new file the code from the function that relates to the formatting and the output.
4. Make your changes to the file's code and save the file.
5. Clear the Theme Registry.

Let's look at an example.

Suppose the developer of Garland had chosen to create a dedicated file for the breadcrumb function (instead of overriding the output in the `template.php` file, as we shall see later). The name of the breadcrumb function is `theme_breadcrumb`. The original function is located at `includes/theme.inc`.

If the Garland developer had decided to create a separate breadcrumb template, he could have done it like this:

1. Create a new file, place it inside the Garland theme directory and name it `breadcrumb.tpl.php`.
2. Enter the following in the new file, and save the file:

```
<div class="breadcrumb"><?php print implode(' > ', $breadcrumb);
                                                        ?></div>
```

Note that the code is basic HTML styling wrapped around a PHP print statement. The PHP statement in this case controls the display of the breadcrumb (as per the original file), and has been modified to include a single right arrow, instead of the default double right arrow. This sort of basic statement should be relatively easier for many people to deal with, as opposed to trying to extract the output statements from the more complicated function code (as you would have to do if you simply dropped all your function overrides into the `template.php` file).

Since the original Garland theme already has a themable function override that affects the breadcrumb trail, we need to take one more step and comment out the breadcrumb themable function so it won't interfere with our new breadcrumb template. So, while you have `template.php` file open, go ahead and comment out (or delete if you prefer), the following lines:

```
function phptemplate_breadcrumb($breadcrumb) {

  if (!empty($breadcrumb)) {

    return '<div class="breadcrumb">'. implode(' > ', $breadcrumb)
.'</div>';

  }

}
```

Save your file and clear the site's Registry. Refresh the browser and you should now see your new breadcrumb styling.

Where to Place Themable Function Overrides

The best practice is to place your themable function overrides inside the individual theme directory. In PHPTemplate, your overrides should be added to the `template.php` file. The appropriate file for your overrides is dictated by the theme engine your site employs, as per the chart below.

Template Engine	Where to place themable function overrides
PHPTal	`template.php`
PHPTemplate	`template.php`
Smarty	`smartytemplate.php`
Xtal	n/a—does not permit this technique

At run time, Drupal searches out themable functions in a specific order. The system will look in the theme files before defaulting to the files included in the Drupal core. This diagram shows the hierarchy of themable functions and templates:

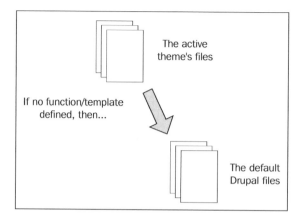

As we saw with CSS earlier, the hierarchy sets an order of precedence that allows you to override functions and templates. However, unlike CSS, where we can override simply by placing a style of the same name in the final CSS file, with themable functions you must understand and employ the naming convention to achieve the most from this powerful feature of the Drupal system.

How to Name Themable Function Overrides

The themable function hierarchy is invoked through the use of a naming convention. The default themable functions can be identified by their names: all employ the nomenclature `theme_functionname()`. For example, the default themable function that controls the output of a Drupal breadcrumb trail is named `theme_breadcrumb()`.

 The default breadcrumb function is located in the `includes/theme.inc` file. We will be looking at this function throughout this chapter, particularly in relation to the way it is overridden in the Garland theme.

At run time, Drupal is designed to look for overrides to themable functions before applying the default functions. The system does this by looking for files in the following order (assuming your site employs the PHPTemplate engine):

1. `themename_functionname` (e.g., `garland_breadcrumb`)
2. `themeengine_functionname` (e.g., `phptemplate_breadcrumb`)
3. `theme_functionname` (e.g., `theme_breadcrumb`)

The naming convention is the key to your files being found and used properly, so it must be followed scrupulously.

If the system does not find a function employing either the specific theme or theme engine namespace, the system will apply the default function.

Note that if your site is not using a theme engine, you must use the theme namespace for your override (e.g., `themename_functionname`). If your site uses a theme engine, common practice is to name the function `themeengine_functionname`, but this is not required; either naming convention (`themename_functionname` or `themeengine_functionname`) will work fine.

The advantage of following the `themeengine_functionname` format is portability. By giving the overrides generic names, you can copy them into other themes or even duplicate an entire theme directory as the first step to writing a new theme, all without having to worry about renaming all the overrides.

Overrides in Action: A Look at Overrides in Garland

Let's have a look at the Garland theme included in the default distro. The author of Garland employs a number of overrides and the ways in which they are implemented provide us with some easily accessible examples of overrides in action. A look inside the `themes/` directory shows the structure employed by Garland and gives us hints to this theme's approach to overrides.

Garland employs the PHPTemplate engine. In addition to the basic `page.tpl.php` file, Garland includes alternative versions of the following default templates:

- `block.tpl.php`
- `comment.tpl.php`
- `maintenance-page.tpl.php`
- `node.tpl.php`

The Garland theme author also includes the `template.php` file.

The presence of the alternative files and the new `template.php` file indicates that the author has specified variations from the default Drupal presentation. This combination of techniques, providing duplicate templates to supersede the default templates and overriding individual themable functions, demonstrates two of the most common approaches to modifying a PHPTemplate theme.

Intercepting the Default Template Files

Garland includes alternative versions of several default template files. The contents of each of those files vary from their counterparts of the same name located elsewhere in the distro.

Here's a list of the default templates the Garland author overrides, along with the locations of the original files:

Template	Original Location
block.tpl.php	modules/system/
comment.tpl.php	modules/comment/
node.tpl.php	modules/node/
maintenance-page.tpl.php	modules/system/

By way of example, let's compare the default version of the block.tpl.php file with Garland's modified version of the block.tpl.php file.

In the default template, you will find the following:

```
<div id="block-<?php print $block->module .'-'. $block->delta; ?>"
class="block block-<?php print $block->module ?>">
<?php if (!empty($block->subject)): ?>
<h2><?php print $block->subject ?></h2>
<?php endif;?>
<div class="content"><?php print $block->content ?></div>
</div>
```

The version of block.tpl.php included in the Garland theme directory looks like this:

```
<div id="block-<?php print $block->module .'-'. $block->delta; ?>"
class="clear-block block block-<?php print $block->module ?>">
<?php if (!empty($block->subject)): ?>
<h2><?php print $block->subject ?></h2>
<?php endif;?>
<div class="content"><?php print $block->content ?></div>
</div>
```

The two versions of the template look very similar, and indeed they are; the only difference between the two versions of the file is the class definition in the highlighted line. The Garland theme author has simply inserted a new CSS class that will be applied to the blocks. When the Garland theme is active, the Drupal system will apply the Garland block.tpl.php, with its new class, and ignore the default file of the same name in the modules/system/ directory. The modified file in the Garland theme takes precedence over the default file of the same name.

The author uses the same technique with the files `comment.tpl.php` and `node.tpl.php`, providing in these files alternative formatting to that included in the default templates. Compare and contrast those files to view the differences.

Overriding Themable Functions

In addition to providing substitutes for some of the default template files, the Garland author has also chosen to override a number of Drupal's default themable functions.

To implement the overrides, the author has created the file `template.php`. If you open the `template.php` file and examine the contents, you will find overrides for several functions, including the themable function affecting the site's breadcrumb trail. The default function, `theme_breadcrumb`, is located at `includes/theme.inc`. The author of Garland has overridden the default function by including a modified version of the function in the `template.php` file. Let's look in more detail at how a themable function override is implemented in the Garland theme.

The default definition for the Drupal breadcrumb trail is given in the file `includes/theme.inc`. The default function looks like this:

```
function theme_breadcrumb($breadcrumb) {
  if (!empty($breadcrumb)) {
    return '<div class="breadcrumb">'. implode(' >> ', $breadcrumb)
.'</div>';
  }
}
```

The Garland theme overrides the default breadcrumb function to provide different styling. The override is contained in the file `garland/template.php`. The override looks like this:

```
function phptemplate_breadcrumb($breadcrumb) {
  if (!empty($breadcrumb)) {
    return '<div class="breadcrumb">'. implode(' > ', $breadcrumb)
.'</div>';
  }
}
```

The differences in the two versions of the functions are subtle, but critical:

- The function has been renamed `phptemplate_breadcrumb` (the developer has adopted the `themeengine_functionname` naming convention in this). The new name alerts Drupal to apply this version of the function, instead of the default `theme_breadcrumb` function.

- Inside the file, the default function decorates the elements in the breadcrumb trail with a double right arrow (>>), while the override changes the decorative element to a single right arrow (>). The result is that the Drupal system recognizes the function placed in the theme file first, and applies a single right arrow to separate the items in the site's breadcrumb trail.

To see this in action, try substituting * for > in the `phptemplate_breadcrumb` code. Save your modified file and reload the page in your browser. You should see the breadcrumb decoration change from a single right arrow to an asterisk.

Summary

Intercepts and overrides are your most powerful techniques for controlling Drupal site output. In this chapter, we covered how to intercept and override both the default Drupal CSS and the themable functions and templates.

The technique requires an understanding of Drupal naming conventions and an appreciation for the hierarchies that dictate precedence. Proper use of the naming conventions will enable you to extensively customize Drupal's appearance.

This chapter also included a discussion of various alternative techniques for handling themable functions, together with the advantages of each. If you engage in a bit of planning, the step-by-step instructions introduced in this chapter should allow you to implement overrides in a variety of manners.

Modifying an Existing Theme

6

In this chapter, we will put together the various techniques we've covered up to this point and demonstrate how to modify and heavily customize an existing theme.

The majority of people who set out to master Drupal theming start out by modifying existing themes and learning from the process; that's exactly what we're going to do in this chapter. We will take an existing theme, look at how it works, then copy it and modify it until we have a very different looking theme. In this case, we will be building a basic fixed width, CSS-based, personal blog theme.

For the purpose of illustrating the examples in this chapter, we start with the Zen theme, which you can download from the Drupal site.

Setting Up the Workspace

There are several software tools that can make your work modifying themes more efficient. Though no specific tools are required to work with Drupal themes, there are a couple of applications that you might want to consider adding to your tool kit.

I work with Firefox as my primary browser, principally due to the fact that I can add into Firefox various extensions that make my life easier. The Web Developer extension, for example, is hugely helpful when dealing with CSS and related issues. I recommend the combination of Firefox and the Web Developer extension to anyone working with Drupal themes. Another extension popular with many developers is Firebug, which is very similar to the Web Developer extension, and indeed more powerful in several regards.

[Pick up Web Developer, Firebug, and other popular Firefox add-ons at
https://addons.mozilla.org/en-US/firefox/]

When it comes to working with PHP files and the various theme files, you will need an editor. The most popular application is probably Dreamweaver, from Adobe, although any editor that has syntax highlighting would work well too. I use Dreamweaver as it helps me manage multiple projects and provides a number of features that make working with code easier (particularly for designers).

If you choose to use Dreamweaver, you will want to tailor the program a little bit to make it easier to work with Drupal theme files. Specifically, you should configure the application preferences to open and edit the various types of files common to PHPTemplate themes. To set this up, open Dreamweaver, then:

1. Go to the **Preferences** dialogue.

2. Open **file types/editors**.

3. Add the following list of file types to Dreamweaver's **open in code view** field:

   .engine

   .info

   .module

   .install

   .theme

4. Save the changes and exit.

With these changes, your Dreamweaver application should be able to open and edit all the various PHPTemplate theme files.

Previewing Your Work

Note that, as a practical matter, previewing Drupal themes requires the use of a server. Themes are really difficult to preview (with any accuracy) without a server environment. A quick solution to this problem is the XAMPP package. XAMPP provides a one step installer containing everything you need to set up a server environment on your local machine (Apache, MySQL, PHP, phpMyAdmin, and more). Visit http://www.ApacheFriends.org to download XAMPP and you can have your own Dev Server quickly and easily.

Another tool that should be on the top of your list is the Theme developer extension for the popular Drupal Devel module. Theme developer can save you untold hours of digging around trying to find the right function or template. When the module is active, all you need to do is click on an element and the Theme developer pop-up window will show you what is generating the element, along with other useful information. In the example later in this chapter, we will also use another feature of the Devel module, that is, the ability to automatically generate sample content for your site.

You can download Theme developer as part of the Devel project at Drupal.org: `http://drupal.org/project/devel`

Note that Theme developer only works on Drupal 6 and due to the way it functions, is only suitable for use in a development environment—you don't want this installed on a client's public site!

 Visit `http://drupal.org/node/209561` for more information on the Theme developer aspects of the Devel module. The article includes links to a screencast showing the module in action—a good quick start and a solid help in grasping what this useful tool can do.

Planning the Modifications

We're going to base our work on the popular Zen theme. We'll take Zen, create a new subtheme, and then modify the subtheme until we reach our final goal. Let's call our new theme "Tao".

The Zen theme was chosen for this exercise because it has a great deal of flexibility. It is a good solid place to start if you wish to build a CSS-based theme. The present version of Zen even comes with a generic subtheme (named "STARTERKIT") designed specifically for themers who wish to take a basic theme and customize it. We'll use the Starterkit subtheme as the way forward in the steps that follow.

 The Zen theme is one of the most active theme development projects. Updated versions of the theme are released regularly. We used version 6.x-1.0-beta2 for the examples in this chapter. Though that version was current at the time this text was prepared, it is unlikely to be current at the time you read this. To avoid difficulties, we have placed a copy of the files used in this chapter in the software archive that is provided on the Packt website. Download the files used in this chapter at `http://www.packtpub.com/files/code/5661_Code.zip`. You can download the current version of Zen at `http://drupal.org/project/zen`.

Any time you set off down the path of transforming an existing theme into something new, you need to spend some time planning. The principle here is the same as in many other areas of life: A little time spent planning at the front end of a project can pay off big in savings later.

A proper dissertation on site planning and usability is beyond the scope of this book; so for our purposes let us focus on defining some loose goals and then work towards satisfying a specific wish list for the final site functionality.

Our goal is to create a two-column blog-type theme with solid usability and good branding. Our hypothetical client for this project needs space for advertising and a top banner. The theme must also integrate a forum and a user comments functionality.

Specific changes we want to implement include:

- Main navigation menu in the right column
- Secondary navigation mirrored at the top and bottom of each page
- A top banner space below top nav but above the branding area
- Color scheme and fonts to match brand identity
- Enable and integrate the Drupal blog, forum, and comments modules

 In order to make the example easier to follow and to avoid the need to install a variety of third-party extensions, the modifications we will make in this chapter will be done using only the default components— excepting only the theme itself, Zen. Arguably, were you building a site like this for deployment in the real world (rather than simply for skills development) you might wish to consider implementing one or more specialized third-party extensions to handle certain tasks.

Creating a New Subtheme

Install the Zen theme if you have not done so before now; once that is done we're ready to create a new subtheme.

 Installing a new theme is covered in Chapter 2.

First, make a copy of the directory named **STARTERKIT** and place the copied files into the directory `sites/all/themes`. Rename the directory "tao".

 Note that in Drupal 5.x, subthemes were kept in the same directory as the parent theme, but for Drupal 6.x this is no longer the case. Subthemes should now be placed in their own directory inside the `sites/all/themes/` directory.

Note that the authors of Zen have chosen to vary from the default stylesheet naming. Most themes use a file named `style.css` for their primary CSS. In Zen, however, the file is named `zen.css`. We need to grab that file and incorporate it into Tao.

Copy the Zen CSS (`zen/zen/zen.css`) file. Rename it `tao.css` and place it in the Tao directory (`tao/tao.css`).

 When you look in the `zen/zen` directory, in addition to the key `zen.css` file, you will note the presence of a number of other CSS files. We need not concern ourselves with the other CSS files. The styles contained in those stylesheets will remain available to us (we inherit them as Zen is our base theme) and if we need to alter them, we can override the selectors as needed via our new `tao.css` file.

In addition to renaming the theme directory, we also need to rename any other theme-name-specific files or functions. Do the following:

- Rename the `STARTERKIT.info` file to `tao.info`.

- Edit the `tao.info` file to replace all occurrences of `STARTERKIT` with `tao`.

- Open the `tao.info` file and find this copy: **The name and description of the theme used on the admin/build/themes page. name = Zen Themer's Starter Kit description = Read the <a href="http://drupal.org/node/226507">online docs</a> on how to create a sub-theme.**

- Replace that text with this copy: **The name and description of the theme used on the admin/build/themes page. name = Tao description = A 2-column fixed-width sub-theme based on Zen.** Make sure the `name=` and `description` = content is not commented out, else it will not register.

- Edit the `template.php` file to replace all occurrences of `STARTERKIT` with `tao`.

- Edit the `theme-settings.php` file to replace all occurrences of `STARTERKIT` with `tao`.

- Copy the file `zen/layout-fixed.css` and place it in the `tao` directory, creating `tao/layout-fixed.css`.

- Include the new `layout-fixed.css` by modifying the `tao.info` file. Change `style sheets[all][] = layout.css` to `style sheets[all][] = layout-fixed.css`.

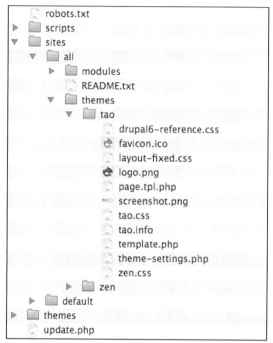

The result of creating our new subtheme and re-naming the files.

The `.info` file functions similar to a `.ini` file: It provides configuration information, in this case, for your theme. A good discussion of the options available within the `.info` file can be found on the Drupal.org site at: `http://drupal.org/node/171205`

Making the Transition from Zen to Tao

The process of transforming an existing theme into something new consists of a set of tasks that can categorized into three groups:

1. Configuring the Theme
2. Adapting the CSS
3. Adapting the Templates & Themable Functions

Configuring the Theme

As stated previously, the goal of this redesign is to create a blog theme with solid usability and a clean look and feel. The resulting site will need to support forums and comments and will need advertising space.

Let's start by enabling the functionality we need and then we can drop in some sample contents. Technically speaking, adding sample content is not 100% necessary, but practically speaking, it is extremely useful; let's see the impact of our work with the CSS, the templates, and the themable functions.

Before we begin, enable your new theme, if you have not done so already. Log in as the administrator, then go to the themes manager (**Administer | Site building | Themes**), and enable the theme **Tao**. Set it to be the default theme and save the changes.

Now we're set to begin customizing this theme, first through the Drupal system's default configuration options, and then through our custom styling.

Enabling Modules

To meet the client's functional requirements, we need to activate several features of Drupal which, although contained in the default distro, are not by default activated. Accordingly, we need to identify the necessary modules and enable them. Let's do that now.

Access the module manager screen (**Administer | Site building | Modules**), and enable the following modules:

- **Blog** (enables blog-type presentation of content)
- **Contact** (enables the site contact forms)
- **Forum** (enables the threaded discussion forum)
- **Search** (enables users to search the site)

Save your changes and let's move on to the next step in the configuration process.

 More detailed information on the use of modules can be found in Chapter 2.

Setting Global and Theme Configuration Options

Navigate to the site information screen (**Administer | Site configuration | Site information**). Rename the site from **Drupal** to **Tao** and then let's add a slogan: **A fixed width blog theme based on Zen.** Save the configuration.

Next, let's deal with the theme-specific configuration settings relevant to our new subtheme Tao. Go to **Administer | Site building | Themes** and click the **configure** link for the Tao theme. Enable the **Site slogan** and the **Search box.** While you're there, disable the **Mission statement**, the **Logo**, and the **Shortcut icon** options; we won't be needing those features. Save your changes.

[More detailed information on the configuration options applicable to themes can be found in Chapter 2.]

Setting User Access

We now need to set the user permissions so that our site visitors can see and use the various functionalities we've set up.

Go to the **Permissions** interface (**Administer | User management | Permissions**) and enable the following for anonymous user access:

- **Access comments**
- **Post comments**
- **Access site-wide contact form**
- **Search content**

Save your new permissions and let's move on to the next step in our preliminary preparations.

Creating Dummy Content

Temporary dummy content allows us to see text on the screen as we make our changes, and helps us to judge more easily our fonts, colors, spacing, and margins.

First, let's create a new page. Name it **About Us** and throw in a few lines of placeholder text. Add it to the Navigation menu by clicking on the **Menu settings** link on page creation screen. Set the **Menu link title** to **About Us** and **Save** your new page.

Next, let's create a couple of blog entries. Go to **Administer | Create content | Create Blog entry** and add two or three pages of dummy text.

We also have a forum to integrate, so we need some sample content. Access the **Forums** option under **Content management**. You will see there a message advising you that you need to create a new forum in order to fully activate this module. Let's add a new forum and name it simply **New**. This is sufficient for our needs at this stage.

Finally, let's create a site wide contact form. To set up your first contact form, go to **Administer | Site building | Contact form** and click on the **Add category** tab. Give the category a name, like **website feedback**, then add one or more email addresses for the form's intended recipient(s). On the same page, change the value for **Selected** to **yes**, then save your work.

Now that we have our modules, some content, a forum, and a contact form in place, it's time to set up the remaining menu choices to connect these items to the navigation.

Auto-Generate Your Dummy Content

While in the example I have set up content manually, there is a faster way. If you have installed the Devel module, you can use it to automatically populate your site with sample data. This is a brilliant little utility that saves time and frustration. When you install the Devel module, enable the option **Devel generate**. Now, when you need sample content, visit the main administration page and look for the heading **Generate items**. Select what you want from the list. Simple, fast, painless—another reason why we love the Devel module.

Setting Up Menus

For this theme, we're going to use the following configuration for the theme's menus:

- Drupal's default **Navigation** menu will hold the site's main navigation items and we're going to assign that to the righthand side of the page.

- We will manually manage the placement of the **Primary Links** menu, placing it at the top of the page inside a new region where it will hold our secondary navigation choices.

- We'll create a footer navigation menu and place that at the bottom of the page. The footer nav will hold secondary menu choices as well as our login/logout link.

To set this up, access the menu manager (**Administer | Site building | Menus**) and make the changes outlined below.

For the **Navigation** menu, make sure the following are enabled (but do not disable the default choices you will see on this menu!):

Name for Link	Path (URL)
Blogs	blog
The Forum	forum
About Us	(link determined by system when you create the page)

Note that you should already have an **About Us** link on the Navigation menu, courtesy of the steps we took when we created the About Us page, in the previous section of this chapter.

For the **Primary Links** menu, we will need to set up the following:

Name for Link	Path (URL)
Home	<front>
Contact Us	Contact

Note that there's an easy shortcut to place the contact form link on the primary nav: When we created the contact form earlier in this chapter, Drupal automatically made a link to the form. The default contact link is on the Navigation menu, so let's just edit that to get it to appear on our Primary links menu.

Go to the Navigation menu (**Administer | Site building | Menus | Navigation**), locate the menu item **Contact**, and click the **Edit** button. On the resulting page, change the setting for the field **Parent item** to **Primary Links**, check the **Enable** option, and then **Save**. The link to the contact form will now appear on your Primary links.

The last step for preparing the Primary links nav is to disable the automatic management feature in Drupal. We want to place this menu manually by assigning the Primary links block to one of the new custom regions we will create in the next section. To disable the default placement, go to the Menu manager (**Administer | Site building | Menus**) and select the **Settings** tab. On the settings page, change **Source for the primary links:** to **No primary links**.

In our design, the plan was to mirror the navigation at the top of the page in the navigation at the bottom (in the footer). Placing menu items on the footer requires an additional step—we have to first create a menu to hold the items.

To set up our footer nav menu, go to the menu manager (**Administer | Site building | Menus**) and select the **Add menu** tab. Drupal requires us to add both a **Menu name** and a **Title**. The menu name is used by the system, while the title is what we'll actually be dealing with on the site. The menu name has to be machine readable, hence it must contain only lowercase letters, numbers or hyphens, and it must be unique; the title field is more forgiving and isn't burdened by these restrictions. Let's give our new menu the name **footer** and the title **Footer Nav**. Once you've added both these fields, click **Save**. Next, let's set up the menu items we want on our new footer nav:

Name for Link	Path (URL)
Home	<front>
Login	user
Contact Us	contact

Adding New Regions

The Tao theme design requires the addition of a horizontal navigation menu that hangs from the top of the page and the ability to insert banner ads at the top of the page. As these areas of the page are planned to be distinct in their usage and in their formatting, it is probably best to create new regions to hold these items.

To provide space for our requirements, we will be adding two new regions, which we shall call **page_top** and **banner**. Before we go any further with the configuration, we need to create these regions so that they are available for block placement.

Adding new regions to a theme is a two-step process: You must modify the theme's `info` file to list the new regions and then you must place the code that includes the regions into the theme's `page.tpl.php` file.

Traditionally, Drupal themes include the following regions, though individual themes are free to vary from this list if they wish to offer additional (or fewer) regions:

- left
- right
- content
- header
- footer

Zen, and by inheritance Tao, varies from the default list of regions. These themes include the following regions:

- left sidebar
- right sidebar
- navigation bar
- content top
- content bottom
- header
- footer
- closure

Here is an unaltered snippet of code from our `tao.info` file, which shows the regions initially available in this theme:

```
regions[left] = left sidebar
regions[right] = right sidebar
regions[navbar] = navigation bar
regions[content_top] = content top
regions[content_bottom] = content bottom
regions[header] = header
regions[footer] = footer
regions[closure_region] = closure
```

> The syntax for the regions statement in the .info file works like this:
> `regions[machine_readable_name_for_region] = name to display to user`

We need to add two regions to this list, so let's open the file `tao/tao.info` with your editor of choice. Add in our two new regions, **page_top** and **banner** as follows:

```
regions[page_top] = page top
regions[banner] = banner
regions[right] = right sidebar
regions[navbar] = navigation bar
regions[content_top] = content top
regions[content_bottom] = content bottom
regions[header] = header
regions[footer] = footer
regions[closure_region] = closure
```

Save the file to conclude the first part of this task.

Note that the contents of the `.info` file are stored in the database by Drupal and are subject to caching. To see your changes immediately, you will need to clear the cache. To do so quickly and easily, use the **clear cached data** button located at **Administrator | Site configuration | Performance**.

The second step is to place the code that produces the regions into the `page.tpl.php` file. For Tao, the plan is to use the region **page top** to hold the primary links nav that hangs from the top of each page. The **banner** region is to be placed below the new **page top** region and above the existing header region, and will be used to hold our banner ads.

The first thing we need to do is create our own `page.tpl.php` file. To do this, simply copy the `page.tpl.php` file of the underlying Zen theme (`zen/zen/page.tpl.php`) and place it in the Tao directory. We will make our changes on the file `tao/page.tpl.php`.

Open Tao's `page.tpl.php` file. Note the following code, immediately after the head of the document:

```
<body class="<?php print $body_classes; ?>">
<div id="page"><div id="page-inner">
<a name="top" id="navigation-top"></a>
<div id="skip-to-nav"><a href="#navigation"><?php print t('Skip to
Navigation'); ?></a></div>
```

We're going to modify that to include our two new regions, as follows:

```
<body class="<?php print $body_classes; ?>">
<div id="page"><div id="page-inner">
<div id="page-top"><?php print $page_top; ?></div>
    <div id="banner"><?php print $banner; ?></div>
```

Note that I have wrapped both the statements that include the new regions with divs. To make them easy to remember, let's name the id of each div to match the region. When we modify the CSS later, we will define these new divs to set the position and formatting of the contents of these regions.

While you have this file open, go ahead and delete or comment out the code that immediately follows our new region, as we won't be needing this:

```
<a name="top" id="navigation-top"></a>
<div id="skip-to-nav"><a href="#navigation"><?php print t('Skip to
Navigation'); ?></a></div>
```

Enabling and Configuring Blocks

Let's enable the blocks we need so we can get the output on the screen. Assign the blocks **Recent comments**, **Syndicate**, and **Who's online** to the region **Right sidebar**. Put them in whatever order you like.

The **Navigation** block currently appears in the left sidebar. We need to move the block to the right sidebar, where it will sit at the top of the column.

Let's also enable the **Footer Nav** block by placing it in the footer region and the **Primary Links** block by placing it in the page top region. Save your changes.

While you're here, hide some of the block titles that we don't want to see on the page. Open the configure dialog for the **Syndicate** block and set the **Block title** to **<none>**. Do the same with the **Primary Links**, **Footer**, and **Navigation** blocks. Save your changes.

One of the requirements for this theme was the provision of space for a banner ad at the top of the pages. While normally you might want to use a dedicated extension to handle ads, for our example we're going to set up the banner the crude way—that is, we're going to create a block for the banner, then hard-code the location of the banner image into the block.

To provide a dummy banner image for us to work with, I downloaded a sample leaderboard-sized ad and then placed it inside our theme folder, in the new directory `images`. I will link to the sample banner image for testing purposes. Later, the user can either employ this banner block or they can find an alternative approach for placing a banner in this position. Either way, the styling will be in place and the site ready to accommodate the ads.

The Internet Advertising Bureau maintains an online collection of sample ad units in various official sizes; this is a good resource for placeholders, like the one used in this example. For our Tao theme, I have downloaded the sample Full Leaderboard ad unit (728 x 90 pixels) from: `http://www.iab.net/iab_products_and_industry_services/1421/1443/Ad_Unit`.

To create our new block, access the block manager and choose **Add Block**. Set the block description to **Banner**. Next, insert a link to the banner image in the **Block body** text field, as follows:

```
<a href="#" ><img src="/sites/all/themes/tao/images/726x90_v2.gif" /></a>
```

Set your input format to **Full HTML**, set the **Block title** field to **<none>,** and then finally choose **Save block**. Assign this block to the region **banner** to complete this operation.

Finally, let's hide two of the default blocks we won't need. Since we added a link to the login function to the footer nav created earlier, let's hide the display of the User login block to keep our screen clear of clutter. To do this, find the **User login** block in the block manager and set the region for the block to **<none>.** Finally, let's hide the **Powered by Drupal** block as well. Save your changes and we have finished this task.

> If this were a production site, rather than a basic demo, I would approach the actual banner management in a different fashion: If I were using Google AdSense on the site, I would use the **Block body** field to input my AdSense code. If, on the other hand, I needed more complete banner management functionality, such as the ability to run my own ads, control display, and generate reports, I would install a third-party extension and follow its instructions for implementing the block. A number of extensions provide extended ad management functionality, see `http://drupal.org/project/Modules/category/55` for a list.

At the conclusion of the process above, your block assignments will look like this:

Name for Block	Region
Primary Links	page top
Banner	banner
Navigation	right sidebar
Recent Comments	right sidebar
Who's Online	right sidebar
Syndicate	right sidebar
Footer Nav	footer

At this point in the process, we have all the basics in place. The system is set up with the basic configuration and the new regions in place. The various modules are enabled, the menus populated, and the output blocks positioned as we want them to be in the final site. While visually the site is a bit of a mess, all the elements are visible and that means we can start on the CSS and the particular customizations required to achieve our final design.

> More detailed information on the use of Blocks can be found in Chapter 3.

Adapting the CSS

We've set up Tao as a subtheme of the Zen theme. As a result, the Tao theme relies upon a number of stylesheets, both in the Tao directory and in the parent theme's directory. The good news is that we do not need to concern ourselves with hacking away at all these various stylesheets, we can instead place all our changes in the `tao.css` file, located in the Tao theme directory. Drupal will give precedence to the styles defined in the theme's `.css` file, in the event of any conflicting definitions.

Precedence and Inheritance

Where one style definition is in an imported stylesheet and another in the immediate stylesheet, the rule in the immediate stylesheet (the one that is importing the other stylesheet) takes precedence.

Where repetitive definitions are in the same stylesheet, the one furthest from the top of the stylesheet takes precedence in the case of conflicts; where repetitive definitions are in the same stylesheet, nonconflicting attributes will be inherited.

Setting the Page Dimensions

For this exercise, the goal is to create a fixed width theme optimized for display settings of 1024 x 768. Accordingly, one of the most basic changes we need to make is to the page dimensions. If you look at the `page.tpl.php` file, you will notice that the entire page area is wrapped with a `div` with the `id=page`. Open up the `tao.css` file and alter it as follows. To help avoid precedence problems, place all your style definitions at the end of the stylesheet.

Let's modify the selector `#page`.

```
#page {
    width: 980px;
    margin: 0 auto;
    border-left: 4px solid #666633;
    border-right: 4px solid #666633;
    background-color: #fff;
}
```

In this case, I set page width to 980 pixels, a convenient size that works consistently across systems, and applied the margin attribute to center the page. I have also applied the `border-left` and `border-right` styles and set the background color.

We also need to add a little space between the frame and the content area as well to keep the presentation readable and clean. The selector #content-area helps us here as a convenient container:

```
#content-area {
    padding: 0 20px;
}
```

Formatting the New Regions

Let's begin by using CSS to position and format the two new regions, page top and banner.

When we placed the code for the two new regions in our page.tpl.php file, we wrapped them both with divs. Page top was wrapped with the div page-top, so let's create that in our tao.css file:

```
#page-top {
    margin: 0;
    background-color: #676734;
    width: 980px;
    height: 25px;
    text-align: right;
}
```

The region banner was wrapped with a div of the same name, so let's now define that selector as well:

```
#banner {
    background-color: #fff;
    width: 980px;
    height: 90px;
    text-align: center;
}
```

Setting Fonts and Colors

Some of the simplest CSS work is also some of the most important—setting font styles and the colors of the elements.

Let's start by setting the default fonts for the site. I'm going to use body tag as follows:

```
body {
    background: #000;
    min-width: 800px;
```

```
    margin: 0;
    padding: 0;
    font: 13px Arial,Helvetica,sans-serif;
    color: #111;
    line-height:1.4em;
}
```

Now, let's add various other styles to cover more specialized text, like links and titles:

```
a, a:link, a:visited {
    color: #666633;
    text-decoration: none;
}

a:hover, a:focus {
    text-decoration: underline;
}

h1.title, h1.title a, h1.title a:hover {
    font-family: Verdana, Arial, Helvetica, sans-serif;
    font-weight: normal;
    color: #666633;
    font-size: 200%;
    margin: 0;
    line-height: normal;
}

h1, h1 a, h1 a:hover {
font-size: 140%;
    color: #444;
    font-family: Verdana, Arial, Helvetica, sans-serif;
margin: 0.5em 0;
}

h2, h2 a, h2 a:hover, .block h3, .block h3 a {
font-size: 122%;
    color: #444;
    font-family: Verdana, Arial, Helvetica, sans-serif;
    margin: 0.5em 0;
}

h3 {
    font-size: 107%;
font-weight: bold;
font-family: Verdana, Arial, Helvetica, sans-serif;
}

h4, h5, h6 {
```

```
  font-weight: bold;
    font-family: Verdana, Arial, Helvetica, sans-serif;
}
#logo-title {
  margin: 10px 0 0 0;
  position: relative;
  background-color: #eaebcd;
  height: 60px;
  border-top: 1px solid #676734;
  padding-top: 10px;
  padding-bottom: 10px;
  border-bottom: 1px solid #676734;
}
#site-name a, #site-name a:hover {
    font-family: Verdana, Arial, Verdana, Sans-serif;
    font-weight: normal;
    color: #000;
    font-size: 176%;
    margin-left: 20px;
    padding: 0;
}
#site-slogan {
    color: #676734;
    margin: 0;
    font-size: 90%;
    margin-left: 20px;
    margin-top: 10px;
}
.breadcrumb {
padding-top: 0;
  padding-bottom: 10px;
padding-left: 20px;
}
#content-header .title {
    padding-left: 20px;
}
```

After you have made the changes, above, remember to go back and comment out any competing definitions that may cause inheritance problems.

Formatting the Sidebars and Footer

The left sidebar is unused in this theme, but the right sidebar region is essential, as it contains the main navigation and several blocks. The way the CSS is written, the style definitions for left and right sidebar are combined; we'll maintain that for convenience.

```
#sidebar-left .block, #sidebar-right .block {
  padding-bottom: 15px;
  margin-bottom: 20px;
}
```

The titles of the blocks in the sidebar are controlled by the h2 tag. Let's add a definition for the h2 tags that appear inside the right sidebar region:

```
#sidebar-right h2 {
  background-color: #676734;
  display: block;
  color: #eaebcd;
  font-size: 110%;
  font-weight: normal;
  font-family: verdana;
  line-height: 1.5em;
  padding-left: 10px;
}
```

I want the footer in this theme to anchor the page and to mirror the look and feel of the page top region we created earlier. The footer region is wrapped with a div of the same name, so I need to modify #footer in my stylesheet, as follows:

```
#footer-wrapper {
   margin: 0;
}
#footer {
   background-color: #676734;
   color: #FFF;
   margin: 0;
   font-size: 100%;
   height: 25px;
}
#footer a {
   color: #fff;
}
```

Formatting the Menus

The top and footer menus require a horizontal presentation, while the main nav in the right column requires a vertical orientation. In all three cases, we also need to make sure the menu style matches the rest of the site.

Creating the Horizontal Menu

First, let's set up horizontal presentation for the primary links menu, which appears at the top of the page. I want the links to appear in a horizontal line, aligned to the right:

```
#page-top li {
    display: inline;
    float: right;
    padding: 5px;
    font-size: 14px;
    font-weight: bold;
    padding: 5px 10px;
}
#page-top li a {
    color: #fff;
}
```

Next, let's do the same for the navigation inside the footer region, again, with right alignment:

```
#footer li {
    display: inline;
    float: right;
    font-size: 14px;
    font-weight: bold;
    padding: 5px 10px;
}
```

Formatting the Vertical Menu

I want to control the styling of the menu in the right sidebar (our Navigation menu), so I will add the following:

```
#sidebar-right ul.menu {
    border-top: 1px solid #676734;
    padding-top: 10px;
    padding-bottom: 10px;
    border-bottom: 1px solid #676734;
```

```
    background-color: #eaebcd;
    color: #676734;
    font-weight: bold;
    font-family: verdana;
    font-size: 14px;
    line-height: 22px;
}
```

Formatting the Search Box and Syndicate Button

The search box formatting needs to be modified to fit our new theme. #search-box handles the formatting and is located in the layout-fixed.css, so let's kill the old selector and substitute ours. Let's set the position:

```
#search-box {
    position: absolute;
    padding: 0;
    top: 20px;
    right: 20px;
}
```

Next, let's adjust the colors to match our new color scheme:

```
#search-box .form-text, #user-login-form .form-text {
    color: #444;
    border: 1px solid #000;
    padding: 2px;
}

#search-box .button,
#search-box .form-submit,
#user-login-form .button,
#user-login-form .form-submit {
    background-color: #676734;
    color: #fff;
    font-weight: bold;
    border: 1px solid #000;
    padding-left: 20px;
    padding-right: 20px;
}
```

The syndicate button will appear on both the right column and the left bottom corner. Let's open some space around it by adding this definition:

```
.feed-icons {
    margin: 20px;
}
```

Formatting the Comments Form and Output

We enabled the comments functionality earlier, let's now set the look and feel. The comments in the default Zen theme are shaded a light blue, consistent with the Zen color scheme. For Tao, we want to make things a little more conservative, a little more somber, so we will change that to a light gray and also apply our font selections.

Make the following changes to the selectors, below:

```
.comment {
  margin: 0 0 10px 0;
  padding: 10px;
  background: #f1f1f1;
}
.comment h3.title, .comment h3.title a {
  font-size: 122%;
  color: #666;
  font-weight: normal;
  font-family: Verdana, Arial, Sans-serif;
  margin-bottom: 3px;
  margin-top: 0;
  padding-left: 0;
}
.comment .new {
  color: #FFC600;
  font-weight: bold;
  font-family: Arial, Verdana, Sans-serif;
}
```

If what you see on your screen at this point is not largely similar to the image at the end of the chapter, odds are you skipped a style definition or have missed commenting out a selector; go back and check the stylesheets to make sure you deleted or commented out any potential inheritance problems.

Adapting the Themable Functions

We don't really need to make a large number of changes to our themable functions to achieve our goals, but we will make some minor modifications to bring more consistency to the new look and feel.

Overriding a Themable Function

The Zen theme includes a themable function for handling the breadcrumb trail. The function is located in the zen/zen/template.php file and looks like this:

```
function zen_breadcrumb($breadcrumb) {
$show_breadcrumb = theme_get_setting('zen_breadcrumb');$show_
breadcrumb_home = theme_get_setting('zen_breadcrumb_home');
   $breadcrumb_separator = theme_get_setting('zen_breadcrumb_
separator');
   $trailing_separator = (theme_get_setting('zen_breadcrumb_trailing')
|| theme_get_setting('zen_breadcrumb_title')) ? $breadcrumb_separator
: '';
   // Determine if we are to display the breadcrumb
   if ($show_breadcrumb == 'yes' || $show_breadcrumb == 'admin' &&
arg(0) == 'admin') {
if (!$show_breadcrumb_home) {
// Optionally get rid of the homepage link
array_shift($breadcrumb);
   }
     if (!empty($breadcrumb)) {
// Return the breadcrumb with separators
return '<div class="breadcrumb">' . implode($breadcrumb_separator,
$breadcrumb) . "$trailing_separator</div>";
     }
   }
   // Otherwise, return an empty string
   return '';
}
```

I want to add a label to help clue people into the function of the breadcrumb. To do this, I must first copy the original function from the Zen directory and paste it into my tao/template.php file. I need to also rename the function to reflect my theme name (from Zen to Tao). The modifications look like this:

```
function tao_breadcrumb($breadcrumb) {
   $show_breadcrumb = theme_get_setting('zen_breadcrumb');$show_
breadcrumb_home = theme_get_setting('zen_breadcrumb_home');
   $breadcrumb_separator = theme_get_setting('zen_breadcrumb_
separator');
   $trailing_separator = (theme_get_setting('zen_breadcrumb_trailing')
|| theme_get_setting('zen_breadcrumb_title')) ? $breadcrumb_separator
: '';
   // Determine if we are to display the breadcrumb
   if ($show_breadcrumb == 'yes' || $show_breadcrumb == 'admin' &&
arg(0) == 'admin') {
if (!$show_breadcrumb_home) {
```

```
// Optionally get rid of the homepage link
array_shift($breadcrumb);
    }
     if (!empty($breadcrumb)) {
// Return the breadcrumb with separators
return '<div class="breadcrumb"><strong>You are here: </strong>' .
implode($breadcrumb_separator, $breadcrumb) . "$trailing_separator</
div>";
    }
  }
  // Otherwise, return an empty string
  return '';
}
```

 Remember to clear the Drupal cache each time you change a themable function or template.

Modifying a Default Template

Our new theme Tao is intended as a blog theme, so let's look at adjusting the formatting of the blog node. To do this, we are going to create a template file to control the output of the blog node; a template file is more specific, and hence preferred over the Zen's default node.tpl.php.

First, duplicate the file zen/zen/node.tpl.php. Paste the file into our tao directory and rename it node-blog.tpl.php; this file will now be used by the system to handle the formatting of the blog node in our theme. Note that you will also need to copy the base template into the theme directory. Suggestions only work when they are in the same directory as the base template. In this case, it means we need to copy into our tao directory Zen's node.tpl.php file. We will not make any changes to the node.tpl.php file, nonetheless it must be in the directory for the suggestion to work properly.

The following variables are available in the node.tpl.php file:

Variable	Purpose
$content	Node content, teaser if it is a summary.
$date	Formatted creation date.
$directory	The directory where the theme is located.
$id	The sequential ID of the node being displayed in a list.
$is_front	True if the front page is currently being displayed.
$links	Node links.

Variable	Purpose
$name	Name of author.
$node	The node object.
$node_url	Link to node.
$page	True if the node is being displayed by itself as a page.
$picture	HTML for user picture.
$sticky	True if the node is sticky.
$submitted	Author and creation date information.
$taxonomy	Array of HTML links for taxonomy terms.
$teaser	Only returns the teaser rather than the full node text.
$terms	HTML for taxonomy terms.
$title	Title of node.
$zebra	Alternates between odd/even in a list.

The default file does not use all these variables, but that doesn't stop us from adding them in. Let's modify and format the information relating to the author and time of posting by modifying the code and adding the $date variable.

 More information on the various variables available can be found in Chapter 4 of this book.

The Zen theme page node is set up to display with each article the text **submitted by:** followed by the author's name; we want to do that differently in Tao. Tao is intended as a personal blog theme, so there's no need for us to display the author name. Additionally, it would be nice to display the date of each entry. Let's break away from the standard Zen "submitted by" language and go with something simple, like showing "posted" followed by the date. To achieve this, I am going to eliminate $submitted from our template file and instead add my preferred language ("posted") and one of the available variables: $date. I will also format the $date output to make it stand out a bit more.

The original statement looked like this:

```
<?php if ($submitted): ?>
<div class="submitted">
<?php print $submitted ?>
</div>
<?php endif; ?>
```

I am going to modify it as follows:

```php
<?php if ($submitted): ?>
<div class="submitted">
<?php print t('Posted ') ?><strong><?php print $date ?></strong>
</div>
<?php endif; ?>
```

Save your file and you're done with this final step.

Before and After

When we started this process, we had the STARTERKIT subtheme in place:

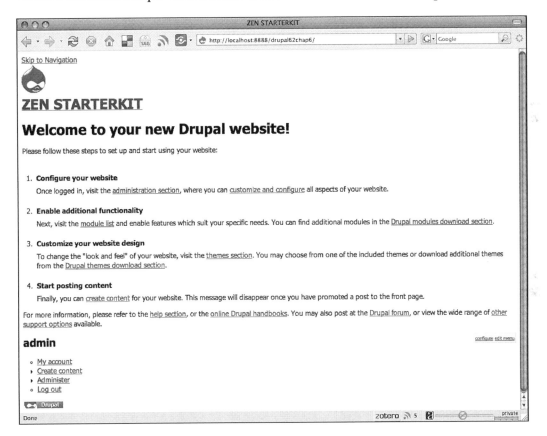

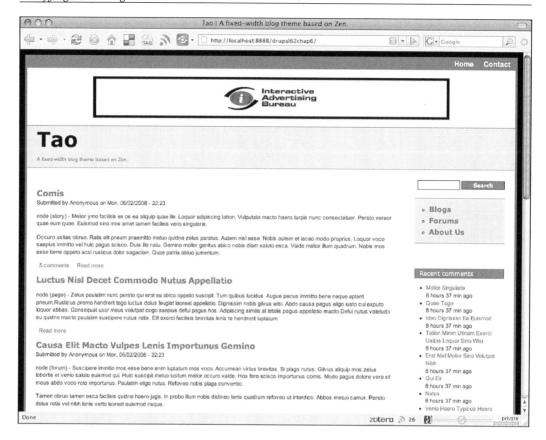

Now, after completing the changes to the CSS, the themable functions, and the default templates, we have Tao:

Summary

This chapter showed Drupal theming in action. We went from the very basic starter theme that comes with the Zen theme to a purpose-built subtheme with a completely different look and feel.

We made the conversion in three steps: configuring the theme, modifying the CSS, and modifying the themable functions and default templates. Along the way, we took default stylesheets and customized them to work with our subtheme and we overrode theme components that were present in the parent theme, Zen.

In addition to a hands-on example of theme customization, we also covered useful tools, such as the Devel module.

7
Building a New Theme

This chapter takes us into the world of building Drupal themes from scratch. While many people may undertake a theme project by copying and then modifying the files of an existing theme, in this chapter we cater to the purists who want to do it all themselves.

Inside, we'll cover the basics of creating a new theme employing the PHPTemplate engine, and step through the various tasks required to produce a fully functional theme. In the last half of the chapter, we take a brief look at creating a pure PHP template, that is, theming Drupal without the use of a theme engine.

To follow fully the examples in this chapter, you will need your favorite web editor (Dreamweaver or another similar program) and, preferably, access to a server upon which to preview your work. In the section dealing with pure PHP themes, we will be using as our example the Chameleon theme from the default Drupal distribution.

Planning the Build

How you go about building a theme is largely framed by your intentions for the theme. If you intend to release the theme for the use of others then it is best to follow certain (albeit largely unwritten) conventions that make the resulting theme more "standard" and therefore, easier for others to use. In contrast, if use by others is not one of your goals, then you can proceed in a fashion that tailors the code more narrowly to your needs. (The latter approach does afford you a bit more flexibility, as you can feel free to take a few shortcuts and save some time.)

For purposes of our discussion in this chapter, I am going to assume you wish others to be able to use your theme and accordingly, our examples will tend towards a best practices approach to Drupal themes. Taking a standardized approach has added advantages: the resulting theme is not only friendly for other users, but also easy to maintain and highly portable.

In terms of features, our goal here is to create a theme with the following attributes:

- Employs PHPTemplate
- Valid XHTML, pure CSS
- Supports one, two, or three columns
- Supports the theme configuration options we usually see in a Drupal PHPTemplate theme (e.g., logo, search box, site slogan, etc.)

Represented visually, the structure of head and body of the `page.tpl.php` file that we will create will look as follows:

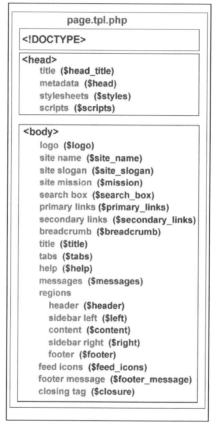

How the functional units will be grouped within the structure of the `page.tpl.php` file.

In terms of the layout that we will impose on the functionality, we will set up a standard three-column layout with a header and a footer, and then create the following structure to hold our functionality:

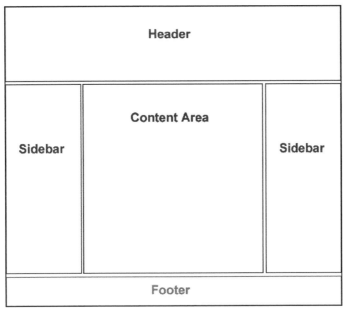

The general page layout we will define with the CSS for this theme

Regions are the primary containers for the placement of content and the functionality. Most frequently, PHPTemplate themes provide the following regions:

- Header
- Content
- Left Sidebar
- Right Sidebar
- Footer

As discussed in previous chapters, you are not restricted to the default regions. You can use all or only some of the regions and you can also define new regions if you so desire. For the example in this chapter, we will employ all the default regions. If you are designing themes for others, it is best to include these common regions, as failing to include them may lead to confusion for users who are less familiar with Drupal.

Regions for a theme are specified in the theme's `.info` file. If no regions are specified in the file, then the system assumes that the default regions (head, content, left sidebar, right sidebar, and footer) are active and available.

Now let's put this all together—here's a graphical representation of how our new theme will place the functional elements, including the regions, relative to the CSS page divisions we will create shortly.

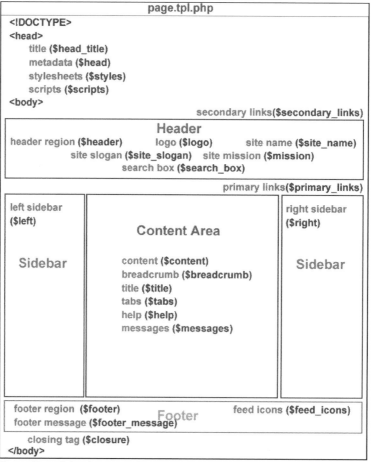

Diagram of the position of the elements relative to the principal divisions of the CSS layout and the main document divisions.

Creating a New PHPTemplate Theme

Let's get started by creating a directory to hold our new theme files. Create a new directory and name it "bluewater"—this will be the home directory and the name of our new theme. Next, let's create the basic files you need for a PHPTemplate-powered theme. Create each of the following (don't worry about the contents right now) and place them inside the Bluewater directory:

- `bluewater.info`
- `page.tpl.php`
- `style.css`

Testing during theme development is easiest if you have access to a server. Unlike straight HTML, it is difficult to preview the PHP files. If you have access to a server with a Drupal installation, go ahead and place the `Bluewater` directory into the `sites/all/themes` directory. Next, copy into that directory a sample logo file we can work with and name it `logo.png`—the default Drupal logo used in the themes included in the distro will work just fine.

 You can grab a copy of the Drupal logo from any of the default themes in the distro. Typically, the logo can be found inside the theme directory and is named `logo.png`, for example, `themes/garland/logo.png`.

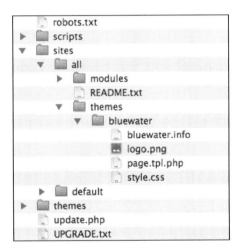

Place the directory and basic files for our new theme, Bluewater, inside `sites/all/themes`.

Building a .info File

As of Drupal 6, a .info file is required as part of a valid theme distribution. The .info file contains a number of pieces of information intended to inform the system about the theme and to set configuration options. The syntax throughout this file is consistent, use key = value. Semicolons can be used to add comments or comment out options. In the event that optional values are not stated, the system will assume default values.

To get started, open up the .info file you created a short while ago and add the following:

First, a name key is required by the system. Note this is a human-readable value. For our theme, this entry will appear as follows:

```
name = Bluewater
```

Next, let's add a description. This data will appear in Drupal's theme manager alongside the theme name and screenshot. This key is optional but as it is very helpful, we're going to include some information here:

```
description = A simple 3 column fixed width theme for Drupal 6.
```

The core key is required to keep the system from disabling our theme due to incompatibility.

```
core = 6.x
```

Add the engine key as follows (in the absence of this key, the system will assume this is a pure PHP theme):

```
engine = phptemplate
```

The regions key sets the regions available for block assignment. Note that this key is not necessary unless you wish to vary from the default set of regions. We've included the regions keys information in this example simply to show the variation in syntax that is required by this key. To set regions, use the following notation: region[machine_readable_name] = human readable name, for example:

```
region[head]    = Head
region[left]    = Left Sidebar
region[right]   = Right Sidebar
region[content] = Content
region[footer]  = Footer
```

The .info file can be also used to enable the various theme configuration features, like the site mission, site name, logo, etc. To specify features use the syntax features[] = name of feature. In the absence of a contrary definition, the system will assume the presence of all the following:

- features[] = logo
- features[] = name
- features[] = slogan
- features[] = mission
- features[] = node_user_picture
- features[] = comment_user_picture
- features[] = search
- features[] = favicon
- features[] = primary_links
- features[] = secondary_links

Should you not want any of these features, simply delineate the ones you wish to see in the .info file and omit the ones you do not wish to see. As we want to enable all the default features, we need to add nothing to our .info file. In this fashion, the system will enable all the default features, above, giving our site administrator the widest number of configurations for Bluewater.

As of Drupal 6, hook_features() is no longer supported.

Finally, note the stylesheets key. In our theme, we intend to use only the default style.css file; in that situation, no notation is required in the .info file. You can, however, use this key to add additional stylesheets or override default stylesheets. Note the variation in syntax, stylesheets[media_type][] = file.name.

To learn more about using the .info file to add or override stylesheets, visit http://drupal.org/node/171209

With all the options above (and more), .info files can be quite lengthy. The garland.info file (themes/garland/garland.info) for example, shows a relatively complex .info file. However, given our new theme's heavy reliance on default values, our .info file will be short and sweet:

```
name = Bluewater
description = A simple 3 column fixed width theme for Drupal 6.
core = 6.x
engine = phptemplate
```

Check that your new .info file contains the code immediately above, and if so, save and close the file and let's move on.

[To learn more about all the options available for the .info file, visit
http://drupal.org/node/171205]

Building a page.tpl.php File

The page.tpl.php file is the key to creating a PHPTemplate theme. This essential file handles the placement of all the major page elements and their output. Accordingly, we will place in this file a mix of HTML and PHP. The HTML supplies the formatting and the PHP supplies the logic and the functionality.

Take note of the ordering of the tags and the relationship between the PHP and the HTML. In this theme, we will typically place the HTML formatting inside the PHP conditional statements, rather than wrapping the PHP with HTML.

For example, we will typically want to order the tags like this (HTML inside the PHP):

```
<!-- slogan -->
<?php if ($site_slogan): ?>
<div class="slogan">
<?php print $site_slogan; ?>
</div>
<?php endif; ?>
```

We generally don't want to do it like this (PHP inside the HTML):

```
<!-- slogan -->
<div class="slogan">
<?php if ($site_slogan): ?>
<?php print $site_slogan; ?>
<?php endif; ?>
</div>
```

The reasoning behind the preference for the first ordering of tags is quite simple: if we place the HTML outside the PHP, then the appearance of the HTML will occur even when the condition contained in the PHP statement is not true, thereby clogging our page with unnecessary code and more importantly, creating unnecessary complexities in dealing with the styling of the page as a whole.

Again by way of example, compare the impact of the different orderings on the resulting source code. First, let's look at what happens when the HTML is placed inside the PHP. Here's the source code with the site slogan functionality enabled by the administrator:

```
<!-- slogan -->
<div class="slogan">
this is the slogan
</div>
```

Compare that with the source code that results when the site slogan function is disabled:

```
<!-- slogan -->
```

In this case, the PHP conditional statement is false (site slogan disabled by the administrator) and, as a result, neither the site slogan nor its accompanying HTML formatting is displayed; the only thing that remains in the resulting source code is the comment tag (the comment tag is located in the template).

Now, let's compare the source code that is produced when the PHP is wrapped with the HTML.

With site slogan enabled, you will see no difference:

```
<!-- slogan -->
<div id="slogan">
this is the slogan
</div>
```

But, when the site slogan is disabled, you do see a difference:

```
<!-- slogan -->
<div id="slogan">
</div>
```

In the latter example, the HTML is visible even though the conditional statement is false. The formatting remains despite the fact that the element the HTML is intended to format is not present. With this ordering of tags, we're always stuck with the presence of styles in the resulting code, regardless of whether the function it is supposed to format appears or not.

The example above makes another point as well, that is, how the use of the PHP conditional statements delivers benefits at run time. With the conditional statements in place, unneeded code is removed at run time. Without the conditional statements, the code remains for the browser to render, regardless of whether it is needed.

As a result of the interaction between the PHP conditional statements and the HTML tags, you will need to make decisions about whether you wish the styles to remain active in the absence of the element that the styling is intended to affect. In some cases, your layout integrity is maintained better by leaving the styling in place, regardless of whether the underlying element is active. In other cases, you will want the formatting to fold away when the element is not active—for example, a sidebar that collapses when no blocks are assigned to a region—and will therefore, want to use the PHP to control the visibility of the HTML.

 For a discussion of theme coding conventions, see the Drupal Theme Handbook at `http://drupal.org/node/1965`.

With that background behind us, let's get started on the `page.tpl.php` file for our new theme.

Insert DocType and Head

Start by declaring the appropriate DocType. XHTML Strict is appropriate for this usage:

```
<!DOCTYPE html PUBLIC "-//W3C//DTD XHTML 1.0 Strict//EN" "http://www.
w3.org/TR/xhtml1/DTD/xhtml1-strict.dtd">
```

Next, place the opening HTML tag and name space. Note that this code also includes the PHP statements that call the appropriate language settings for your site, and should not be altered.

```
<html xmlns="http://www.w3.org/1999/xhtml" xml:lang="<?php print
$language->language ?>" lang="<?php print $language->language ?>"
dir="<?php print $language->dir ?>">
```

As the opening tag, above, is an HTML declaration, go ahead and add the closing HTML tag now.

```
</html>
```

The rest of the code, discussed below, will be placed inside these two HTML tags.

Next, let's set up the head of the document. The various statements that compose the head of the document (including the metadata, the links to the stylesheets, and any scripts) are produced by the following lines of code:

```
<head>
   <title>
      <?php print $head_title; ?>
   </title>
```

```
    <?php print $head; ?>
    <?php print $styles; ?>
    <?php print $scripts; ?>
</head>
```

Here is a description of each of the variables:

string name	function
$head_title	Produces the site title (not the page title).
$head	Includes the Drupal head code.
$styles	Includes the various stylesheets.
$scripts	Includes any necessary scripts.

There is no need to alter any of these, unless you have special needs.

Note that due to a quirk in the Internet Explorer browser that can result in a flash of unstyled content, you may wish to add an empty <script> tag to your document head, e.g., <script type="text/javascript"></script>.

For more on this phenomenon, visit http://www.bluerobot.com/web/css/fouc.asp/

Insert Body Tags

Immediately after the </head> tag, open the <body> tag. With Drupal 6, we have the ability to insert into the body tag a bit of code that aids immensely with creating dynamic styling—that is, styling that can be changed easily depending on the page conditions:

```
<body class="<?php print $body_classes; ?>">
```

Then add a closing </body> tag:

```
</body>
```

All the code discussed in the section below will be placed inside the body tag.

The use of $body_classes to enable dynamic CSS styling is discussed at length in Chapter 8.

Taken together, at this stage, you should now have the template's bare skeleton, like this:

```
<!DOCTYPE html PUBLIC "-//W3C//DTD XHTML 1.0 Strict//EN" "http://www.
w3.org/TR/xhtml1/DTD/xhtml1-strict.dtd">
<html xmlns="http://www.w3.org/1999/xhtml" xml:lang="<?php print
$language->language ?>" lang="<?php print $language->language ?>"
dir="<?php print $language->dir ?>">
<head>
<title>
<?php print $head_title; ?>
</title>
<?php print $head; ?>
<?php print $styles; ?>
<?php print $scripts; ?>
<script type="text/javascript"></script>
</head>
<body class="<?php print $body_classes; ?>">
</body>
</html>
```

Into this document outline, we will now place the basic HTML that defines the layout of the output on the page. Once we have the basic HTML in place, we will then insert the functional elements into the appropriate areas.

Lay Out the Page Divisions

The next step is to outline the general divisions that will define the layout of the page.tpl.php output. Between the <body> tags, add the following:

```
<div id="page-wrapper">
   <div id="header-wrapper">
      <div id="header-region">
      </div>
   </div>
   <div id="primary-links">
   </div>
   <div id="main-wrapper">
      <div id="sidebar-left-region">
      </div>
      <div id="content-region-<?php print $layout ?>">
      </div>
      <div id="sidebar-right-region">
      </div>
   </div>
   <div id="footer-region">
   </div>
</div>
```

Before we get started with placing the functional flesh on this HTML formatting skeleton, note that the organization of divs, above, wraps the entire body section inside `<div id="page-wrapper">`. Within that main div, we create separate styling for the header, the primary links, the main content area, and finally, the footer. We have also set up dedicated styling for each of the five regions—all nested inside the primary div.

Now, let's look at this in more detail as we add the functionality.

Place the Functional Elements

With our formatting in place, we can now go back and place the functional elements where we want them to appear inside the layout.

Insert the Secondary Links

For this theme, I have placed the secondary links at the very top righthand side of the page, before the header area. The placement is a subjective decision and here, instead of treating the secondary links as subnavigation to the primary links (which some templates do), I have separated them from the primary links, in order to create a distinct area in which secondary navigation can be positioned.

Let's use a conditional statement to control the placement of the secondary links (`$secondary_links`). The conditional statement allows this area of the layout to compress and disappear from view when the secondary links are disabled.

```
<!-- secondary links -->
<?php if ($secondary_links): ?>
<div id="secondary-links">
<?php print theme('links', $secondary_links); ?>
</div>
<?php endif; ?>
```

Inside the Header Wrapper

We've designated the next area of our page layout as "header". This page division will appear below the secondary navigation on our final page. This area of the page will hold a number of elements related to the site's identity, as well as some basic functionality. Note that this area comes in the code before the header region, which is discussed below.

Let's open this section of the code with a comment statement and a div to wrap this section of the page:

```
<!-- BEGIN Header -->
<div id="header-wrapper">
```

Logo

The following snippet includes the logo ($logo), with a hyperlink to the homepage. Note that the title and alt attributes are set by the code below. In this snippet, the image attributes are set to Click to return to the Homepage, but you can change this to whatever wording you wish. Note also the t function, which enables the translation feature of Drupal.

Wrap the logo inside a div with the id logo. We want this area of the layout to be stable and not changing size in response to the logo settings, so in this case, we'll place the div outside the PHP (instead of placing the styling inside the conditional statement).

```
<!-- logo -->
<div id="logo">
<?php if ($logo): ?>
<a href="<?php print $base_path; ?>" title="<?php print t('Click
to return to the Homepage'); ?>"><img src="<?php print $logo; ?>"
alt="<?php print t('Click to return to the Homepage '); ?>" /></a>
<?php endif; ?>
</div>
```

 The logo code in the example calls the system default logo image. The logo setting is controlled by the administrator in the theme and global configuration settings. If you intend to distribute your theme to others, you must place a logo file in the proper location (inside the directory), with the proper name (i.e., logo.png) and include it with your theme files. The Drupal logo is commonly used for this purpose in distributed themes.

Site Name

To include the site name ($site_name) on the page, together with a hyperlink to the homepage, add the code below. The title attribute of the a tag is set dynamically and tied to the translate functions (t). You can change the text from "Home" to whatever you wish.

A div named sitename is used to wrap the functionality. Unlike the logo, above, the formatting here is inside the PHP conditional statement, so that the formatting is disabled if the site name feature is disabled by the administrator.

```
<!-- site name -->
<?php if ($site_name): ?>
<div id="sitename">
<h1><a href="<?php print $base_path ?>" title="<?php print t('Home')
?>"><?php print $site_name; ?></a></h1>
</div>
<?php endif; ?>
```

Theme Search Box

The theme search box is inserted with the following snippet wrapped in a div with the id `searchbox`.

```
<!-- theme search box -->
<?php if ($search_box): ?>
<div id="searchbox">
<?php print $search_box; ?>
</div>
<?php endif; ?>
```

Site Slogan

Next comes the site slogan wrapped with a div with the id `site-slogan`:

```
<!-- slogan -->
<?php if ($site_slogan): ?>
<div id="site-slogan">
<?php print $site_slogan; ?>
</div>
<?php endif; ?>
```

Site Mission

The site mission statement is included with `$mission`. Wrap it in a div with the id `mission`:

```
<!-- mission statement -->
<?php if ($mission): ?>
<div id="mission">
<?php print $mission; ?>
</div>
<?php endif; ?>
```

Header Region

Despite the confusing name, this has nothing to do with the header of the HTML page — this is a region named "Header", which will be used for the placement of blocks.

`$header` prints the region to the page. Note that we employ a conditional statement, which allows the space for the region to compress if nothing is assigned to the region.

I have wrapped the region with a div. The id here is `header-region`.

```
<!-- Region: header -->
<?php if ($header): ?>
<div id="header-region">
<?php print $header; ?>
</div>
<?php endif; ?>
```

Insert the Primary Links

I am going to place the primary links in the space between the header wrapper and the main wrapper. In this fashion, it is easy for me to control the formatting of this area, which will span the width of the design.

The primary links for the site are included by the following. Note that the div is inside the conditional statement so if the user decides not to use the primary links, then the area compresses and is hidden from sight.

```
<!-- Primary Links -->
<?php if ($primary_links): ?>
<div id="primary-links">
<?php print theme('links', $primary_links); ?>
</div>
<?php endif; ?>
```

Inside the Main Wrapper

There is a bit more styling involved here, given that three columns and a wide range of functionality will be included in this critical area of the page. For this theme, in addition to placing the main content region inside the area between the two sidebars, we're also placing the breadcrumb trail, title, tabs, help, messages, and feed icons. To control all this, we will wrap the entire set of tags with one div (with the id `main-content-wrapper`), and then create inside of that the formatting for each column and its constituent elements.

Sidebar Left

Let's place first the left sidebar (`$sidebar_left`), using a conditional statement to wrap the entire thing. We want this to compress and fold up if nothing is assigned to this region, thereby allowing us to create a one- or two-column layout. Note the div controlling this region has been named `sidebar-left-region`.

```
<div id="main-wrapper">
<!-- Region: Sidebar Left -->
<?php if ($left): ?>
<div id="sidebar-left-region">
<?php print $left; ?>
</div>
<?php endif; ?>
```

The Main Content Area

For the main content area of this design, I've created a div to wrap all the following elements. In a three-column layout, the area inside this div would be the center column. Regardless of how many columns are used, this area will hold the main content of the site by default.

Breadcrumb Trail

The breadcrumb functionality is placed on the screen with $breadcrumb. Note that while you can style this from within the page.tpl.php file, the creation of the breadcrumb trail is controlled by a themable function. You can obtain the best control over the display and formatting settings by overriding the themable function, rather than by styling this PHP statement.

```
<!-- breadcrumb trail -->
<?php if ($breadcrumb): ?>
<?php print $breadcrumb; ?>
<?php endif; ?>
```

 A list of all the themable functions is included in Chapter 4.

Title

Insert the following conditional statement to place the page title on the screen. Style the title with the H2 tag and a dedicated class, content-title.

```
<!-- title -->
<?php if ($title): ?>
<h2 class="content-title"><?php print $title; ?></h2>
<?php endif; ?>
```

Tabs

$tabs controls the placement of the tabs-based navigation. Note that while the default front-end settings do not employ tabs, the default administration interface does; therefore, omitting the placement of this feature can cause you problems in the administration interface. Wrap the PHP print statement with a div and a class, tabs.

```
<!-- tabs -->
<?php if ($tabs): ?>
<div class="tabs">
<?php print $tabs; ?>
</div>
<?php endif; ?>
```

Help

$help controls the output of the context-sensitive help information. The help link typically only appears in the admin interface. You can style this statement if you choose, but in this example, I have added no extra styling and left it to the system to provide the default styling.

```
<!-- help -->
<?php print $help; ?>
```

Messages

Insert $messages wherever you wish the system status and alerts messages to appear on your page. Note that you can style this statement if you choose. In this example, I have added no extra styling and left it to the system to provide the default styling.

```
<!-- messages -->
<?php print $messages; ?>
```

Content Region

The content region ($content) is the primary region used by the Drupal system to hold a variety of information, including nodes, the administration interface, and more. I have not used a conditional statement for this region as the system does not give the user the option to omit output to this region; this region is required for your theme to function properly. The formatting for this area is governed by a div that wraps the entire column; in our example, no additional styling is needed as we will be able to independently control the styling of the various elements that appear within this area of the page.

```
<!-- Region: content -->
<?php print $content; ?>
```

Sidebar Right

Let's close out this section of our page layout by including the right sidebar region ($sidebar_right). Wrap this with a conditional statement so it will compress out of sight in the event nothing is assigned to the right sidebar. The div sidebar-right-region is used to wrap the region itself.

```
<!-- Region: Sidebar Right -->
<?php if ($right): ?>
<div id="sidebar-right-region">
<?php print $right; ?>
</div>
<?php endif; ?>
```

Inside the Footer

Lastly, at the bottom of our layout, is the footer. Let's wrap this with a div and name it appropriately. Inside the div, we will place the footer region, the feed icon, and the footer message.

```
<!-- Region: Footer -->
<div id="footer-region">
<?php print $footer; ?>
```

Feed Icons

Place the RSS feed icon (`$feed_icons`) inside the div for the footer and wrap it in a div named `feed-icons`:

```
<!-- feed icons -->
<div id="feed-icons">
<?php print $feed_icons; ?>
</div>
```

Footer Message

The footer message is set by the administrator in the site information manager. The message typically appears in or near the footer region, hence the name. Let's wrap `$footer_message` in a div so we can style it easily.

```
<!-- footer text -->
<div id="footer-text">
<?php print $footer_message; ?>
</div>
```

 Note that as of Drupal 6, `$footer_message` is used only for placing the footer message (set in the site configuration by the administrator). The footer region will instead be controlled by `$footer`.

Insert the Template Closing Tag

The final snippet we will need to include produces no output but is required by the Drupal system to close the logic of the template. Add this statement immediately before the closing body tag. No styling is needed.

```
<?php print $closure; ?>
```

The Final page.tpl.php File

At this stage, we've assembled all the necessary pieces of a fully functional PHPTemplate theme. All the elements you need are in place, though the styling is lacking as we have yet to define the selectors in our `style.css` file.

Let's stop here for a moment and get the big picture. Below is our raw `page.tpl.php` file, with only comment tags added to enhance readability:

```php
<!DOCTYPE html PUBLIC "-//W3C//DTD XHTML 1.0 Strict//EN" "http://www.
w3.org/TR/xhtml1/DTD/xhtml1-strict.dtd">
<html xmlns="http://www.w3.org/1999/xhtml" xml:lang="<?php print
$language->language ?>" lang="<?php print $language->language ?>"
dir="<?php print $language->dir ?>">

<head>
<title>
<?php print $head_title; ?>
</title>

<?php print $head; ?>
<?php print $styles; ?>
<?php print $scripts; ?>
<script type="text/javascript"></script>
</head>

<body class="<?php print $body_classes; ?>">

<div id="page-wrapper">

<!-- secondary links -->
<?php if ($secondary_links): ?>
<div id="secondary-links">
<?php print theme('links', $secondary_links); ?>
</div>
<?php endif; ?>

<!-- BEGIN Header -->
<div id="header-wrapper">

<!-- logo -->
<div id="logo">
<?php if ($logo): ?>
<a href="<?php print $base_path; ?>" title="<?php print t('Click
to return to the Home page'); ?>"><img src="<?phpprint $logo; ?>"
alt="<?php print t('Click to return tothe Home page '); ?>" /></a>
<?php endif; ?>
</div>

<!-- site name -->
<?php if ($site_name): ?>
```

```
<div id="sitename">
<h1><a href="<?php print $base_path ?>" title="<?php printt('Home')
?>"><?php print $site_name; ?></a></h1>
</div>
<?php endif; ?>

<!-- theme search box -->
<?php if ($search_box): ?>
<div id="searchbox">
<?php print $search_box; ?>
</div>
<?php endif; ?>

<!-- slogan -->
<?php if ($site_slogan): ?>
<div id="site-slogan">
<?php print $site_slogan; ?>
</div>
<?php endif; ?>

<!-- mission statement -->
<?php if ($mission): ?>
<div id="mission">
<?php print $mission; ?>
</div>
<?php endif; ?>

<!-- Region: header -->
<?php if ($header): ?>
<div id="header-region">
<?php print $header; ?>
</div>
<?php endif; ?>

</div>

<!-- primary links -->
<?php if ($primary_links): ?>
<div id="primary-links">
<?php print theme('links', $primary_links); ?>
</div>
<?php endif; ?>

<!-- BEGIN Center Content -->
<div id="main-wrapper">

<!-- Region: sidebar left -->
<?php if ($left): ?>
<div id="sidebar-left-region">
<?php print $left; ?>
```

```
</div>
<?php endif; ?>

<div id="content">

<!-- breadcrumb trail -->
<?php if ($breadcrumb): ?>
<?php print $breadcrumb; ?>
<?php endif; ?>

<!-- title -->
<?php if ($title): ?>
<h2 class="content-title"><?php print $title; ?></h2>
<?php endif; ?>

<!-- tabs -->
<?php if ($tabs): ?>
<div class="tabs">
<?php print $tabs; ?>
</div>
<?php endif; ?>

<!-- help -->
<?php print $help; ?>

<!-- messages -->
<?php print $messages; ?>

<!-- Region: content -->
<?php print $content; ?>

</div>

<!-- Region: sidebar right -->
<?php if ($right): ?>
<div id="sidebar-right-region">
<?php print $right; ?>
</div>
<?php endif; ?>

</div>
<!-- END Content Area -->

<!-- BEGIN Footer -->
<!-- Region: footer -->
<div id="footer-region">
<?php print $footer; ?>

<!-- feed icons -->
<div id="feed-icons">
<?php print $feed_icons; ?>
</div>
```

```
<!-- footer text -->
<div id="footer-text">
<?php print $footer_message; ?>
</div>

</div>
</div>
<?php print $closure; ?>

</body>
</html>
```

The style.css File

Let's go back now and open up the `style.css` file we created at the beginning of this chapter. We will use this file to define the various selectors we've placed in the `page.tpl.php` file. In addition to the selectors we've used to control the placement of the functionality, you will need to define various tags, classes, and IDs to specify fonts and style the information hierarchy. You may also wish to add decorative touches via some creative CSS. All the theme-specific styles should be defined in this document, along with any overrides of existing selectors.

Because an exhaustive CSS tutorial is beyond the scope of this text, we're not going to go through all the various styling. The file is included, below, for your review:

```css
/** global styles **/
body {
font: 13px/16px Verdana, Arial, Helvetica, sans-serif;
color: #CCCCCC;
background-color: #CCCCCC;
}

#page-wrapper {
position:relative;
width:974px;
text-align:left;
background-color: #336699;
border: solid 12px #FFFFFF;
margin: 0 auto;
}

a, a:link, a:visited {
  color: #FFFFFF;
  text-decoration: none;
}

a:hover, a:focus {
  color: #6191C5;
```

```
      text-decoration: underline;
    }
  a:active, a.active {
    color: #89A3E4;
  }
  h1.title, h1.title a, h1.title a:hover {
    font-family: "Trebuchet MS", Arial, Helvetica, sans-serif;
    font-weight: normal;
    color: #6191C5;
    font-size: 200%;
    margin:0;
    line-height:normal;
  }
  h1, h1 a, h1 a:hover {
    font: 20px/20px Arial, Helvetica, sans-serif;
    color: #FFFFFF;
    margin: 0;
  }
  h2,  h3 {
    font: 18px/18px Arial, Helvetica, sans-serif;
  color: #FFFFFF;
    margin: 2px 0 0 0;
    padding: 2px 5px;
    border: dashed 1px #FFFFFF;
  }
  h2 a, h2 a:hover, .block h3, .block h3 a {
    font: 18px/22x Arial, Helvetica, sans-serif;
    color: #FFFFFF !important;
    margin: 0;
    padding: 0;
  }
  #sidebar-left-region h2,
  #sidebar-left-region h3,
  #sidebar-right-region h2,
  #sidebar-right-region h3 {
    font: 16px/16px Arial, Helvetica, sans-serif;
    color: #FFFFFF;
    margin: 0;
    padding: 20px 0 0 0;
    border: none;
  }
  h4, h5, h6 {
```

```css
    font-weight: bold;
font-family: Arial, Helvetica, sans-serif;
}
/** header styles **/
#header-wrapper {
    position: relative;
    display: block;
    background-color: #336699;
    height: 120px;
}

#header-region {
}

#logo {
    float: left;
    width: 50px;
    margin: 12px 0 0 12px;
    padding: 8px 12px;
    border: 10px solid#FFFFFF;
    background-color: #6699CC;
}

#sitename {
    float: left;
    margin-top: 20px;
}

#sitename h1 a{
    font: 28px/28px Arial, "Century Gothic", Verdana;
    color: #FFFFFF;
    margin-left: 7px;
    text-decoration: none;
}

#searchbox {
    float:right;
    width:210px;
    height: 20px;
    margin-top:55px;
    margin-right:0px;
}

#search .form-text {
  width: 137px;
  vertical-align: middle;
  border: 1px solid #6699CC;
}
```

```css
#search .form-submit {
  padding: 0 3px;
  vertical-align: middle;
  border-top: 1px solid #FFFFFF;
  border-right: 1px solid #666666;
  border-bottom: 1px solid #666666;
  border-left: 1px solid #FFFFFF;
}
.submitted {
  color: #333333;
}
.submitted a{
  color: #000000;
}
#primary-links {
position: relative;
display: block;
height:20px;
width:974px;
border-top: solid 12px #FFFFFF;
background-color: #666666;
}
#primary-links ul {
  padding:0;
  margin:0;
  list-style:none;
  float: right;
}
#primary-links ul li {
  display:inline;
}
#primary-links ul li a, #primary-links ul li a:visited {
  padding: 3px 10px 0 10px;
  font: 10px/13px Verdana, Arial, Helvetica, sans-serif;
  color: #FFFFFF;
}
#primary-links ul li a:hover {
  color: #000000;
}
#secondary-links {
position: relative;
display: block;
```

```
height:20px;
width:974px;
margin-top: 0;
border-bottom: solid 12px #FFFFFF;
background-color: #666666;
}
#secondary-links ul {
list-style: none;
  float: right;
}
#secondary-links ul li {
    display: inline;
}
#secondary-links ul li a, #secondary-links ul li a:visited {
  padding: 3px 10px 0 10px;
  font: 10px/13px Verdana, Arial, Helvetica, sans-serif;
  color: #FFFFFF;
}
#secondary-links ul li a:hover {
  color: #000000;
}
#mission {
    position: absolute;
    left: 113px;
    width: 650px;
    top: 68px;
}
#site-slogan {
    position: absolute;
    left: 113px;
    top: 50px;
}
/** content area styles **/
#main-wrapper{
    position: relative;
    width:auto;
    height: 100%;
    border-top: solid 12px #FFFFFF;
    background-color: #336699;
}
 .no-sidebars #content {
    padding: 12px 10px 10px 10px;
```

```css
    position: relative;
 }
.sidebar-left #content {
    width: 743px;
    padding:12px 0 10px 10px;
    position: relative;
    float:left;
}
.sidebar-right #content {
    width: 743px;
    padding:12px 10px 10px 10px;
    position: relative;
    float:left;
}
.two-sidebars #content {
    width: 533px;
    padding:12px 10px 10px 10px;
    position: relative;
    float:left;
}
/** sidebar styles **/
#sidebar-left-region{
    position:relative;
    float:left;
    width:200px;
    padding: 0 0 0 10px;
}
#sidebar-right-region{
    position:relative;
    float:right;
    width:200px;
    padding: 0 10px 0 0;
}
/** footer styles **/
#footer-region {
    position:relative;
    width: auto;
    height:40px;
    margin:0 auto;
    clear:both;
    border-top:12px solid #FFFFFF;
}
```

```
#feed-icons {
   float:right;
   padding: 8px;
}
#footer-text {
   position:relative;
   display: block;
   height: 30px;
   float:left;
   color: #FFFFFF;
   font-size: 10px;
   line-height: 35px;
   left: 10px;
}
/** Admin Style **/
/* Tabs */
ul.primary {
   border-bottom: solid 1px #18324B;
}
ul.secondary {
   border-bottom: solid 1px #18324B;
}
ul.primary li.active a.active {
   background-color:#2B5986;
   border: solid 1px #18324B;
}
ul.primary li a {
   background-color:#6699CC;
}
ul.secondary li  {
   margin-bottom: 5px;
}
/* Region: content */
#content-region-both table  {
   width: 530px;
}
table thead {
   color: #FFFFFF;
}
table tbody tr.odd,
table tbody tr.odd td.menu-disabled{
   background: #2B5986;
   border-bottom: solid 1px #336699;
```

```
}
table tbody tr.even,
table tbody tr.even td.menu-disabled{
    background: #2D5E8D;
    border-bottom: solid 1px #336699;
}
table tr td.region{
    font-weight: normal;
    color:#FFFFFF;
    background:   #6699CC;
}
ul.secondary li.active a.active {
    border-bottom: solid 1px #18324B;
}
```

 In addition to your theme-specific selectors, you may wish to redefine the portions of the /modules/system/admin.css file that affects the administrator's interface.

While the vast majority of the selectors defined in our style.css are basic (we used a bare minimum for this example), you should note the following, which relate to the implementation of the three-column layout:

```
.no-sidebars #content {
    padding: 12px 10px 10px 10px;
    position: relative;
 }
.sidebar-left #content {
    width: 743px;
    padding:12px 0 10px 10px;
    position: relative;
    float:left;
}
.sidebar-right #content {
    width: 743px;
    padding:12px 10px 10px 10px;
    position: relative;
    float:left;
}
.two-sidebars #content {
    width: 533px;
    padding:12px 10px 10px 10px;
    position: relative;
    float:left;
}
```

These selectors work together with the dynamic styling we applied to the body tag (`<body class="<?php $body_classes;?>"`) to create a center column that expands to fill either the right or left column when either of the sidebars carry no blocks. The styles, in other words, are critical to creating a template that can support a one-, two- or three-column layout.

The technique used to create the fluid columns structure is discussed in the next chapter, in the section on *Creating Dynamic CSS Styling*.

 As of Drupal 6, best practice for themes would have us include a separate stylesheet to handle those sites that use right-to-left oriented text. The additional stylesheet is normally named `styles-rtl.css`. Examples of this file can be found in both the Garland and Bluemarine themes in the default Drupal distribution.

A Look at Our New Theme

With the completion of the `style.css` file, the new theme is ready for use.

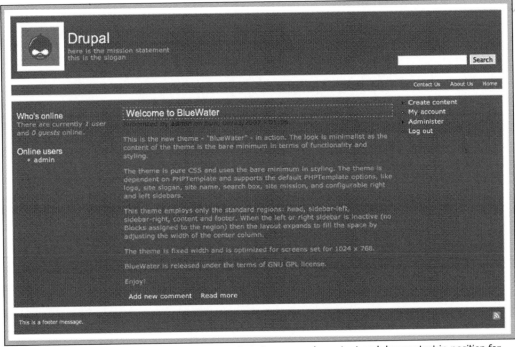

Our new theme in action. Note that this screenshot shows sample content and dummy text in position for testing the primary links, the main content area, the site slogan, site mission, and footer message. The Who's Online block has also been assigned to the left region.

If you wish to distribute your theme and share it with the Drupal community (something we strongly encourage!), you will need to include a thumbnail of the theme in action. Take note of Drupal's guidelines for theme screenshots, as they are rather specific http://drupal.org/node/11637.

Build a New Pure PHP Theme

It is possible to build pure PHP templates without the use of PHPTemplate (or any other theme engine). In this section, we will look at the basics behind this approach to theming, and give you the information you need to get started, should you decide this is how you want to proceed.

Given the popularity of the PHPTemplate engine, and the extent that it eases the difficulties attendant to theming, it is probably no surprise that few people choose to build their themes without the use of the theme engine. Moreover, pure PHP themes tend to be more difficult to maintain over time and there are fewer help resources available in the Drupal community (as most people employ one of the theme engines). Given the advantages of PHPTemplate, and the drawbacks of building without it, it is very hard to recommend that you build a pure PHP theme; indeed, without some special circumstance, I would recommend against it.

If you wish to build a pure PHP theme, there is an example bundled with the default Drupal distro: Chameleon. Neither the Chameleon theme, nor its subtheme Marvin, use a theme engine. Note, that while we use Chameleon as a convenient reference, the theme does employ tables and is starting to look a bit old school at this stage. Should you choose to use Chameleon as the starting point of your own PHP theme, you may want to revisit the formatting.

Building a theme in pure PHP requires a slightly different approach to theming. A number of the functions that would normally be automatically handled by the PHPTemplate engine must be coded manually into your PHP theme. Open up the file `chameleon.theme` (inside the Chameleon theme directory) with your editor. When you examine the code, it will be immediately apparent that this is radically different from what we've seen so far in this chapter.

The learning process associated with building PHP themes for Drupal can be challenging unless you have strong PHP skills. For most people, the correct first step will be to crack open the Chameleon directory and copy the elements you need. Copying the code from the Chameleon theme and modifying it to fit your needs is not only a great way to learn but also a huge time saver, as it cuts down dramatically on the chance for errors.

Required Elements

Pure PHP themes, like their PHPTemplate counterparts, require a `.info` file. The syntax and options available are the same as those discussed above. Accordingly, one of your first steps should be the creation of a `.info` file for your new theme. Here's the `chameleon.info` file:

```
; $Id: chameleon.info,v 1.4 2007/07/01 23:27:31 goba Exp $
name = Chameleon
description = Minimalist tabled theme with light colors.
regions[left]  = Left sidebar
regions[right]  = Right sidebar
features[]  = logo
features[]  = favicon
features[]  = name
features[]  = slogan
stylesheets[all][]  = style.css
stylesheets[all][]  = common.css
version = VERSION
core = 6.x
; Information added by drupal.org packaging script on 2008-04-09
version = "6.2"
project = "drupal"
datestamp = "1207776008"
```

 Note that the code at the top, behind the comment tags, is used as an identifier in CVS. Similarly, the code at the bottom, behind the comment tags, is supplied automatically by the Drupal packaging script when this theme was prepared for distribution. You do not need to worry about either of those areas.

The only other required file for a pure PHP theme is the `.theme` file. This is a plain PHP file and will be placed into the `sites/all/themes/themename` directory. For development purposes, you should also copy into that directory a sample logo; the Drupal logo will work just fine.

The `themename.theme` file begins with a function to autodiscover the features you have set in your `.info` file. This function is required. Let's use the Chameleon theme, with the `chameleon.theme` file, as our example. Here's the code:

```
function chameleon_theme($existing, $type, $theme, $path) {
    return drupal_find_theme_functions($existing, array($theme));
}
```

This tells the system to enable the functions registered in your `.info` file. You can add or delete other optional theme functions from within the `.info` file without having to make changes to your `.theme` file.

Note that the Chameleon author also handles a couple of housekeeping matters at the top of the file. First, `$title` is defined in order to incorporate the Drupal site name, and `$blocks_left` and `$blocks_right` are provided for use in placing the themed blocks.

HTML Headers

Placing the necessary HTML headers is done with two `$output` statements, as below:

```
$output  = "<!DOCTYPE html PUBLIC \"-//W3C//DTD XHTML 1.0 Strict//EN\"
\"http://www.w3.org/TR/xhtml1/DTD/xhtml1-strict.dtd\">\n";
$output .= "<html xmlns=\"http://www.w3.org/1999/xhtml\" lang=\
"$language\" xml:lang=\"$language\" dir=\"$direction\">\n";
```

Head of Document

The header of the resulting web page needs to incorporate the Drupal head elements, along with the various stylesheets and scripts. The code below does this, as well as invoking `$title` (set earlier in the document), the site name, and the site slogan.

```
$output .= "<head>\n";
$output .= " <title>". ($title ? strip_tags($title) ." | ". variable_
get("site_name", "Drupal") : variable_get("site_name", "Drupal") ." |
". variable_get("site_slogan", "")) ."</title>\n";
$output .= drupal_get_html_head();
$output .= drupal_get_css();
$output .= drupal_get_js();
$output .= "</head>";
```

Implementing the Features

At the top of the document, the author declared the function `chameleon_features()`. In addition to declaring the features you must also insert the code to implement the conditions attached to those features and display the resulting output.

Favicon

The author deals with the setting of the favicon early in the document, prior to the output of the head of the document, and thereby makes the `<link rel>` tag available to the document head when it is output. All the other features, below, are placed in the body of the page where they will appear in the layout.

```
if (theme_get_setting('toggle_favicon')) {    drupal_set_html_
head('<link rel="shortcut icon" href="'. check_url(theme_get_
setting('favicon')) .'" type="image/x-icon" />');}
```

Logo

The following conditional statement enables the logo to be toggled on or off, wraps the image in an `<a>` tag and also sets the `title` and `alt` attributes.

```
if ($logo = theme_get_setting('logo')) {
    $output .= "  <a href=\"". url() ."\" title=\"". t('Home')
."\"><img src=\"$logo\" alt=\"". t('Home') ."\" /></a>";
}
```

Site Name

This snippet enables the site name to be toggled on or off, and wraps it with an `H1` tag and a `class`.

```
if (theme_get_setting('toggle_name')) {
    $output .= "  <h1 class=\"site-name title\">". l(variable_
get('site_name', 'drupal'), "") . "</h1>";
}
```

You have probably noticed by now the recurrence of the `t()` function. This function is the key to tying into Drupal's language system and enables the system to support multiple languages. Preserve the `t()` function in your overrides and code to be able to maintain the system's support for multilingual labels, error messages, and alerts.

Site Slogan

The following statement enables the site slogan to be toggled on or off, and wraps it with a div and a class for styling.

```
if (theme_get_setting('toggle_slogan')) {
    $output .= "  <div class=\"site-slogan\">". variable_get(
'site_slogan', '') ."</div>";
}
```

Primary and Secondary Links

Chameleon combines the placement of the primary and secondary links, basically locking the secondary links into a subnavigation role. You don't have to group these two items together in this fashion, but it is one logical option.

Note the snippet below. In both cases, the display of the links is conditional (depending on what is enabled by the administrator). If either one is enabled, then it will appear inside a div with the class navlinks. Additionally, to be able to style each set of links individually, both $primary_links and $secondary_links are provided with a unique class and id.

```
$primary_links = theme('links', menu_primary_links(), array('class' =>
'links', 'id' => 'navlist'));
$secondary_links = theme('links', menu_secondary_links(),
array('class' => 'links', 'id' => 'subnavlist'));
if (isset($primary_links) || isset($secondary_links)) {
    $output .= ' <div class="navlinks">';
    if (isset($primary_links)) {
        $output .= $primary_links;      }
    if (isset($secondary_links)) {
        $output .= $secondary_links;      }
    $output .= " </div>\n";
}
```

Sidebars

The placement of the sidebars is split in the code (reflecting the placement within the table structure) with the left sidebar appearing first, followed by the main content area (discussed below), then the footer (see below) and finally the right sidebar. The author only declared two regions for this theme, left and right; as you might expect, those two regions are placed in the left and right sidebars, respectively.

Sidebar Left

The following places the blocks designated for the left region into a table cell. Note the conditional statement; this allows the output to be hidden in the event that no blocks are assigned to the region. For styling, the table cell (td) is given an id name to reflect the placement (sidebar-left).

```
if ($show_blocks && !empty($blocks_left)) {
   $output .= "    <td id=\"sidebar-left\">$blocks_left</td>\n";
}
```

Sidebar Right

This snippet places the blocks designated for the right region into a table cell. Note the conditional statement; this allows the output to be hidden in the event that no blocks are assigned to the region. For styling, the table cell (td) is given an id name to reflect the placement (sidebar-right).

```
if ($show_blocks && !empty($blocks_right)) {
   $output .= "    <td id=\"sidebar-right\">$blocks_right</td>\n";
}
```

Main Content Area

The author of Chameleon has set up a number of critical elements to appear inside the main content area. The section will appear as the middle column where there are blocks assigned to both left and right sidebars. The entire set of elements is placed inside a table cell and styled with the id main:

```
$output .= "    <td id=\"main\">\n";
```

Title and Breadcrumb Trail

The author places the title and breadcrumb together on the page and makes both subject to the appearance of the title; the title is also wrapped with the<h2> tag.

```
if ($title) {
   $output .= theme("breadcrumb", drupal_get_breadcrumb());
   $output .= "<h2>$title</h2>";
}
```

Tabs

This conditional statement controls the tabs.

```
if ($tabs = theme('menu_local_tasks')) {
$output .= $tabs;
}
```

Help

This excerpt prints the help link:

```
$output .= theme('help');
```

Messages

This excerpt places the output of the messages:

```
$output .= theme('status_messages');
```

Content Region

The content region is placed below, wrapped by a comment statement:

```
$output .= "\n<!-- begin content -->\n";
$output .= $content;
$output .= drupal_get_feeds();
$output .= "\n<!-- end content -->\n";
```

Footer

Though the author only declared two regions, left and right, he includes the footer region in the code. This provides us with a good example of the function `chameleon_regions()` in action. The function defines which regions will be available for the administrator to use for the assignment of blocks. In this case, only left and right are options for the administrator, despite the presence of the footer region in the code. Had the function `chameleon_regions()` been written so as to include `'footer' => t('footer')`, then the region would be accessible to the administrator for block assignment. As it stands, however, the only output of the code below is the footer message, wrapped with a div.

```
if ($footer = variable_get('site_footer', '')) {
    $output .= " <div id=\"footer\">$footer</div>\n";
}
```

Theme Closure

You must close the page properly, adding the `theme_closure()` function and the closing `<body>` and `<html>` tags. The final line renders the page.

```
$output .= theme_closure();
$output .= " </body>\n";
$output .= "</html>\n";
return $output;
```

Overriding Functions

You can override Drupal's default theme functions in your pure PHP theme. The process of creating overrides is almost identical to that used in a PHPTemplate theme: copy the function, rename it, and make your changes. The only difference is where you place the overrides. In a pure PHP theme you place the overrides in the `themename.theme` file.

Turning to `chameleon.theme` again for an example, we find that the theme provides overrides for the node, comment, and help functions.

Themable function	Name of override
theme_comment	chameleon_comment
theme_help	chameleon_help
theme_node	chameleon_node

In each case, the original function has been copied from its source, then pasted into the `chameleon.theme` file, renamed, and modified as desired.

Summary

This chapter has taken us from a blank page to a completely functional theme. We've covered how to build a PHPTemplate-powered theme from scratch, including the creation of the all required files and their contents. While the theme created, Bluewater, is a basic theme and intended for example purposes, the concepts and techniques employed are applicable to all PHPTemplate themes and provide you with the building blocks for doing greater things.

This chapter also touched on building themes without the use of a theme engine, though as stated, this is probably not the optimal course for building themes for Drupal 6.

8
Dynamic Theming

The Drupal system, when combined with the PHPTemplate engine, gives you the ability to create logic that will automatically display templates or specific elements in response to the existence of certain conditions. In previous chapters, we have seen some of this logic in action. In this section, we take the discussion one step further and look at running multiple templates, and at creating dynamic elements and styles.

Among the techniques covered in this chapter are: using suggestions—naming conventions—to control template display, the use of $body_classes to create dynamic styling, and the implementation of the preprocessor function.

Using Multiple Templates

Most advanced sites built today employ multiple page templates. In this section, we will look at the most common scenarios and how to address them with a PHPTemplate theme.

While there are many good reasons for running multiple page templates, you should not create additional templates solely for the purpose of disabling regions to hide blocks. While the approach will work, it will result in a performance hit for the site, as the system will still produce the blocks, only to then wind up not displaying them for the pages. The better practice is to control your block visibility using the techniques discussed in Chapter 2.

Using a Separate Admin Theme

With the arrival of Drupal 5, one of the most common Drupal user requests was satisfied; that is, the ability to easily designate a separate admin theme. In Drupal, designating a separate theme for your admin interface remains a simple matter that you can handle directly from within the admin system.

To designate a separate theme for your admin section, follow these steps:

1. Log in and access your site's admin system.

2. Go to **Administer | Site configuration | Administration theme**.

3. Select the theme you desire from the drop-down box listing all the installed themes.

4. Click **Save configuration**, and your selected theme should appear immediately.

 Instructions for installing new themes for your Drupal site are provided in Chapter 2.

Multiple Page or Section Templates

In contrast to the complete ease of setting up a separate administration theme is the comparative difficulty of setting up multiple templates for different pages or sections.

The bad news is that there is no admin system shortcut—you must manually create the various templates and customize them to suit your needs. The good news is that creating and implementing additional templates is not difficult and it is possible to attain a high degree of granularity with the techniques described below. Indeed, should you be so inclined, you could literally define a distinct template for each individual page of your site.

As discussed in Chapter 5, Drupal employs an order of precedence based on a naming convention (or "suggestions" as they are now being called on the Drupal site). You can unlock the granularity of the system through proper application of the naming convention. It is possible, for example, to associate templates with every element on the path, or with specific users, or with a particular functionality—all through the simple process of creating a new template and naming it appropriately.

The system will search for alternative templates, preferring the specific to the general, and failing to find a more specific template, will apply the default `page.tpl.php`. Consider the following example of the order of precedence and the naming convention in action.

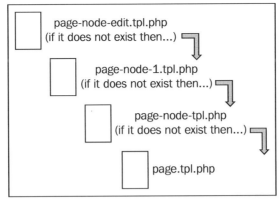

The custom templates above could be used to override the default `page.tpl.php` and theme either an entire node (`page-node.tpl.php`), or simply the node with an ID of 1 (`page-node-1.tpl.php`), or the node in editmode (`page-node-edit.tpl.php`), depending on the name given the template.

> In the example above, the page-node templates would be applied to the node in full page view. In contrast, should you wish to theme the node in its entirety, you would need to intercept and override the default `node.tpl.php`. See the discussion later in this chapter for more on this topic.

The fundamental methodology of the system is to use the first template file it finds and ignore other, more general templates (if any). This basic principle, combined with proper naming of the templates, gives you control over the template used in various situations.

> The default suggestions provided by the Drupal system should be sufficient for the vast majority of theme developers. However, if you find that you need additional suggestions beyond those provided by the system, it is possible to extend your site and add new suggestions. See `http://drupal.org/node/223440` for a discussion of this advanced Drupal theming technique.

Let's take a series of four examples to show how this feature can be used to provide solutions to common problems:

1. Create a unique homepage template.
2. Use a different template for a group of pages.
3. Assign a specific template to a specific page.
4. Designate a specific template for a specific user.

Create a Unique Homepage Template

Let's assume that you wish to set up a unique template for the homepage of a site. Employing separate templates for the homepage and the interior pages is one of the most common requests web developers hear.

With Drupal, you can, without having to create a new template, achieve some variety within a theme by controlling the visibility of blocks on the homepage. If that simple technique does not give you enough flexibility, you will need to consider using a dedicated template that is purpose-built for your homepage content.

The easiest way to set up a distinct front page template is to copy the existing `page.tpl.php` file, rename it, and make your changes to the new file. Alternatively, you can create a new file from scratch. In either situation, your front-page-specific template must be named `page-front.tpl.php`. The system will automatically display your new file for the site's homepage, and use the default `page.tpl.php` for the rest of the site.

> Note that `page-front.tpl.php` is whatever page you specify as the site's front page via the site configuration settings. To override the default homepage setting visit **Administer | Site configuration | Site information**, then enter the URL you desire into the field labeled **Default home page**.

Use a Different Template for a Group of Pages

Next, let's associate a template with a group of pages. You can provide a template to be used by any distinct group of pages, using as your guide the path for the pages. For example, to theme all the user pages you would create the template `page-user.tpl.php`.

To theme according to the type of content, you can associate your page template with a specific node, for example, all blog entry pages can be controlled by the file `page-blog-tpl.php`. The table below presents a list of suggestions you can employ to theme various pages associated with the default functionalities in the Drupal system.

Suggestion	Affected page
`page-user.tpl.php`	user pages
`page-blog.tpl.php`	blog pages (but not the individual node pages)
`page-forum.tpl.php`	forum pages (but not the individual node pages)
`page-book.tpl.php`	book pages (but not the individual node pages)
`page-contact.tpl.php`	contact form (but not the form content)

Assign a Specific Template to a Specific Page

Taking this to its extreme, you can associate a specific template with a specific page. By way of example, assume we wish to provide a unique template for a specific content item. Let's assume our example page is located at `http://www.demosite.com/node/2/edit`. The path of this specific page gives you a number of options. We could theme this page with any of the following templates (in addition to the default `page.tpl.php`):

- `page-node.tpl.php`
- `page-node-2.tpl.php`
- `page-node-edit.tpl.php`

A Note on Templates and URLs

Drupal bases the template order of precedence on the default path generated by the system. If the site is using a module like pathauto, which alters the path that appears to site visitors, remember that your templates will still be displayed based on the original paths. The exception here being `page-front.tpl.php`, which will be applied to whatever page you specify as the site's front page via the site configuration settings (**Administer | Site configuration | Site information**).

Designate a Specific Template for a Specific User

Assume that you want to add a personalized theme for the user with the ID of 1 (the Drupal equivalent of a Super Administrator). To do this, copy the existing `page.tpl.php` file, rename it to reflect its association with the specific user, and make any changes to the new file. To associate the new template file with the user, name the file: `page-user-1.tpl`.

Now, when user 1 logs into the site, they will be presented with this template. Only user 1 will see this template and only when he or she is logged in and visiting the account page.

The official Drupal site includes a collection of snippets relating to the creation of custom templates for user profile pages. The discussion is instructive and worth review, though you should always be a bit cautious with user-submitted code snippets as they are not official releases from the Drupal Association. See, `http://drupal.org/node/35728`

Dynamically Theming Page Elements

In addition to being able to style particular pages or groups of pages, Drupal and PHPTemplate make it possible to provide specific styling for different page elements.

Associating Elements with the Front Page

Drupal provides `$is_front` as a means of determining whether the page currently displayed is the front page.

`$is_front` is set to true if Drupal is rendering the front page; otherwise it is set to false. We can use `$is_front` in our `page.tpl.php` file to help toggle display of items we want to associate with the front page.

To display an element on only the front page, make it conditional on the state of `$is_front`. For example, to display the site mission on only the front page of the site, wrap `$mission` (in your `page.tpl.php` file) as follows:

```php
<?php if ($is_front): ?>
  <div id="mission">
    <?php print $mission; ?>
  </div>
<?php endif; ?>
```

To set up an alternative condition, so that one element will appear on the front page but a different element will appear on other pages, modify the statement like this:

```php
<?php if ($is_front): ?>
    //whatever you want to display on front page
<?php else: ?>
     //what is displayed when not on the front page
<?php endif; ?>
```

 `$is_front` is one of the default baseline variables available to all templates. For a complete list of these variables, see Chapter 4. See also, the discussion below concerning `$body_classes`.

Dynamically Styling Modules and Blocks

In Chapter 5, we discussed at length the process of intercepting and overriding default templates and themable functions. Those templates and functions supply much of the key output on a Drupal site and many are positioned on the page through the assignment of blocks to regions. In this chapter, we want to look at how you can control the formatting of a site's various modules and blocks.

Remember, suggestions only work when placed in the same directory as the base template. In other words, to get `block-user.tpl.php` to work, you must also place `block.tpl.php` inside in the same directory.

Dynamically Styling Blocks

Block output is controlled by the `block.tpl.php` template. As we have seen in other areas, PHPTemplate will look to the names given to multiple template files to determine which template to display. The order of precedence used for the block template is consistent with that used elsewhere:

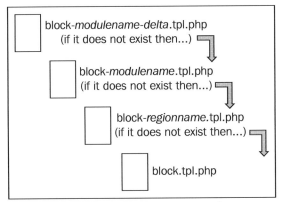

The naming convention determines what is displayed. At the most specific, you can provide a template to apply to the blocks of a specific module of a specific delta (`block-modulename-delta.tpl.php`). You can also attach a template to blocks of a module by module name (`block-modulename.tpl.php`), or to the blocks of a particular region (`block-regionname.tpl.php`). Failing the presence of any of the above, the system applies the default `block.tpl.php` template.

Note that the order of precedence includes the name of the module that produces the output being displayed in the block. Delta is a system-generated value that provides a unique identifier for each block.

 All blocks manually created by the user share the module name "block.".

If you are not certain of the provenance of your block, that is, the name of the module that produces the block or the block's delta, try using the Theme Developer feature of the Devel module. If you have the Devel module installed on your site, you can harvest this information in the form of a list of suggestions quite easily. To use this feature:

1. Install the Devel module.
2. Activate the Theme Developer option.
3. Open your browser and go to the page where your block appears.
4. Click the **Themer Info** checkbox on the bottom left of the screen, then click on the block in question.

When you click on the element, a pop up will appear, like the one in the following illustration:

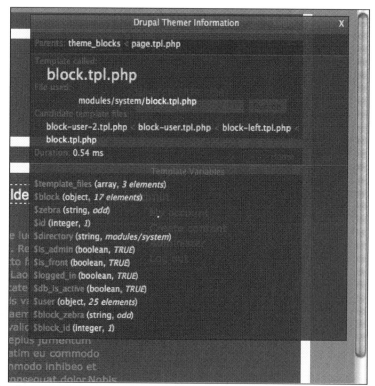

The Theme Developer module in action. After clicking on the Who's Online block in our Bluewater theme, we see the information above appear in a pop-up window.

Looking at the above screenshot, you can see the suggestions relevant to the block in our example:

Template	Will apply to...
block-user-2.tpl.php	The Who's Online block (in our example)
block-user.tpl.php	All blocks output by the User module
block-left.tpl.php	All blocks in the sidebar-left region
block.tpl.php	All blocks

 You can also use the Theme Developer extension to help you identify potential suggestions for page templates.

Dynamically Styling the Comment Module

The base template of the comment module can be dynamically styled using the suggestions provided by the system. The principal comment template, comment.tpl.php, can be styled according to the node type with which the comment is associated by using the syntax comment-[type].tpl.php. The default comment wrapper template (comment-wrapper.tpl.php) can also be styled according to the node with the syntax comment-wrapper-[type].tpl.php.

Dynamically Styling the Forum Module

The base templates of the forum module is forums.tpl.php. There are several options open for suggestions for both forum containers and topics:

Suggestion	Will apply to...
forums-topics.tpl.php	Forum topics
forums-topics-[forumID].tpl.php	Forum topics belonging to a forum of a specific ID
forums-containers.tpl.php	Forum containers
forums-containers-[forumID].tpl.php	Forum containers belonging to a forum of a specific ID
forums-[forumID].tpl.php	Forum of a specific ID.

Dynamically Styling the Polls Module

The Polls module is the subject of a number of default templates. There are default suggestions available for all the key templates:

Default template	Suggestion syntax
poll-results.tpl.php	poll-results-[block].tpl.php
poll-vote.tpl.php	poll-vote-[block].tpl.php
poll-bar.tpl.php	poll-bar-[block].tpl.php

Dynamically Styling Nodes

PHPTemplate provides a specific template for nodes—node.tpl.php. Using the same principles of precedence we've seen throughout, you can provide alternative node templates to suit your needs. To provide a template for the blog node, for example, create node-blog.tpl.php; for the story node, node-story.tpl.php. In the absence of a more specific template, the system will apply the default node.tpl.php file. The table below shows the suggestions for the default system:

Suggestion	Affected node
node-blog.tpl.php	blog entries
node-forum.tpl.php	forum entries
node-book.tpl.php	book entries
node-story.tpl.php	story entries
node-page.tpl.php	page entries

 Note that you cannot use node-admin.tpl.php to theme your admin pages. As noted elsewhere in this chapter, you can style the admin section either by setting an admin-specific theme or by creating the page-admin.tpl.php template.

Creating Dynamic CSS Styling

In addition to creating dynamic templates, the Drupal system also enables you to apply CSS dynamically. Drupal creates unique identifiers for various elements of the system and you can use those identifiers to create specific CSS selectors. As a result, you can provide styling that responds to the presence (or absence) of specific conditions on any given page. Two of the most common uses of this technique are covered below: The creation of node-specific styles and the use of $body_classes.

Using Dynamic Selectors for Nodes

In the discussion above, we looked at applying node templates dynamically. Using a similar process, we can create individual node styling through the use of dynamic CSS selectors.

The system generates a unique ID for each node on the website. We can use that unique ID to activate a unique selector by applying this nomenclature for the selector:

```
#node-[nid] {
}
```

For example, assume you wish to add a border to the node with the ID of 2. Simply create a new div in `style.css` with the name:

```
#node-2 {
border: 1px solid #336600
}
```

Changing the Body Class Based on $body_classes

One of the most useful dynamic styling tools introduced in Drupal 6 is the implementation of `$body_classes`. This variable is intended specifically as an aid to dynamic CSS styling. It allows for the easy creation of CSS selectors that are responsive to the layout of the page. This technique is typically used to control the styling where there may be one, two or three columns displayed, depending on the page and the content.

 Prior to Drupal 6, `$layout` was used to detect the page layout, that is, one, two or three columns. While `$layout` can technically still be used, the better practice is to use `$body_classes`.

Implementing `$body_classes` is a simple matter; just add `$body_classes` to the body tag of your `page.tpl.php` file—the Drupal system will do the rest. Once the body tag is altered to include this variable, the class associated with the body tag will change automatically in response to the conditions on the page at that time. Now, all you have to do is create the CSS selectors that you wish to see applied in the various situations.

Let's step through this with a quick example. Open up your `page.tpl.php` file and modify the body tag as follows:

```
<body class="<?php print $body_classes; ?>">
```

This will now automatically create a class for the page based on the conditions on the page. The chart below shows the options this presents:

Condition	Class available
no sidebars	`.no-sidebar`
one sidebar	`.one-sidebar`
left sidebar visible	`.sidebar-left`
right sidebar visible	`.sidebar-right`
two sidebars	`.two-sidebars`
front page	`.front`
not front page	`.not-front`
logged in	`.logged-in`
not logged in	`.not-logged-in`
page visible	`.page-[page type]`
node visible	`.node-type-[name of type]`

If you'd like to see this technique in action (without having to create it from scratch), take a look at the Bluewater theme we created in the previous chapter. In the `page.tpl.php` file you will find the `$body_classes` variable added to the body tag.

Enable the theme and then open the site with your browser. View the source code for your front page. Find the body tag in your source code. It now reads:

```
<body class="front not-logged-in page-node one-sidebar sidebar-left">
```

 This above example from the Bluewater source code assumes you are running the default implementation with no modification and that you are not logged in!

`$body_classes` provides the key to easily creating a theme that includes collapsible sidebars. To set up this functionality, modify the `page.tpl.php` file to include `$body_classes`.

Now, go to the `style.css` file and create the following selectors:

```
.one-sidebar {
}
.sidebar-left {
}
.sidebar-right {
}
.no-sidebar {
}
.two-sidebars {
}
```

The final step is to create the styling for each of the selectors above (as you see fit).

When the site is viewed, the system-generated value of `$body_classes` will determine which selector is applied. You can now specify, through the selectors above, exactly how the page appears—whether the columns collapse, the resulting widths of the remaining columns, and so on , and so on

 This technique is used in the previous chapter to handle the columns in the example theme Bluewater.

Working with Template Variables

As we have seen, above, Drupal produces variables that can be used to enhance the functionality of themes. Typically, a theme-related function returns values reflecting the state of the page on the screen. A function may indicate, for example, whether the page is the front page of the site, or whether there are one, two, or three active columns (for example, the variable `$body_classes`). Tapping into this information is a convenient way for a theme developer to style a site dynamically.

The default Drupal variables cover the most common (and essential) functions, including creating unique identifiers for items. Some of the Drupal variables are unique to particular templates; others are common to all. In addition to the default variables, you can also define your own variables.

 Using the function `theme_preprocess()`, you can either set new variables, or unset existing ones that you do not want to use.

In Drupal 6, preprocess functions have made working with variables easier and cleaner. By using the preprocessor, you can set up variables within your theme that can be accessed by any of your templates. The code for the preprocess function is added to your `template.php` file, thereby keeping the actual template files (the `.tpl.php` files) free of unnecessary clutter. Note that the preprocess functions only apply to theming hooks implemented as templates; plain theme functions do not interact with the preprocessors.

 In Drupal 5 and below, the function `_phptemplate_variables` served the same purpose as the preprocess function. For a list of the expected preprocess functions and their order of precedence, see `http://drupal.org/node/223430`

Typically, if you wish to implement a preprocessor applicable to your theme, you will use one of the following:

Name of preprocessor	Application
`[engineName]_preprocess`	This namespace should be used for your base theme. Should be named after the theme engine used by the theme. Will apply to all hooks.
`[engineName]_preprocess_[hookname]`	Should be used for your base theme. Also named after the theme engine applicable to the theme but note that it is specific to a single hook.
`[themeName]_preprocess`	This namespace should be used for subthemes. Will apply to all hooks.
`[themeName]_preprocess_[hookname]`	Should be used for subthemes. Note that it is specific to a single hook.

Let's look first at intercepting and overriding the default variables and then at creating your own variables.

Intercepting and Overriding Variables

You can intercept and override the system's existing variables. Intercepting a variable is no different in practice from intercepting a themable function: you simply restate it in the `template.php` file and make your modifications there, leaving the original code in the core intact.

 The basic principles behind intercepts and overrides are discussed at length in Chapter 5.

To intercept an existing variable and override it with your new variable, you need to use the function _phptemplate_preprocess(). Add this to your template.php file according to the following syntax:

```php
<?php
function phptemplate_preprocess(&$vars) {
$vars['name'] = add your code here...;
}
?>
```

Note that nothing should be returned from these functions. The variables have to be passed by reference, as indicated by the ampersand before variables, e.g., &$vars.

Let's take a very basic example and apply this. Let's override $title in page.tpl. php. To accomplish this task, add the following code to the template.php file:

```php
<?php
function phptemplate_preprocess(&$vars) {
    $vars['title'] = 'override title';
    }
?>
```

Remember to clear your theme registry!

With this change made and the file saved to your theme, the string **override title** will appear, substituted for the original $title value.

Making New Variables Available

The preprocess function also allows you to define additional variables in your theme. To create a new variable, you must declare the function in the template.php file. In order for your theme to have its preprocessors recognized, the template associated with the hook must exist inside the theme. If the template does not exist in your theme, copy one and place it in the theme directory.

The syntax is the same as that just used for intercepting and overriding a variable, as seen above. The ability to add new variables to the system is a powerful tool and gives you the ability to add more complex logic to your theme.

Summary

This chapter covers the basics needed to make your Drupal theme responsive to the contents and the users. By applying the techniques discussed in this chapter, you can control the theming of pages based on content, state of the page or the users viewing them. Taking the principles one step further, you can also make the theming of elements within a page conditional. The ability to control the templates used and the styling of the page and its elements is what we call dynamic theming.

This chapter covered not only the basic ideas behind dynamic theming, but also the techniques needed to implement this powerful tool. Among the items discussed at length were the use of suggestions to control template display, and the implementation of $body_classes. Also covered in this chapter, was the use of the preprocess function to work with variables inside your theme.

9
Dealing with Forms

In this chapter, we look at the forms generated by the Drupal core and how they can be themed. We'll cover all the default forms available on the front end of a Drupal website, including the various search, login, and contact forms, as well as the polls module.

It's worth noting at the outset that this chapter is about theming forms, not about creating custom forms; accordingly, the contents of this chapter are concerned with presentation, not with adding or deleting form elements or creating new forms.

There are no additional files to download or install for this chapter; all examples are based on the default Garland theme or new code contained in this chapter. You will, however, need access to your favorite editor to make the modifications discussed here, as well as a Drupal installation on which to preview your work.

How Forms Work in Drupal

The forms in Drupal are tightly integrated with the core. Forms are always displayed either inside nodes or blocks, therefore, working with forms also means working with the area surrounding the form. Moreover, many of the Drupal forms are closely associated with modules. As a result of these various complications, theming the Drupal forms requires awareness of a variety of techniques and can, frankly, be a bit of a chore.

For developers, there is a dedicated API for Drupal forms. The API makes it possible to access the full functionality of the forms and to create your own forms. While it is not necessary to dig into the API to theme your forms, if you wish to do more, for example adding new fields or deleting mandatory fields, you will need to reference the API. See, `http://api.drupal.org/api/file/developer/topics/forms_api.html/6` and `http://api.drupal.org/api/file/developer/topics/forms_api_reference.html/6`

Unlike other areas of the system, most forms do not include a selection of default templates and themable functions. Instead, if you wish to theme a form you are typically left with the choice of either working directly with the form functions in the Drupal core or with following the well-trodden path of intercepting and overriding the form output using the power of the PHPTemplate template engine.

While you will note that a number of functions are mentioned in this chapter, most of them are specific to a particular form. The global function `drupal_render` is, however, worthy of particular mention. The function `drupal_render` produces form output throughout the system and is one of the keys to dealing with forms.

At first glance, the `drupal_render` function doesn't volunteer much information. Look at this bare-bones implementation of the function; the code below provides the output of the Login Block Form:

```
function phptemplate_user_login_block($form) {
    $output = drupal_render($form);
return $output;
}
```

`drupal_render` supersedes the old function `form_render`, which was used in the earlier Drupal systems.

The code above, when placed in the `template.php` file, will override the default form function and produce the output of the form. This is useful for simple modifications, for example, adding HTML around the form. However, if your goal is the styling of individual form elements, you will have to do more.

To achieve a greater degree of control over the styling, we need to go behind the scenes a bit, to look at what goes on when the system invokes this function. For the sake of discussion, let's take a look at an example of an unaltered Drupal form function and examine it in more detail.

Here's the function that produces the Login Block form. The original code can be found in `modules/user/user.module`:

```
function user_login_block() {
    $form = array(
        '#action' => url($_GET['q'], array('query' =>drupal_get_
destination())),
        '#id' => 'user-login-form',
        '#validate' => user_login_default_validators(),
        '#submit' => array('user_login_submit'),
    );
    $form['name'] = array('#type' => 'textfield',
        '#title' => t('Username'),
        '#maxlength' => USERNAME_MAX_LENGTH,
        '#size' => 15,
        '#required' => TRUE,    );
    $form['pass'] = array('#type' => 'password',
        '#title' => t('Password'),
        '#maxlength' => 60,
        '#size' => 15,
        '#required' => TRUE,
    );
    $form['submit'] = array('#type' => 'submit',
        '#value' => t('Log in'),
    );
    $items = array();
    if (variable_get('user_register', 1)) {
        $items[] = l(t('Create new account'), 'user/register',
array('title' => t('Create a new user account.')));
    }
    $items[] = l(t('Request new password'), 'user/password',
array('title' => t('Request new password via e-mail.')));
    $form['links'] = array('#value' => theme('item_list', $items));
    return $form;
}
```

Note how this function sets the attributes for the various fields, including field lengths and data labels. For example, the excerpt below produces the password field and its related attributes (text, maximum length, size of the box displayed, and whether it is a required field):

```
$form['pass'] = array('#type' => 'password',
    '#title' => t('Password'),
    '#maxlength' => 60,
    '#size' => 15,
    '#required' => TRUE,
);
```

The use of an array to hold the values for these attributes is typical of the way the system deals with the information needed to create the various elements in a form.

Here is a simpler example, which produces the submit button, including the text for the button ("log in"):

```
$form['submit'] = array('#type' => 'submit',
  '#value' => t('Log in'),
);
```

The appearance of all of these items can be modified by intercepting and overriding this function, as discussed below. The trick is locating the form ID of the original item you wish to change and then identifying the elements (for example, the password field or the submit button) that you wish to modify.

Finding the Form ID

Note that the name of our function, above, was derived from the form ID. The form ID for the example above is `user_login_block` and our function was accordingly named `function user_login_block()`. You will need to obtain the ID of the form you wish to modify for many of the techniques in this chapter. Finding the form ID is relatively simple, as all forms in Drupal have a unique ID. To locate this information, view the HTML source code of the page upon which your form appears. Look for some hidden fields near the top of the form. One will have the `name="form_id"`. You want to use the `value` of that `form_id` input field. In our example above, the code we want looks like this:

```
<input type="hidden" name="form_id" id="edit-user-
login-block" value="user_login_block"  />
```

How to Approach Modifying Forms

There are five ways to modify the appearance of a Drupal form. You can:

1. Work with the existing CSS styling
2. Modify the page or block holding the form
3. Override a default template associated with the form
4. Use a theme function
5. Modify the form with a custom module

Of those five techniques, the first two are the most limited, as they do not involve changing the form output itself. The third technique, overriding the default template associated with the form, is useful, but limited by the fact that not all the forms are the subject of existing templates.

Of the five, the last two techniques are the most powerful as they deal with the form itself. Unfortunately, the last two techniques are also the most complex to implement.

Working with the CSS Styling

This is the most limited option available to you, but sometimes all you need. As noted in Chapter 4, and again later in this chapter, there are default styles in place for all the system forms. You can achieve a degree of customization by intercepting and overriding the relevant selectors with your own definitions. The technique is no different than that discussed elsewhere; simply add the selectors to your theme's `style.css` file, thereby overriding the original definitions.

Modifying the Page or Block Holding the Form

With the help of PHPTemplate, we can create custom templates for either the pages, or the blocks in which the forms are displayed.

Templates for Pages Containing Forms

Many of the forms in the default Drupal system appear inside the content area of pages. For those forms, it is sometimes desirable to provide dedicated page templates. In most cases, this is a straightforward matter; we treat it like any other page template override.

 Overriding page templates is discussed in depth in Chapter 7.

By way of example, let's set up a dedicated page template for the site-wide contact form.

First, create the page template where your form will appear. It's easiest just to copy the existing `page.tpl.php`, rename it `page-contact.tpl.php`, and save it to the root directory of your theme. Make your changes to the new template file and you are done. The system will automatically give precedence to the more specific `page-contact.tpl.php` and display it instead of the default `page.tpl.php`.

Templates for Blocks Containing Forms

Just as you can create a custom template for a page, you can also create a custom template for a block. Where a form appears inside the block, we are able to achieve a degree of control over the theming of the form by way of the block template.

As we discussed in Chapter 5, overriding a block template is a relatively simple matter. We need to create the template, name it properly, and then let Drupal do the rest.

 Overriding templates is discussed in depth in Chapter 5.

The Polls module, the Search Block Form, and the Login Block Form are all forms that are displayed as blocks. It is conceivable that you may want to provide a dedicated block template for any of them.

By way of example, let's assume you want to provide a customized template for the block containing the Search Block Form.

First, create your new template file. Name it `block-search.tpl.php`. For the contents of the file, let's copy and paste the contents of the default `block.tpl.php` file and then insert a custom style (highlighted below):

```
<div id="block-<?php print $block->module .'-'. $block->delta; ?>"
class="block block-<?php print $block->module ?>">
<?php if ($block->subject): ?>
<h2><?php print $block->subject ?></h2>
<?php endif;?>
<div class="search-block">
        <?php print $block->content ?>
    </div>
</div>
```

Save this file to your theme directory and you are done; the presentation of the block containing the Search Block Form is now controlled by your new template.

 Remember for your new template to work properly, you must include the base template in the same directory. For example, if you want to style `block-search.tpl.php`, you must include the base template (`block.tpl.php`) in the same directory. You have to have the base template in your folder even if you are not making any changes to it.

While PHPTemplate allows us to set up page and block templates with very little coding, we can go a step further and with a bit of additional work, gain control over the elements of the forms themselves (independent of the page or block containing the form). As we'll see later in this chapter, creating functions or modules for forms allows us the freedom to modify the output with greater granularity.

Override the Default Template Associated with the Form

There exist in the system several templates applicable to forms. These templates can be intercepted and overridden with your own versions—just like in other areas of Drupal theming.

As an example, let's modify the Search Block Form again, but this time we'll affect the form directly, rather than just the block containing the form (as we did in the section immediately above). To do this, we will need to create a custom template file dedicated to our Search Block Form.

To begin, let's copy the default template file associated with the Search Block Form. That template is named `search-block-form.tpl.php`, and it can be found in the `modules/search/` directory. Copy the file to your theme directory.

Open up the file and note the code:

```
<div class="container-inline">
  <?php print $search_form; ?>
</div>
```

The `php print` statement is the default key used to produce the output that displays on the screen, together with the hidden fields that are necessary for this form to work properly.

Note also the comment information near the top of the file:

```
* Available variables:
* - $search_form: The complete search form ready for print.
* - $search: Array of keyed search elements. Can be used to print each
            form element separately.
* Default keys within $search:
* - $search['search_block_form']: Text input area wrapped in a div.
* - $search['submit']: Form submit button.
* - $search['hidden']: Hidden form elements. Used to validate forms
                      when submitted.
```

The information above helps help us modify the form. We're going to replace the original `$search_form` with the following code, which exposes the form's elements and thereby gives us a little more control:

```
<div class="container-inline">
    <?php print $search['search_block_form']; ?>
    <?php print $search['submit']; ?>
    <?php print $search['hidden']; ?>
</div>
```

We can now add into this form whatever we need, for example additional text or wrapping the elements with the styles of our choosing.

 Remember to clear your theme registry!

Using a Theme Function to Control Elements

The most flexible way to achieve control over the look and feel of a form is through the manipulation of a theme function. This is a two step process: You must both create the function and then register it with the system. Both steps occur within the `template.php` file.

Registering a new function is a simple—almost clerical—task. To accomplish this, add the following to your `template.php` file. (Note, you need to replace `themename` with the name of your theme and `form_id` with the ID of the form you wish to modify):

```
function themename_theme() {
  return array(
    'form_id' => array(
      'arguments' => array('form' => NULL),
    ),
  );
}
```

Next, let's create the function that allows us to access the form elements, again in your `template.php` file. (Note that you need to replace `themename_form_id` with your theme's name and the ID of the form you wish to modify):

```
function themename_form_id($form) {
  //add your modifications here
  $output .= drupal_render($form);
  return $output;
}
```

It is good practice to call `drupal_render` at the end of your modifications (on the entire `$form`), as the function will render any remaining elements that you have not specified—including any hidden elements, which may be necessary for the form to function properly.

With those two items done, we now have our function registered, and ready to receive our changes.

 For a discussion of the technical niceties behind why we have to register these sorts of items, please see `http://drupal.org/node/223463`

Let's step through a complete example using the User Login Form. In this example, we will make two changes to the form: We will change the wording that appears below the username field and we will change the wording on the submit button.

The key steps to executing this strategy are identifying the elements that need to be changed and implementing the changes via a new function. We will need to:

1. Add the function to `template.php` and register it.
2. Enable viewing the `$form` array.
3. Visit the page in order to see the contents of the `$form` array.
4. Add the modifications to the function we created.

The first step is to open up the `template.php` file and add in our function and register it. Here's the code to register our function (note I am using the Garland theme and the form ID is `user_login`):

```php
function garland_theme() {
  return array(
    'user_login' => array(
      'arguments' => array('form' => NULL),
    ),
  );
}
```

Next, let's add in the function itself:

```php
function garland_user_login($form) {
  $output .= drupal_render($form);
  return $output;
}
```

Clear your registry and you are set—the new function is controlling the form, though at this stage, you will not see any difference as the function above only prints the default form as a whole.

The second step is to find the identity of the elements we wish to change. The information we want is kept in an array (specifically, the $form array) and you will need to extract that data to be able to set up the modifications.

You can get a list of the contents of the array associated with a form by using the print_r() function. We'd modify our function, above, as follows:

```
function garland_user_login($form) {
  print_r($form);
  return $form;
  $output .= drupal_render($form);
  return $output;
}
```

This function will print on the page you are viewing the contents of the $form array(s) on that page. All you need to do to identify the element you wish to change is go to the page containing your form and view the output on the screen.

For the third step, visit the page /user. You should see something similar to the following exhibit:

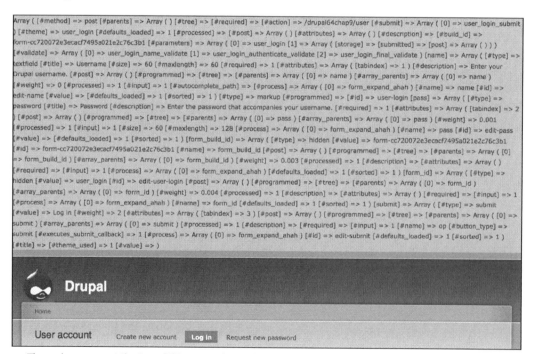

The code you see at the top of this screenshot is the $form array associated with the User Login Form (this is the /user page). The information was revealed through the addition of the function print_r() to the theme's template.php file.

Our goal here is to make two changes to the form: The wording that appears below the username field (**Enter your Drupal username**) and the wording on the submit button (**log in**). From the print out of the array above, we can see that the text **Enter your Drupal username** is associated with `username[#description]` and the wording for the submit button is associated with `submit[#value]`. We simply take that information and slot it into our function and add our chosen language, as per the code below:

```
function garland_user_login($form) {
    $form['username']['#description'] = t('Enter your username');
    $form['submit']['#value'] = t('Let me in!');
    $output .= drupal_render($form);
    return $output;
}
```

Once you save your file and reload the page in your browser, you will be able to see the changes to your form.

> The Drupal Forms API has a good reference page on elements and their attributes: `http://api.drupal.org/api/file/developer/topics/forms_api_reference.html/6/source`

Modifying Forms with Custom Modules

Another alternative for modifying forms is the use of custom modules. The function `form_alter()` is the key to this technique; it allows you to add to, subtract from, and modify the contents of a form. This is a powerful tool and is not dependent upon the use of PHPTemplate; it works directly with the Drupal core. At its most basic, `form_alter` is useful for modifying the presentation of one or more forms (e.g., data labels and text that appear with the form). At a more advanced level, you can use this function to modify the functionality of the form (e.g., adding or subtracting fields).

`form_alter` opens up some intriguing possibilities, but the use of the function requires a different approach than what we have used elsewhere in this book; to implement this function, you will need to create a new module.

> Using a module to make theming changes may seem counterintuitive, but remember this is simply one option for making changes to a form's appearance. If you are not comfortable with this approach, consider one of the other techniques discussed in this chapter. There are, however, situations in which you must use a module to change a form, for example, to change the functionality of a form or to completely remove a required form element.

Creating a new module to hold your form modifications may sound like a lot of extra work, but it's not as bad as you might think. While a detailed discussion of building modules is beyond the scope of this book, let's take a run at illustrating this technique as it is relevant to the task at hand.

Assume we wish to make the following modifications to the forms on our site:

1. Change the data labels on the User Login Form.
2. Change the wording on the submit button of the User Login Form.
3. Change the wording on the submit button of the User Registration Form.
4. Change the data labels for the Request Password Form.

To accomplish these basic changes, we can either isolate and modify the user_login function, the user_register function, and the user_pass function, or we can create one new module, implement form_alter(), and make all our required changes in one place.

Let's work through an example. We will create a new module and implement form_alter(), using it to make changes to several forms simultaneously.

First, create a new directory to hold the custom module. If it does not already exist, create a directory named modules and place it inside sites/all. Now, create a directory with your module name and place it inside sites/all/modules. Let's name this new module formmod.

Next, modules, like themes, need to be accompanied by a .info file. Name the file formmod.info and save it to our formmod directory. The contents of the file should be as follows:

```
; $Id$
name = Form mod
description = Contains modifications to the site forms.
package = Packt
core = 6.x
```

Note in the code above that I have specified our new module's name for the name field. I have added a description as well, which will appear in the administration interface (in the module manager's listing of all the installed modules). The value for package is used to determine where this module will appear in the groupings of modules inside the module manager. In this case, instead of running the risk of confusion by placing our custom module within the listing of modules in the Drupal core, I have specified a new group (named Packt) that will hold our custom module. The core field is required and should indicate which version of Drupal this module supports.

The `.info` file for modules has only three required fields: name, description, and core. There are several optional fields. To learn more, visit the Drupal 6.x Module Developer's Guide page on `.info` files: http://drupal.org/node/231036

Next, let's create a new file and name it `formmod.module`—this is where we will add the function and our modifications. Here are the contents of the file:

```php
<?php
//$Id$
/**
 *
 * Adds modifications to various site forms.
 *
 */
function formmod_form_alter(&$form, $form_state, $form_id) {
    // This part changes the user login form
    if ($form_id == 'user_login') {
        // Change the text below the username field to 'Enter your
username.'
        $form['name']['#description'] = t('Enter your username.');
        // Change the text on the submit button to 'enter'
        $form['submit']['#value'] = t('let me in!');
    }
    // This part changes the user registration form
    if ($form_id == 'user_register') {
        // Change the text on the submit button to 'submit registration'
        $form['submit']['#value'] = t('submit registration');
    }
    // This part changes the request password form
    if ($form_id == 'user_pass') {
        // Changes the data label to add basic instructions to form
        $form['name']['#title'] =
t('Enter your username or email address, then click the request
password button');
        // Change the text on the submit button to 'request password'
        $form['submit']['#value'] = t('request password');
    }
}
```

Note that this module file opens with a php tag, but *does not* include a closing tag; this is intentional and necessary to avoid formatting problems.

After you have entered the contents, save the file to the `formmod` directory. You are done. That's all there is to creating a new module!

> Our example, above, uses a single module to hold a single function, which contains changes to multiple forms. If you wished instead to implement a single module containing separate functions for each form, you could easily do so. For an example of the code involved, see,
> `http://drupal.org/node/144132#form-id-alter`

Next, let's go activate our new module. Log in to the admin system and head over to the module manager (**Administer | Site building | Modules**). Scroll down the list of modules and you will find a new section named **Packt**, along with our new module, **Form mod**. You must activate the module and click on **Save** to enable this module. Once you have completed this step, the changes made to the forms will be immediately visible.

Adding HTML via Function Attributes

The Drupal form API makes provisions for you to be able to add basic HTML to a form via a limited set of attributes named `#prefix`, `#suffix`, and `#markup`. These attributes are invoked from inside the function; accordingly, this approach to modifying forms is used most frequently by developers when they create the form.

- `#prefix` is used to add HTML before a form element.
- `#suffix` is used to add HTML after an element.
- `#markup` allows you to declare HTML as type `#markup` in the form.

This approach is generally less preferred, as it is less flexible and harder to maintain going forward. If you are looking to modify an existing form, the better practice is to create a function, as per the discussions above.

Solutions to Common Form Issues

Following are the solutions to some of the common form issues:

Modifying Data Labels and Other Text

One of the most commonly requested form modifications is the ability to change the data labels and the explanatory text built into the default forms. There are several alternative ways to modify the text elements. The choice of which technique to apply depends largely on the number, and extent of the changes you wish to make.

Using form_alter()

As we saw earlier in this chapter, you can create a custom module and use the function `form_alter` to make changes to one or more forms. This approach is very useful where you want to make changes across several forms or if you wish to combine text changes with more extreme form modifications (for example, adding or deleting fields). However, if your goal is simply to insert new text not related to a specific field, or if you wish to modify only one form, you are probably better served by one of the other approaches outlined below.

Using a Function

If you have only limited changes to make to one form, creating a specific function is one option. Basic modifications can be managed easily from within `template.php`, without the need to create a custom module or a dedicated template.

Using a Template

If you wish to add new text or HTML around your form, the creation of a new page or block template is likely to be your best solution. A separate dedicated `.tpl.php` file is easy to theme. If the form you are working with is subject to one of the default templates, you may find the solution is achieved easiest through overriding that template.

Modifying the Styling of a Form

All of the forms, excepting the contact forms, have dedicated stylesheets. The primary selectors affecting each form are defined in their respective stylesheets.

Form	Primary stylesheet
contact us	`modules/system/system.css`
login	`modules/user/user.css`
request password	`modules/user/user.css`
polls	`modules/poll/poll.css`
search	`modules/search/search.css`
user edit	`modules/user/user.css`
user registration	`modules/user/user.css`

Overriding the CSS styling for forms is no different than overriding the CSS for other areas of your Drupal site. Simply identify the elements that need to be modified and place your new definitions in your theme's `style.css` file.

Using form_alter()

You can use `form_alter()` to inject custom style definitions inside your form, but this approach is probably not the best way to deal with this issue. Apart from special needs, your best approach is to either create a function override from within `template.php` and include your changes or to create a new template.

Using a Function

Using a function to alter individual form elements is the most direct method for adding styling to elements (though it may not be the simplest path).

Using a Template

If the form you are working with is subject to one of the default templates, you may find the solution is achieved easiest through overriding that template. Note that if your styling can be achieved by wrapping the form with selectors, the manipulation of a page or block template is likely to be your easiest solution.

Using Images for Buttons

If you wish to use images for the buttons on a form, there are several alternative solutions. The method described below creates a new generic theme function that enables the use of images for the submit buttons throughout your site. This approach requires you to make two changes to your `template.php` file (and of course, you need to provide an image).

The first bit of code is necessary to overcome several issues in the system and to provide proper IDs for the image. The code:

```
function phptemplate_button($element) {
// following lines are copied directly from form.inc core file:
// Make sure not to overwrite classes
  if (isset($element['#attributes']['class'])) {
    $element['#attributes']['class'] = 'form-'. $element['#button_
type'] .' '. $element['#attributes']['class'];
  }
  else {
    $element['#attributes']['class'] =
            'form-'. $element['#button_type'];
  }
  // My change is type="' . (($element['#button_type'] == "image") ?
// 'image' : 'submit' ) . '"
  return '<input type="' . (($element['#button_type'] == "image") ?
'image' : 'submit' ) . '" '. (empty($element['#name']) ? '' :
```

```
'name="'. $element['#name'] .'" ')  .'id="'. $element['#id'].'"
value="'. check_plain($element['#value']) .'" '. drupal_attributes($el
ement['#attributes']) ." />\n";
}
```

The second bit of code is required to place the button on the form. If you wanted, for example, to now use an image for the submit button of your Theme Search Form, you would add the following to your `template.php` file:

```
function phptemplate_search_theme_form($form) {
    $form['submit']['#theme'] = 'button';
    $form['submit']['#button_type'] = 'image';
    $form['submit']['#attributes'] = array(
        'src' => base_path() . path_to_theme() . '/images/btn-search-
        submit.png',
        'alt' => t('Search')
    );
return drupal_render($form);
}
```

Now, assuming you have an image file named properly and uploaded to the proper directory (that is, `/images/btn-search-submit.png`), you should be done. Note that you will need to repeat this exercise for each form where you wish to use an image for the submit button.

> The code for the function `phptemplate_button`, above, was originally published on the Drupal.org site and is included in the snippets section. This is worth watching for additional discussion and revisions from the community. Visit `http://drupal.org/node/144758`.

The Default Forms

The default Drupal distribution includes a number of forms for the front-end user. Some are active at installation, others need to be enabled and configured by the administrator. On the following pages, we go through the default forms and provide a quick look at each, highlighting any special concerns unique to each particular form.

The User Forms

The user forms consist of the Login Forms, the User Registration Form, the Request Password Form, and the User Profile Form.

The Login Forms

The Login Form exists in two varieties: The Login Block Form and the Login Page Form.

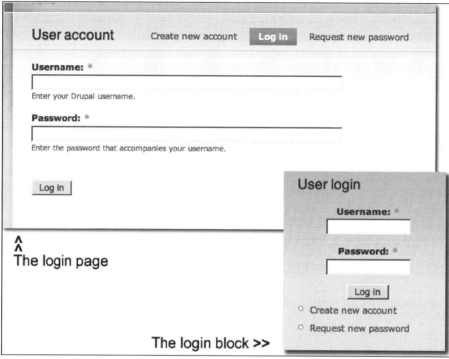

The Login Form appears both as a block (aka, the Login Block Form) and in the content region (aka, the Login Page Form). Note that the Login Page also includes links to new account registration (aka, the User Registration Form) and the Request Password Form.

The Login Block Form

The function that builds this form is `user_login_block`, which is located at `modules/user/user.module`.

The styling of the Login Block Form is predominantly managed by the selectors defined in the file `modules/user/user.css`. See Appendix A for a listing of the contents of that file.

The Login Page Form

In addition to the block position, the Login Form can also occupy a page position. In the page position, the Login Form is controlled by the function `user_login`, located at `modules/user/user.module`.

The styling of the Login Page form is predominantly managed by the selectors defined in the file `modules/user/user.css`. See Appendix A for a listing of the contents of that file.

 You can find a good discussion of theming the Login Form on the official Drupal site at `http://drupal.org/node/266591`

The User Registration Form

The User Registration Form appears in the content region and can be reached from either the link in the Login block or from the links at the top of the Login Form and the Request Password Form.

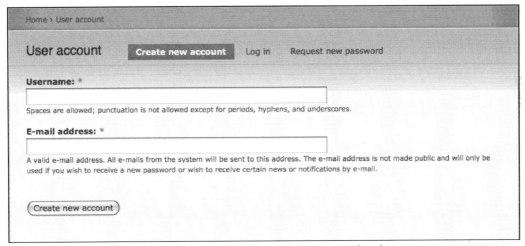

The user registration form appears in page mode only.

This form is generated by the function `user_register`, found at `modules/user.module`.

The styling of the User Registration Form is predominantly managed by the selectors defined in the file `modules/user/user.css`. See Appendix A for a listing of the contents of that file.

The Request Password Form

The Request Password Form appears in the content region and can be reached from either the link in the Login Block or from the links at the top of the Login Form and the User Registration Form.

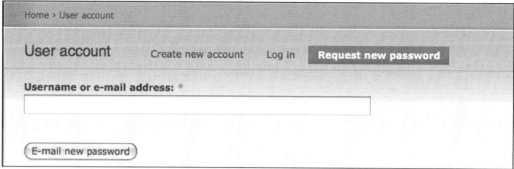

The Request Password Form appears in the content region.

The function that controls the output of the Request Password Form is `user_pass` at `modules/user/user.pages.inc`.

The styling of the Request Password Form is predominantly managed by the selectors defined in the file `modules/user/user.css`. See Appendix A for a listing of the contents of that file.

The User Profile Form

Registered users of a Drupal site are able to maintain their personal information themselves via the account information screen.

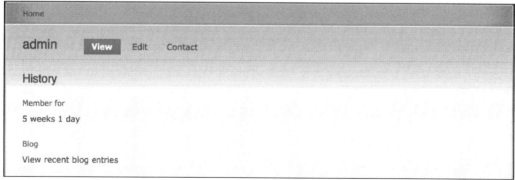

The User Profile Form is accessible by registered users and appears in the content region. The particular form shown here is for the admin user and includes options not visible to users with lesser privileges.

The function that controls the output of the User Profile Form is `user_edit_form` found at `modules/user.module`.

The styling of the User Profile Form is predominantly managed by the selectors defined in the file `modules/user/user.css`. See Appendix A for a listing of the contents of that file.

The Default Contact Form

Drupal includes a contact module that can be used to generate one or more contact forms for your site.

Contact Us
You can leave a message using the contact form below.

Your name: *

Your e-mail address: *

Subject: *

Message: *

☐ Send yourself a copy.

Send e-mail

The default Drupal Contact Form.

The function that controls the output of the Contact Form is `contact_site_page` found at `modules/contact/contact.pages.inc`.

The styling of the Contact Form is predominantly managed by the selectors defined in the file `modules/system/system.css`. See Appendix A for a listing of the contents of that file.

The Search Forms

The Search Forms have several unique characteristics that set them apart from the other forms in Drupal. The first unique characteristic is their number and variety: There are multiple variations of the Search Form in the system. The second is the fact that we also have output to consider, that is, the Search Results page.

There are four versions of the Search Form in the default Drupal distribution:

1. The **Theme Search Form** is generally placed near the top of the page (a decision made by the theme developer) and subsequently enabled/disabled by the configuration settings.

2. The **Block Search Form** is produced by the search module and is typically placed in a sidebar region. (Before the search block will appear on the site, the corresponding module must be enabled by the administrator and the search block assigned to an active region.)

3. The **Page Search Form** appears in the content region of a page. While the search page is just a basic one-line search box, the search page also has a link to the advanced search functionality, which is a more complex variation on the basic Search Form.

4. The **Advanced Search Form** always appears in the content area in search page format (assuming the user has been granted access to the advanced search functionality by the administrator).

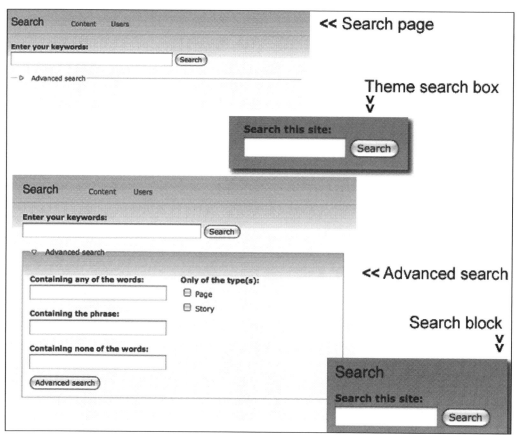

The various Search Forms as they appear in the default Garland theme.

The Theme Search Form

The Theme Search Form typically appears somewhere near the top of the theme (or wherever it has been placed by the theme developer).

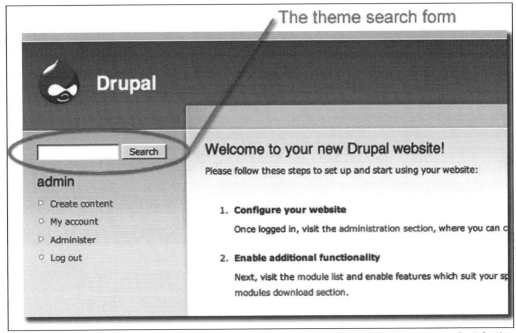

In Garland, the Theme Search Form appears at the top of the left column, making it easy to mistake it for the search block (as though the search block was assigned to the left sidebar region).

The output of this form is handled by the default template `search-theme-form.tpl.php`, located at `modules/search`.

The styling of the Search Forms is predominantly managed by the selectors defined in the file `modules/search/search.css`. See Appendix A for a listing of the contents of that file.

[For a discussion on how to modify Drupal's theme search form, see
`http://drupal.org/node/224183`]

The Block Search Form

The Block Search Form is often visually similar to the Theme Search Form, but the key point to note here is that this is controlled by the search module and must be assigned to a block position. Like other blocks, a title can also be specified by the administrator via the block manager.

The Block Search Form often visually differs from the Theme Search Form in only one regard: the option to display the block title (in the default Garland implementation, above, "Search").

The Block Search Form is produced by the default template `search-block-form.tpl.php`, located at `modules/search`.

The styling of the Search Forms is predominantly managed by the selectors defined in the file `modules/search/search.css`. See Appendix A for a listing of the contents of that file.

 A broad-ranging discussion of a number of alternative approaches (some recommended, some not!) to modifying the Block Search Form can be found on the official Drupal site at `http://drupal.org/node/232874`

The Page Search Form

The Page Search Form provides a basic search box, but with the addition of an advanced search link and the option to search for other content or users.

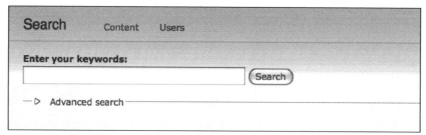

The Page Search Form always appears in the content region.

The Page Search Form is produced by the function `search_form`, located at `modules/search/search.module`.

The styling of the Search Forms is predominantly managed by the selectors defined in the file `modules/search/search.css`. See Appendix A for a listing of the contents of that file.

The Advanced Search Form

Clicking on the advanced search link on the Page Search Form brings the user to the Advanced Search Form, which includes a number of additional options for searching the site.

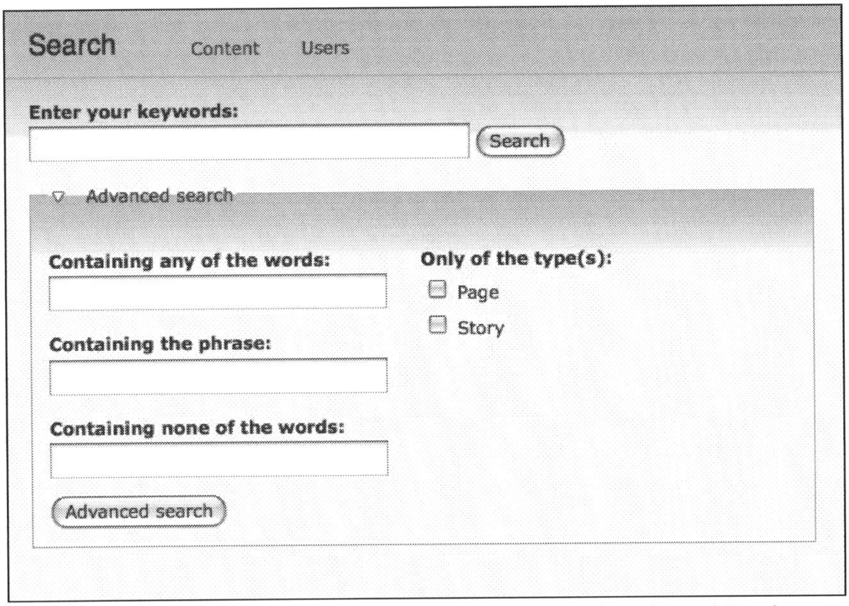

More options appear here—and more formatting issues. The Advanced Search Form appears in the content region.

The Advanced Search Form is produced by the function `search_form` (same as the form above) working in conjunction with the code in the `node.module` file, located at `modules/node/node.module`.

The styling of the Search Forms is predominantly managed by the selectors defined in the file `modules/search/search.css`. See Appendix A for a listing of the contents of that file.

The Search Results Page

The search results page is produced by the action of the various Search Forms. The functions that control the output are contained in `modules/search/search.pages.inc`. The function `search_view` collects the results and provides the page titles and related info.

The default Drupal system also includes two templates affecting the search results; one for the individual results (`search-result.tpl.php`), the other for the result set as a whole (`search-results.tpl.php`).

The styling of the search results is predominantly managed by the selectors defined in the file `modules/search/search.css`. See Appendix A for a listing of the contents of that file.

The Poll Module Forms

The poll module involves several forms. The two we will deal with here are the Poll Block Form and the Poll Page Form. You will note that there are several default templates associated with the poll module. If you look at those templates you will find that they cover the functionality very well. There are default templates for the theming of the particular elements (`poll-bar.tpl.php`, `poll-bar-block.tpl.php`), and for the presentation of the search results (`poll-results.tpl.php`, `poll-results-block.tpl.php`) and for the actual voting form (`poll-vote.tpl.php`).

Still, if you want to do more, you can dig into the function associated with the form, as per below:

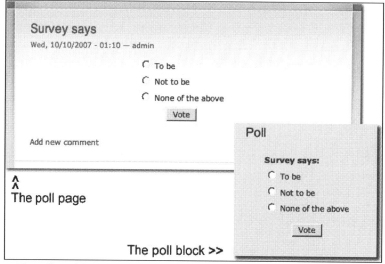

The poll module forms come in two varieties—a page form and a block form.

Drupal provides only one themable function for the poll module. The function `theme_poll_view_results` is located at `modules/poll/poll.module` and helps with theming the poll results view.

The Poll Block Form

The Poll Block Form appears when the administrator has enabled both the Poll module and assigned the Poll Block to an active region.

The Poll Block Form is produced by the function `poll_block`, which is located at `modules/poll/poll.module`, but note as well the default templates mentioned at the beginning of the section on polls.

The styling of the Poll Block Form is predominantly managed by the selectors defined in the file `modules/poll/poll.css`. See Appendix A for a listing of the contents of that file.

The Poll Page Form

The Poll Page Form appears whenever a visitor clicks on the poll or if the administrator has provided a menu item linking to a page containing the poll content item.

The Poll Page Form is produced by the function `poll_form`, which is located at `modules/poll/poll.module`, but note as well the default templates mentioned at the beginning of the section on polls.

The styling of the Poll Page Form is predominantly managed by the selectors defined in the file `modules/poll/poll.css`. See Appendix A for a listing of the contents of that file.

Summary

This chapter has covered one of the more challenging areas of Drupal theming, that is, dealing with forms in Drupal. The default forms covered in this chapter can be styled through the application of a variety of techniques, both with and without the assistance of PHPTemplate.

In this chapter, we looked at the various theming techniques and identified the key components associated with each task and where to find them. We also introduced the idea of creating a module to control form modifications, via the function `form_alter`.

A
Drupal CSS Map

All of the HTML output in Drupal comes from various functions, many of which are themable. The styling of the output is controlled by various stylesheets. Accordingly, one of the keys to controlling your site's look and feel is having a good command of the stylesheets.

The Drupal system contains a large number of stylesheets. In this chapter, we'll take you on a guided tour of all the various stylesheets.

A Guide to Drupal Stylesheets

A typical Drupal installation will include more than forty stylesheets, and may also include a certain number of embedded styles. If you have installed additional extensions, you may well find that they come with their own stylesheets, pushing the count up even higher.

The Drupal approach to stylesheets may initially appear to be overkill in the extreme, or at the very least a rather literal application of modularization, but there is a method behind this madness. The use of multiple stylesheets not only makes it easier for the individual module maintainers of the Drupal development team, but also helps you find what you need more quickly than having to deal with one or two massive files. The net result is an approach that is actually quite effective—once you get past the initial shock!

In order to reduce the potential threats of conflicting stylesheets and absurd loading times, Drupal provides a CSS pre-processing engine. This engine identifies the required stylesheets, strips out the line breaks and spaces from all the files, and delivers the styles in a combined single file. The use of this feature is disabled by default; if you wish to use it, you must access **Administer | Site configuration | Performance** and enable the **Bandwidth** optimization option labeled **Aggregate and compress CSS files**.

While working on the themes of your Drupal site, you should make sure the CSS compression is *disabled*. If the compression is enabled, you may not be able to immediately see the impact of changes to your site's CSS.

In the section below, we list the default Drupal stylesheets, where they are found, and briefly explain their function.

admin.css

`/modules/system`

Concerns the admin system interface, status reports, and theme configuration.

```
admin.css
        ├── .date-container
        ├── .date-container .custom-container
        ├── .date-container .form-item
        ├── .date-container .select-container, .date-container .custom-container
        ├── .theme-info h2
        ├── .theme-info p
        ├── .theme-settings-bottom
        ├── .theme-settings-left
        ├── .theme-settings-right
        ├── div.admin
        ├── div.admin .expert-link
        ├── div.admin .left
        ├── div.admin .right
        ├── div.admin-dependencies, div.admin-required
        ├── div.admin-panel
        ├── div.admin-panel .body
        ├── div.admin-panel .description
        ├── div.admin-required
        ├── html.js .custom-container label
        ├── span.admin-disabled
        ├── span.admin-enabled
        ├── span.admin-missing
        ├── table.package
        ├── table.package .description
        ├── table.screenshot
        ├── table.system-status-report th
        ├── table.system-status-report tr.error th
        ├── table.system-status-report tr.merge-up td, table.system-status-report th
        ├── table.system-status-report tr.ok th
        └── table.system-status-report tr.warning th
```

admin-rtl.css

/modules/system

Additional styles needed for proper display in character sets that read right-to-left.

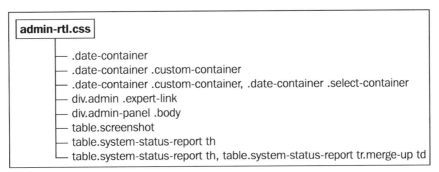

aggregator.css

/modules/aggregator

Affects the RSS/Newsfeed Aggregator Module and its contents.

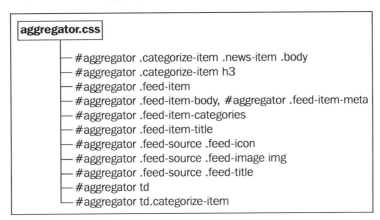

aggregator-rtl.css

/modules/aggregator

Additional styles needed for proper display in character sets that read right-to-left.

block.css

`/modules/block`

Controls Block formatting.

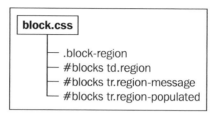

book.css

`/modules/book`

Controls the formatting of Book node content.

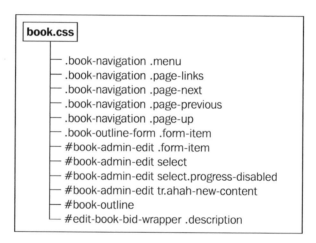

book-rtl.css

`/modules/book`

Additional styles needed for proper display in character sets that read right-to-left.

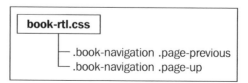

color.css

`/modules/color`

Controls the Color module used with some themes.

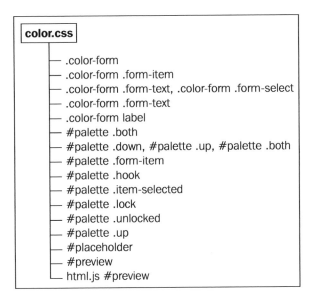

color-rtl.css

`/modules/color`

Additional styles needed for proper display in character sets that read right-to-left.

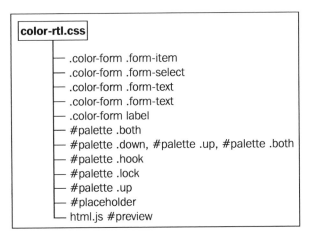

comment.css

/modules/comment

Provides the indent style for Comments.

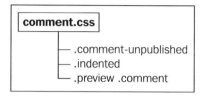

comment-rtl.css

/modules/comment

Additional styles needed for proper display in character sets that read right-to-left.

dblog.css

/modules/dblog

Styles related to the display of the DB Log functionality.

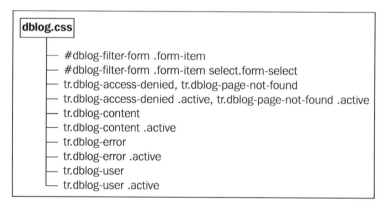

dblog-rtl.css

`/modules/dblog`

Additional styles needed for proper display in character sets that read right-to-left.

defaults.css

`/modules/system`

Provides styling for basic default HTML elements used throughout the system.

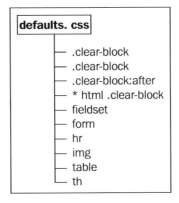

defaults-rtl.css

`/modules/system`

Additional styles needed for proper display in character sets that read right-to-left.

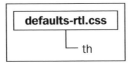

forum.css

`/modules/forum`

Affects the contents of the Forum module.

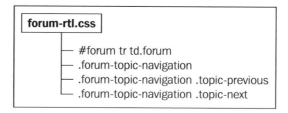

```
forum.css

        .forum-topic-navigation
        .forum-topic-navigation .topic-next
        .forum-topic-navigation .topic-previous
        #forum .description
        #forum div.indent
        #forum td.created, #forum td.posts, #forum td.topics, #forum td.last-reply, #forum td.replies, #forum td.pager
        #forum td.posts, #forum td.topics, #forum td.replies, #forum td.pager
        #forum tr td.forum
        #forum tr.new-topics td.forum
```

forum-rtl.css

`/modules/forum`

Additional styles needed for proper display in character sets that read right-to-left.

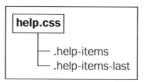

```
forum-rtl.css

        #forum tr td.forum
        .forum-topic-navigation
        .forum-topic-navigation .topic-previous
        .forum-topic-navigation .topic-next
```

help.css

`/modules/help`

Styles Help items.

```
help.css

        .help-items
        .help-items-last
```

help-rtl.css

`/modules/help`

Additional styles needed for proper display in character sets that read right-to-left.

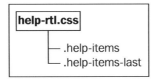

locale.css

`/modules/locale`

Provides a selector for the Locale module.

maintenance.css

`/modules/system`

Provides styling for the Maintenance page. This controls the "site offline" page.

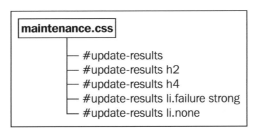

node.css

`/modules/node`

Provides selectors for Nodes.

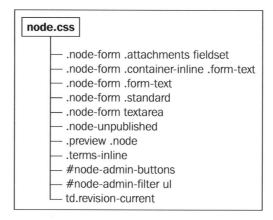

```
node.css
        ├── .node-form .attachments fieldset
        ├── .node-form .container-inline .form-text
        ├── .node-form .form-text
        ├── .node-form .standard
        ├── .node-form textarea
        ├── .node-unpublished
        ├── .preview .node
        ├── .terms-inline
        ├── #node-admin-buttons
        ├── #node-admin-filter ul
        └── td.revision-current
```

node-rtl.css

`/modules/node`

Additional styles needed for proper display in character sets that read right-to-left.

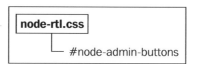

```
node-rtl.css
        └── #node-admin-buttons
```

openid.css

`/modules/openid`

Styling for the OpenID module.

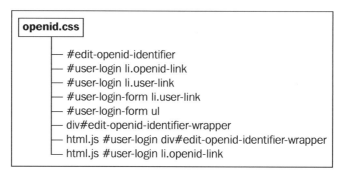

```
openid.css
        ├── #edit-openid-identifier
        ├── #user-login li.openid-link
        ├── #user-login li.user-link
        ├── #user-login-form li.user-link
        ├── #user-login-form ul
        ├── div#edit-openid-identifier-wrapper
        ├── html.js #user-login div#edit-openid-identifier-wrapper
        └── html.js #user-login li.openid-link
```

poll.css

/modules/poll

Styling for Polls.

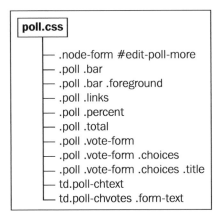

poll-rtl.css

/modules/poll

Additional styles needed for proper display in character sets that read right-to-left.

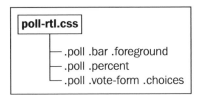

profile.css

/modules/profile

Styling for the Profile module.

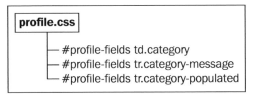

search.css

`/modules/search`

Styling for the Search module.

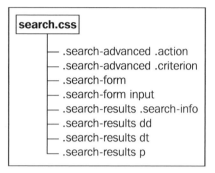

search-rtl.css

`/modules/search`

Additional styles needed for proper display in character sets that read right-to-left.

style.css

Theme-specific styles—located in the `theme` directory. This is the most critical file in a PHPTemplate theme and is the highest in the order of precedence; styles placed here will override conflicting selectors located in any other default CSS file. See the end of this Appendix for a listing of the stylesheets for the themes included in the default distribution.

system.css

`/modules/system`

Covers a wide variety of common styles, and also includes menus, tabs, and progress bars.

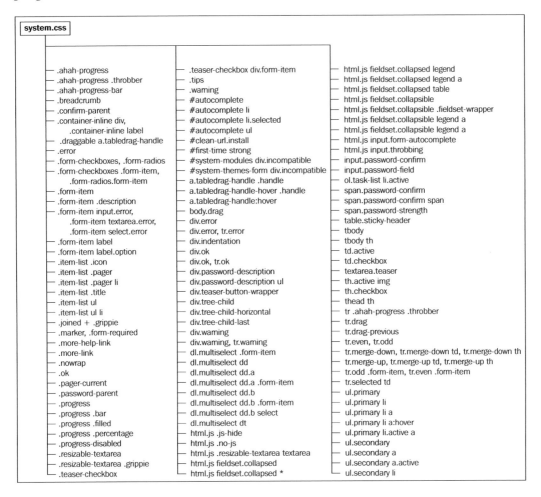

system.css

- .ahah-progress
- .ahah-progress .throbber
- .ahah-progress-bar
- .breadcrumb
- .confirm-parent
- .container-inline div,
  - .container-inline label
- .draggable a.tabledrag-handle
- .error
- .form-checkboxes, .form-radios
- .form-checkboxes .form-item,
  - .form-radios.form-item
- .form-item
- .form-item .description
- .form-item input.error,
  - .form-item textarea.error,
  - .form-item select.error
- .form-item label
- .form-item label.option
- .item-list .icon
- .item-list .pager
- .item-list .pager li
- .item-list .title
- .item-list ul
- .item-list ul li
- .joined + .grippie
- .marker, .form-required
- .more-help-link
- .more-link
- .nowrap
- .ok
- .pager-current
- .password-parent
- .progress
- .progress .bar
- .progress .filled
- .progress .percentage
- .progress-disabled
- .resizable-textarea
- .resizable-textarea .grippie
- .teaser-checkbox

- .teaser-checkbox div.form-item
- .tips
- .warning
- #autocomplete
- #autocomplete li
- #autocomplete li.selected
- #autocomplete ul
- #clean-url.install
- #first-time strong
- #system-modules div.incompatible
- #system-themes-form div.incompatible
- a.tabledrag-handle .handle
- a.tabledrag-handle-hover .handle
- a.tabledrag-handle:hover
- body.drag
- div.error
- div.error, tr.error
- div.indentation
- div.ok
- div.ok, tr.ok
- div.password-description
- div.password-description ul
- div.teaser-button-wrapper
- div.tree-child
- div.tree-child-horizontal
- div.tree-child-last
- div.warning
- div.warning, tr.warning
- dl.multiselect .form-item
- dl.multiselect dd
- dl.multiselect dd.a
- dl.multiselect dd.a .form-item
- dl.multiselect dd.b
- dl.multiselect dd.b .form-item
- dl.multiselect dd.b select
- dl.multiselect dt
- html.js .js-hide
- html.js .no-js
- html.js .resizable-textarea textarea
- html.js fieldset.collapsed
- html.js fieldset.collapsed *

- html.js fieldset.collapsed legend
- html.js fieldset.collapsed legend a
- html.js fieldset.collapsed table
- html.js fieldset.collapsible
- html.js fieldset.collapsible .fieldset-wrapper
- html.js fieldset.collapsible legend a
- html.js fieldset.collapsible legend a
- html.js input.form-autocomplete
- html.js input.throbbing
- input.password-confirm
- input.password-field
- ol.task-list li.active
- span.password-confirm
- span.password-confirm span
- span.password-strength
- table.sticky-header
- tbody
- tbody th
- td.active
- td.checkbox
- textarea.teaser
- th.active img
- th.checkbox
- thead th
- tr .ahah-progress .throbber
- tr.drag
- tr.drag-previous
- tr.even, tr.odd
- tr.merge-down, tr.merge-down td, tr.merge-down th
- tr.merge-up, tr.merge-up td, tr.merge-up th
- tr.odd .form-item, tr.even .form-item
- tr.selected td
- ul.primary
- ul.primary li
- ul.primary li a
- ul.primary li a:hover
- ul.primary li.active a
- ul.secondary
- ul.secondary a.active
- ul.secondary li

system-rtl.css

/modules/system

Additional styles needed for proper display in character sets that read right-to-left.

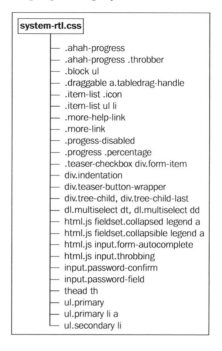

system-rtl.css
- .ahah-progress
- .ahah-progress .throbber
- .block ul
- .draggable a.tabledrag-handle
- .item-list .icon
- .item-list ul li
- .more-help-link
- .more-link
- .progess-disabled
- .progress .percentage
- .teaser-checkbox div.form-item
- div.indentation
- div.teaser-button-wrapper
- div.tree-child, div.tree-child-last
- dl.multiselect dt, dl.multiselect dd
- html.js fieldset.collapsed legend a
- html.js fieldset.collapsible legend a
- html.js input.form-autocomplete
- html.js input.throbbing
- input.password-confirm
- input.password-field
- thead th
- ul.primary
- ul.primary li a
- ul.secondary li

system-menus.css

/modules/system

Provides the styling for the menus in the admin system.

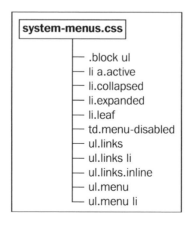

system-menus.css
- .block ul
- li a.active
- li.collapsed
- li.expanded
- li.leaf
- td.menu-disabled
- ul.links
- ul.links li
- ul.links.inline
- ul.menu
- ul.menu li

system-menus-rtl.css

`/modules/system`

Additional styles needed for proper display in character sets that read right-to-left.

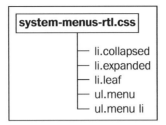

taxonomy.css

`/modules/taxonomy`

Styles used by the Taxonomy module.

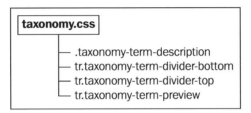

tracker.css

`/modules/tracker`

Table styles used by the Tracker module.

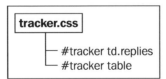

update.css

`/modules/update`

Styles necessary for the Update module.

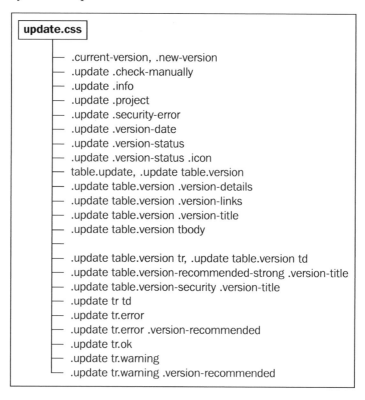

update-rtl.css

`/modules/update`

Additional styles needed for proper display in character sets that read right-to-left.

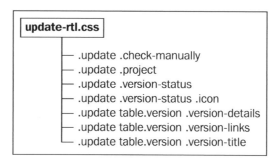

user.css

`/modules/user`

Styles for the User module and Profile module; includes styles for user administration.

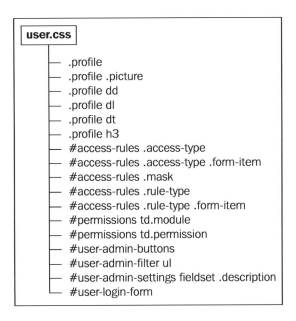

user-rtl.css

`/modules/user`

Additional styles needed for proper display in character sets that read right-to-left.

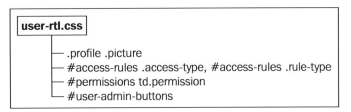

The Stylesheets of the Default Themes

In the following section we show the key stylesheets for each of the themes in the default Drupal distribution.

Marvin

`/themes/chameleon/marvin`

Styles for the theme, Marvin.

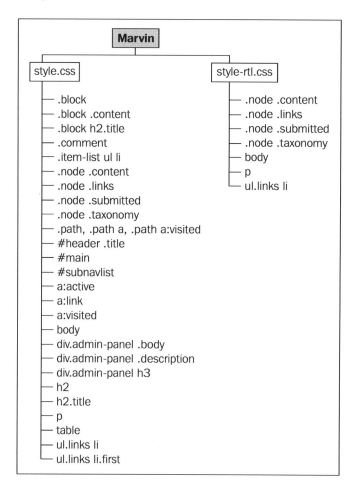

Bluemarine

`/themes/bluemarine`

Styles for Bluemarine theme.

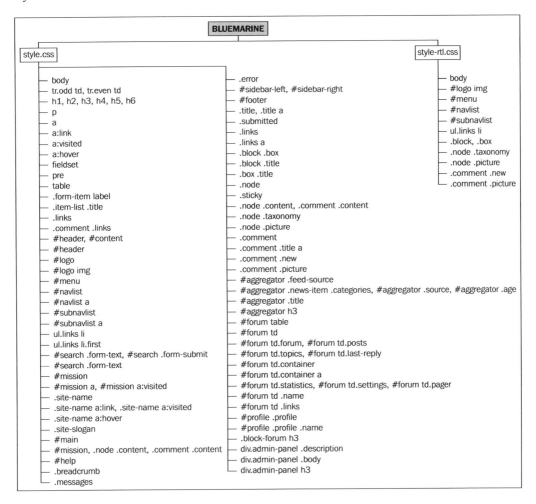

Pushbutton

`/themes/pushbutton`

Styles for the Pushbutton theme.

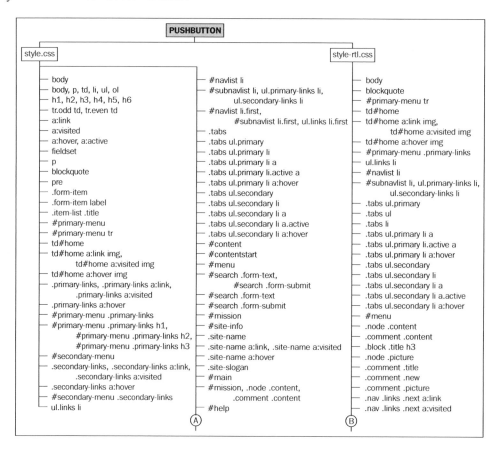

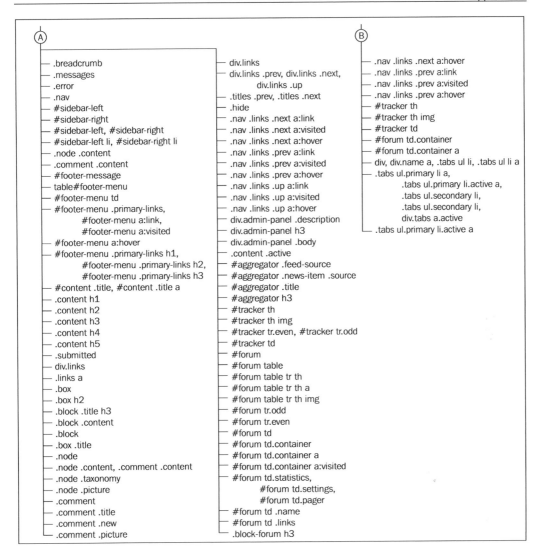

Ⓐ

- .breadcrumb
- .messages
- .error
- .nav
- #sidebar-left
- #sidebar-right
- #sidebar-left, #sidebar-right
- #sidebar-left li, #sidebar-right li
- .node .content
- .comment .content
- #footer-message
- table#footer-menu
- #footer-menu td
- #footer-menu .primary-links,
    #footer-menu a:link,
    #footer-menu a:visited
- #footer-menu a:hover
- #footer-menu .primary-links h1,
    #footer-menu .primary-links h2,
    #footer-menu .primary-links h3
- #content .title, #content .title a
- .content h1
- .content h2
- .content h3
- .content h4
- .content h5
- .submitted
- div.links
- .links a
- .box
- .box h2
- .block .title h3
- .block .content
- .block
- .box .title
- .node
- .node .content, .comment .content
- .node .taxonomy
- .node .picture
- .comment
- .comment .title
- .comment .new
- .comment .picture

- div.links
- div.links .prev, div.links .next,
    div.links .up
- .titles .prev, .titles .next
- .hide
- .nav .links .next a:link
- .nav .links .next a:visited
- .nav .links .next a:hover
- .nav .links .prev a:link
- .nav .links .prev a:visited
- .nav .links .prev a:hover
- .nav .links .up a:link
- .nav .links .up a:visited
- .nav .links .up a:hover
- div.admin-panel .description
- div.admin-panel h3
- div.admin-panel .body
- .content .active
- #aggregator .feed-source
- #aggregator .news-item .source
- #aggregator .title
- #aggregator h3
- #tracker th
- #tracker th img
- #tracker tr.even, #tracker tr.odd
- #tracker td
- #forum
- #forum table
- #forum table tr th
- #forum table tr th a
- #forum table tr th img
- #forum tr.odd
- #forum tr.even
- #forum td
- #forum td.container
- #forum td.container a
- #forum td.container a:visited
- #forum td.statistics,
    #forum td.settings,
    #forum td.pager
- #forum td .name
- #forum td .links
- .block-forum h3

Ⓑ

- .nav .links .next a:hover
- .nav .links .prev a:link
- .nav .links .prev a:visited
- .nav .links .prev a:hover
- #tracker th
- #tracker th img
- #tracker td
- #forum td.container
- #forum td.container a
- div, div.name a, .tabs ul li, .tabs ul li a
- .tabs ul.primary li a,
    .tabs ul.primary li.active a,
    .tabs ul.secondary li,
    .tabs ul.secondary li,
    div.tabs a.active
- .tabs ul.primary li.active a

Garland

`/themes/garland`

Styles specific to the Garland theme.

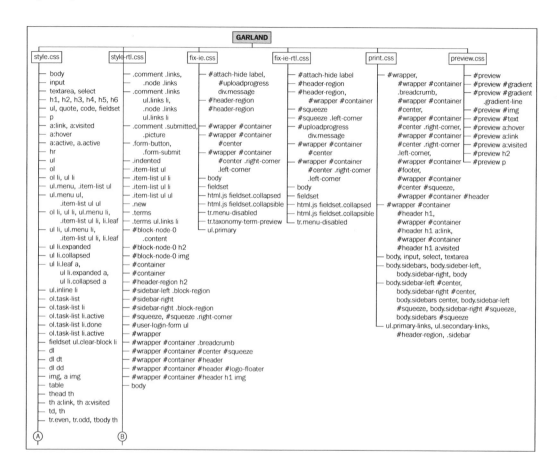

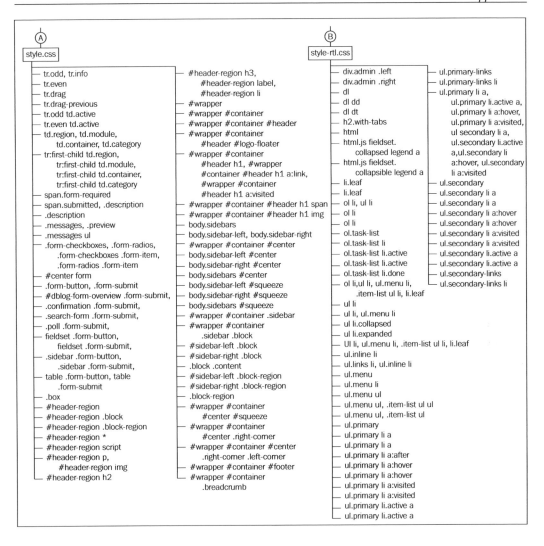

(A) style.css

- tr.odd, tr.info
- tr.even
- tr.drag
- tr.drag-previous
- tr.odd td.active
- tr.even td.active
- td.region, td.module,
  td.container, td.category
- tr:first-child td.region,
  tr:first-child td.module,
  tr:first-child td.container,
  tr:first-child td.category
- span.form-required
- span.submitted, .description
- .description
- .messages, .preview
- .messages ul
- .form-checkboxes, .form-radios,
  .form-checkboxes .form-item,
  .form-radios .form-item
- #center form
- .form-button, .form-submit
- #dblog-form-overview .form-submit,
  .confirmation .form-submit,
  .search-form .form-submit,
  .poll .form-submit,
  fieldset .form-button,
  fieldset .form-submit,
  .sidebar .form-button,
  .sidebar .form-submit,
  table .form-button, table
  .form-submit
- .box
- #header-region
- #header-region .block
- #header-region .block-region
- #header-region *
- #header-region script
- #header-region p,
  #header-region img
- #header-region h2

- #header-region h3,
  #header-region label,
  #header-region li
- #wrapper
- #wrapper #container
- #wrapper #container #header
- #wrapper #container
  #header #logo-floater
- #wrapper #container
  #header h1, #wrapper
  #container #header h1 a:link,
  #wrapper #container
  #header h1 a:visited
- #wrapper #container #header h1 span
- #wrapper #container #header h1 img
- body.sidebars
- body.sidebar-left, body.sidebar-right
- #wrapper #container #center
- body.sidebar-left #center
- body.sidebar-right #center
- body.sidebars #center
- body.sidebar-left #squeeze
- body.sidebar-right #squeeze
- body.sidebars #squeeze
- #wrapper #container .sidebar
- #wrapper #container
  .sidebar .block
- #sidebar-left .block
- #sidebar-right .block
- .block .content
- #sidebar-left .block-region
- #sidebar-right .block-region
- .block-region
- #wrapper #container
  #center #squeeze
- #wrapper #container
  #center .right-corner
- #wrapper #container #center
  .right-corner .left-corner
- #wrapper #container #footer
- #wrapper #container
  .breadcrumb

(B) style-rtl.css

- div.admin .left
- div.admin .right
- dl
- dl dd
- dl dt
- h2.with-tabs
- html
- html.js fieldset.
  collapsed legend a
- html.js fieldset.
  collapsible legend a
- li.leaf
- li.leaf
- ol li, ul li
- ol li
- ol li
- ol.task-list
- ol.task-list li
- ol.task-list li.active
- ol.task-list li.active
- ol.task-list li.done
- ol li,ul li, ul.menu li,
  .item-list ul li, li.leaf
- ul li
- ul li, ul.menu li
- ul li.collapsed
- ul li.expanded
- Ul li, ul.menu li, .item-list ul li, li.leaf
- ul.inline li
- ul.links li, ul.inline li
- ul.menu
- ul.menu li
- ul.menu ul
- ul.menu ul, .item-list ul ul
- ul.menu ul, .item-list ul
- ul.primary
- ul.primary li a
- ul.primary li a
- ul.primary li a:after
- ul.primary li a:hover
- ul.primary li a:hover
- ul.primary li a:visited
- ul.primary li a:visited
- ul.primary li.active a
- ul.primary li.active a

- ul.primary-links
- ul.primary-links li
- ul.primary li a,
  ul.primary li.active a,
  ul.primary li a:hover,
  ul.primary li a:visited,
  ul secondary li a,
  ul.secondary li.active
  a,ul.secondary li
  a:hover, ul.secondary
  li a:visited
- ul.secondary
- ul.secondary li a
- ul.secondary li a
- ul.secondary li a:hover
- ul.secondary li a:hover
- ul.secondary li a:visited
- ul.secondary li.active a
- ul.secondary li.active a
- ul.secondary-links
- ul.secondary-links li

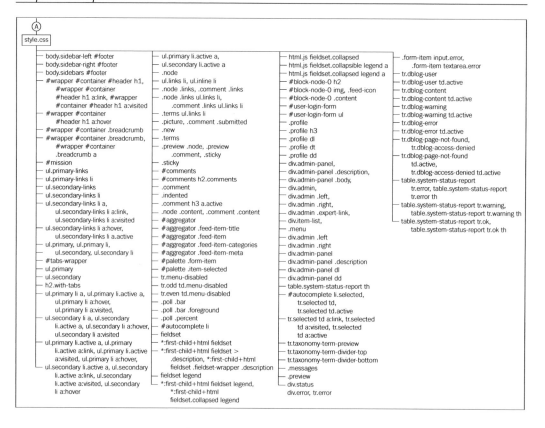

(A) style.css

- body.sidebar-left #footer
- body.sidebar-right #footer
- body.sidebars #footer
- #wrapper #container #header h1,
    #wrapper #container
    #header h1 a:link, #wrapper
    #container #header h1 a:visited
- #wrapper #container
    #header h1 a:hover
- #wrapper #container .breadcrumb
- #wrapper #container .breadcrumb,
    #wrapper #container
    .breadcrumb a
- #mission
- ul.primary-links
- ul.primary-links li
- ul.secondary-links
- ul.secondary-links li
- ul.secondary-links li a,
    ul.secondary-links li a:link,
    ul.secondary-links li a:visited
- ul.secondary-links li a:hover,
    ul.secondary-links li a.active
- ul.primary, ul.primary li,
    ul.secondary, ul.secondary li
- #tabs-wrapper
- ul.primary
- ul.secondary
- h2.with-tabs
- ul.primary li a, ul.primary li.active a,
    ul.primary li a:hover,
    ul.primary li a:visited,
- ul.secondary li a, ul.secondary
    li.active a, ul.secondary li a:hover,
    ul.secondary li a:visited
- ul.primary li.active a, ul.primary
    li.active a:link, ul.primary li.active
    a:visited, ul.primary li a:hover,
- ul.secondary li.active a, ul.secondary
    li.active a:link, ul.secondary
    li.active a:visited, ul.secondary
    li a:hover

- ul.primary li.active a,
- ul.secondary li.active a
- .node
- ul.links li, ul.inline li
- .node .links, .comment .links
- .node .links ul.links li,
    .comment .links ul.links li
- .terms ul.links li
- .picture, .comment .submitted
- .new
- .terms
- .preview .node, .preview
    .comment, .sticky
- .sticky
- #comments
- #comments h2.comments
- .comment
- .indented
- .comment h3 a.active
- .node .content, .comment .content
- #aggregator
- #aggregator .feed-item-title
- #aggregator .feed-item
- #aggregator .feed-item-categories
- #aggregator .feed-item-meta
- #palette .form-item
- #palette .item-selected
- tr.menu-disabled
- tr.odd td.menu-disabled
- tr.even td.menu-disabled
- .poll .bar
- .poll .bar .foreground
- .poll .percent
- #autocomplete li
- fieldset
- *:first-child+html fieldset
- *:first-child+html fieldset >
    .description, *:first-child+html
    fieldset .fieldset-wrapper .description
- fieldset legend
- *:first-child+html fieldset legend,
    *:first-child+html
    fieldset.collapsed legend

- html.js fieldset.collapsed
- html.js fieldset.collapsible legend a
- html.js fieldset.collapsed legend a
- #block-node-0 h2
- #block-node-0 img, .feed-icon
- #block-node-0 .content
- #user-login-form
- #user-login-form ul
- .profile
- .profile h3
- .profile dl
- .profile dt
- .profile dd
- div.admin-panel,
- div.admin-panel .description,
- div.admin-panel .body,
- div.admin,
- div.admin .left,
- div.admin .right,
- div.admin .expert-link,
- div.item-list,
- .menu
- div.admin .left
- div.admin .right
- div.admin-panel
- div.admin-panel .description
- div.admin-panel dl
- div.admin-panel dd
- table.system-status-report th
- #autocomplete li.selected,
    tr.selected td,
    tr.selected td.active
- tr.selected td a:link, tr.selected
    td a:visited, tr.selected
    td a:active
- tr.taxonomy-term-preview
- tr.taxonomy-term-divider-top
- tr.taxonomy-term-divider-bottom
- .messages
- .preview
- div.status
    div.error, tr.error

- .form-item input.error,
    .form-item textarea.error
- tr.dblog-user
- tr.dblog-user td.active
- tr.dblog-content
- tr.dblog-content td.active
- tr.dblog-warning
- tr.dblog-warning td.active
- tr.dblog-error
- tr.dblog-error td.active
- tr.dblog-page-not-found,
    tr.dblog-access-denied
- tr.dblog-page-not-found
    td.active,
    tr.dblog-access-denied td.active
- table.system-status-report
    tr.error, table.system-status-report
    tr.error th
- table.system-status-report tr.warning,
    table.system-status-report tr.warning th
- table.system-status-report tr.ok,
    table.system-status-report tr.ok th

Minnelli

/themes/garland/minnelli

Styles for the Minnelli theme.

Minnelli

minnelli.css

- body #wrapper #container
- body.sidebar-left #wrapper #container, body.sidebar-right #wrapper #container
- body.sidebars #wrapper #container

Chameleon

`/themes/chameleon`

Styles for the Chameleon theme.

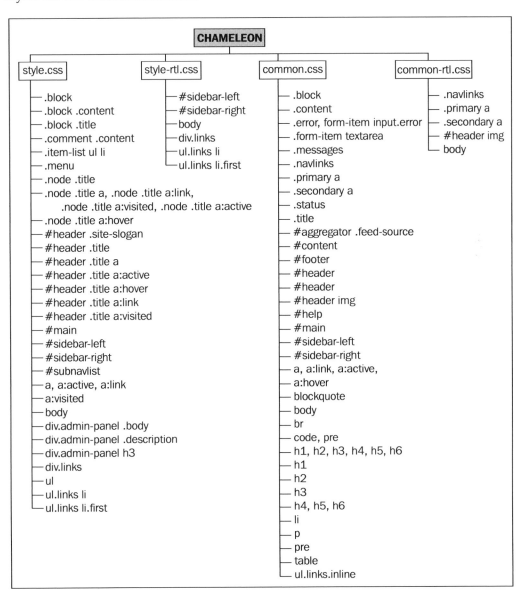

B

The Themers' Toolkit

Throughout this book, I have used a variety of tools to demonstrate the various chapters. In addition to a basic toolset made up of an HTML editor, an FTP program, and a browser, I also used several specialized tools. In this Appendix, I have rounded up a listing of all the specialized tools used in this book, along with several additional items that you may find useful when working on your themes.

The tools fall into two categories: Drupal modules and extensions to the Firefox browser. Each is listed along with a brief synopsis and a URL to the relevant project site:

- Content Construction Kit
- Devel Module
- Firebug
- Panels Module
- Views Module
- The Web Developer Extension

Drupal Modules

Following are the Drupal modules:

Content Construction Kit

The Content Construction Kit (CCK) is a Drupal module that allows for the easy creation of custom content types with custom fields. While this module is not in itself a theming tool, it does allow for more flexible layout of your site. There are a number of options that can be combined to extend the functionality of CCK, making this a very powerful—and widely used—extension.

The Content Templates (Contemplate) module can be combined with CCK to enable easy control of the Drupal teaser and body fields.

Learn more: `http://drupal.org/project/cck` see also, `http://drupal.org/project/contemplate`

Devel Module

The Devel module is a suite of tools that are useful to both module and theme developers. This extension was used for several purposes in this book: revealing information about themes, providing dummy content, and identifying recommendations for overrides.

When creating intercepts and overrides, you will find the Theme Developer option particularly useful, as it provides quick access to key information about the templates and functions being used by each page. The Theme Developer option is included with the Devel module, but must be activated separately.

The option to create dummy content quickly and to your specifications is also a real time-saver. No more time wasted, spent creating dummy users, content items, and comments by hand. Again, the Create Content option is included with the Devel module, but must be activated separately.

 This extension is intended for use during development and should not be employed on a production site.

Learn more: `http://drupal.org/project/devel`

Panels Module

The Panels module makes the creation of multi-column layouts a breeze. With Panels, you are able to divide a page into content areas and control the content in each area. Blocks and nodes can be mixed freely.

The system comes with several default 2 and 3 column formats, but you can do virtually anything you want with a little configuration work.

Learn more: `http://drupal.org/project/panels`

Views Module

The Views module enhances your control over the listing of content items (nodes). With views you can create custom lists that contain the content you want, sorted in the manner you want. Views makes it easy to make blog-site type lists of the most recent articles, most recent comments, top posts in a category, most popular posts, etc.

Learn more: `http://drupal.org/project/views`

Firefox Extensions

Following are the Firefox extensions:

Firebug Firefox Extension

Those of you using the Firefox browser will want to check out the Firebug extension. Firebug allows you to pop up an inspection pane that contains information about the page in the browser. You can then click on elements and see the details of their formatting in the inspection window.

Firebug is a great time-saver for CSS work as you can not only view the styles at work but also edit them to see the impact on the page element. Firebug also eases work with JavaScript and, with the YSlow extension (a separate add-on you must install), you can even measure and benchmark page performance.

Learn more: `https://addons.mozilla.org/en-US/firefox/addon/1843`

The Web Developer Extension

Like Firebug, the Web Developer Extension is an add-on for the Firefox browser. Web Developer provides a wide variety of information about web pages as well as the ability to identify selectors and to edit active stylesheets. Web Developer also provides useful tools for forms and even links into different validation engines.

Whether you prefer Firebug or Web Developer is up to you. Firebug is faster and easier to use, but Web Developer provides a great deal of information. Both are installed in my Firefox browser.

Learn more: `https://addons.mozilla.org/firefox/addon/60`

Index

E

existing theme, modifying
about 143
modifications, planning 145, 146
new sub-theme, creating 146-148
workspace, setting up 143-145

F

Filter Module, theming
theme_filter_admin_order, themable
    functions 102
theme_filter_admin_overview, themable
    functions 102
theme_filter_tips, themable functions 102
theme_filter_tips_more_info, themable
    functions 102
themable functions 101
Firefox extensions
Firebug Firefox extension 283
web developer extension 283
flexibility, Drupal theme 13, 15
form, modifying
block templates 231, 232
CSS styling, working with 231
custom modules used 237, 238, 240
custom templates, creating 231
default template, overriding 233
form_alter() used 237, 238, 240
HTML, adding via function attributes 240
page templates 231
theme function, using to control elements
    234-237
form functionality, theming
theme_button, themable functions 102
theme_checkbox, themable functions 102
theme_checkboxes, themable
    functions 102
theme_date, themable functions 102
theme_fieldset, themable functions 102
theme_file, themable functions 102
theme_form, themable functions 102
theme_form_element, themable
    functions 103
theme_hidden, themable functions 103
theme_image_button, themable
    functions 103

theme_item, themable functions 103
theme_markup, themable functions 103
theme_password, themable functions 103
theme_password_confirm, themable
    functions 103
theme_radio, themable functions 103
theme_radios, themable functions 103
theme_select, themable functions 103
theme_submit, themable functions 103
theme_textarea, themable functions 103
theme_textfield, themable functions 103
theme_token, themable functions 103
themable functions 102
form issues, Drupal
data labels, form_alter() used 241
data labels, function used 241
data labels, modifying 240
data labels, template used 241
images, using for buttons 242, 243
styling of form, form_alter() used 242
styling of form, function used 242
styling of form, modifying 241
styling of form, template used 242
text, modifying 240
forms, working
about 227, 228
form functions, login form 228-230
form functions, override creating 228
form ID, finding 230
forum module, theming
default stylesheets 105
default templates 104
forum-icon.tpl.php, default templates 104
forum-list.tpl.php, default templates 104
forum-rtl.css, default stylesheets 105
forum-submitted.tpl.php, default
    templates 104
forum-topic-list.tpl.php, default
    templates 105
forum-topic-navigation.tpl.php, default
    templates 105
forum.css, default stylesheets 105
forums.tpl.php, default templates 105
functional elements, page.tpl.php file
breadcrumb trail, main wrapper 187
content region, main wrapper 188
feed icons, footer 189

Thank you for buying
Drupal 6 Themes

Packt Open Source Project Royalties

When we sell a book written on an Open Source project, we pay a royalty directly to that project. Therefore by purchasing Drupal 6 Themes, Packt will have given some of the money received to the Drupal Project.

In the long term, we see ourselves and you — customers and readers of our books — as part of the Open Source ecosystem, providing sustainable revenue for the projects we publish on. Our aim at Packt is to establish publishing royalties as an essential part of the service and support a business model that sustains Open Source.

If you're working with an Open Source project that you would like us to publish on, and subsequently pay royalties to, please get in touch with us.

Writing for Packt

We welcome all inquiries from people who are interested in authoring. Book proposals should be sent to authors@packtpub.com. If your book idea is still at an early stage and you would like to discuss it first before writing a formal book proposal, contact us; one of our commissioning editors will get in touch with you.

We're not just looking for published authors; if you have strong technical skills but no writing experience, our experienced editors can help you develop a writing career, or simply get some additional reward for your expertise.

About Packt Publishing

Packt, pronounced 'packed', published its first book "Mastering phpMyAdmin for Effective MySQL Management" in April 2004 and subsequently continued to specialize in publishing highly focused books on specific technologies and solutions.

Our books and publications share the experiences of your fellow IT professionals in adapting and customizing today's systems, applications, and frameworks. Our solution-based books give you the knowledge and power to customize the software and technologies you're using to get the job done. Packt books are more specific and less general than the IT books you have seen in the past. Our unique business model allows us to bring you more focused information, giving you more of what you need to know, and less of what you don't.

Packt is a modern, yet unique publishing company, which focuses on producing quality, cutting-edge books for communities of developers, administrators, and newbies alike. For more information, please visit our website: www.PacktPub.com.

Drupal 5 Themes

ISBN: 978-1-847191-82-3   Paperback: 250 pages

Create a new theme for your Drupal website with a clean layout and powerful CSS styling

1.   Learn to create new Drupal 5 Themes

2.   No experience of Drupal 5 theming required

3.   Set up and configure themes

4.   Understand Drupal 5's themeable functions

Drupal for Education and E-Learning

ISBN: 978-1-847195-02-9   Paperback: 333 pages

Teaching and learning in the classroom using the Drupal CMS

1.   Use Drupal in the classroom to enhance teaching and engage students with a range of learning activities

2.   Create blogs, online discussions, groups, and a community website using Drupal.

3.   Clear step-by-step instructions throughout the book

4.   No need for code! A teacher-friendly, comprehensive guide

Please check **www.PacktPub.com** for information on our titles

6986909R0

Made in the USA
Lexington, KY
08 October 2010